Kate Gregory

D0860920

Microsoft
Visual C++
.NET 2003

KICK START

SAMS

800 East 96th Street, Indianapolis, Indiana 46240

Microsoft Visual C++ .NET 2003 Kick Start

International Standard Book Number: 0-672-32600-0

Library of Congress Catalog Card Number: 2003111832

Printed in the United States of America

First Printing: December 2003

06   05   04   03   4   3   2   1

Trademarks

All terms mentioned in this book that are known to be trademarks or service marks have been appropriately capitalized. Sams Publishing cannot attest to the accuracy of this information. Use of a term in this book should not be regarded as affecting the validity of any trademark or service mark.

Warning and Disclaimer

Every effort has been made to make this book as complete and as accurate as possible, but no warranty or fitness is implied. The information provided is on an "as is" basis. The author and the publisher shall have neither liability nor responsibility to any person or entity with respect to any loss or damages arising from the information contained in this.

Bulk Sales

Sams Publishing offers excellent discounts on this book when ordered in quantity for bulk purchases or special sales. For more information, please contact

U.S. Corporate and Government Sales
1-800-382-3419
corpsales@pearsontechgroup.com

For sales outside of the U.S., please contact

International Sales
1-317-428-3341
international@pearsontechgroup.com

Associate Publisher
Michael Stephens

Executive Editor
Candace Hall

Acquisitions Editor
Todd Green

Development Editor
Songlin Qiu

Managing Editor
Charlotte Clapp

Project Editor
Dan Knott

Copy Editor
Kezia Endsley

Indexer
Mandie Frank

Proofreader
Kathy Bidwell

Technical Editor
Benjamin Garcia

Publishing Coordinator
Cindy Teeters

Designer
Gary Adair

Page Layout
Kelly Maish

Contents at a Glance

Table of Contents

About the Author

Kate Gregory, Microsoft Regional Director for Toronto, Ontario, is a founding partner of Gregory Consulting Limited. For the past 17 years her firm has been developing software using tools like .NET, XML, Web Services, VC++, VB, C#, ASP, Java, and Perl. Kate teaches and develops courses for a variety of corporate clients and is an adjunct faculty member at Trent University. She is in demand as an expert speaker, with five cross-country tours for Microsoft Canada in the past two years, and talks at Tech Ed USA and Europe. Kate is the author of numerous books for Que Publishing, including four editions of *Special Edition Using Visual C++*. She also writes a Visual C++ column at CodeGuru.

Dedication

To Brian, for your support and care through all we take on together.

Acknowledgments

A book is a team effort, and this one is no exception to that rule. Candace Hall and Todd Green have been with me through this process from outline to the finished product, and like any author I doubt I would have finished it without their midwifery skills. Songlin Qiu made sure that what I typed was what I really wanted everyone to read, and insisted on clarity throughout—the book is better for her influence. My technical editor this time is Ben Garcia, and his patience checking every line of code and every screen shot is deeply appreciated. While I cheerfully share the credit for the accurate and educational aspects of this book, the mistakes and omissions I have to claim as mine alone. Please bring them to my attention so that they can be corrected in subsequent printings and editions. I am as grateful as ever to readers who have done so for my previous books, and improved this book in the process.

I am lucky enough to be married to my business partner (and a fellow geek) and so I always have someone to bounce ideas or sample code at, or to run explanations past. Brian, where would I be without you? My children, Beth and Kevin, understand that the rhythm of a writer's life is not like everyone else's and I thank them for supporting me—and for distracting me when I needed to be distracted.

Microsoft people who contributed to my understanding of Visual C++, interoperability, and runtime internals include Nick Hodapp, Anson Tsao, Scott Currie, and Jan Gray. I thank you all for your insight and patience.

All that I have learned about C++, the .NET runtime, and interoperability has come from questions. Sometimes the questions have been my own, born of curiosity or a programming problem I've faced. Other times they've been asked by clients, readers, or someone from the audience at a presentation. These questions have tremendous value to me; I thank all those who've asked them. Keep asking!

We Want to Hear from You!

As the reader of this book, *you* are our most important critic and commentator. We value your opinion and want to know what we're doing right, what we could do better, what areas you'd like to see us publish in, and any other words of wisdom you're willing to pass our way.

As an associate publisher for Sams Publishing, I welcome your comments. You can email or write me directly to let me know what you did or didn't like about this book—as well as what we can do to make our books better.

Please note that I cannot help you with technical problems related to the topic of this book. We do have a User Services group, however, where I will forward specific technical questions related to the book.

When you write, please be sure to include this book's title and author as well as your name, email address, and phone number. I will carefully review your comments and share them with the author and editors who worked on the book.

Email: feedback@samspublishing.com

Mail: Michael Stephens
         Associate Publisher
         Sams Publishing
         800 East 96th Street
         Indianapolis, IN 46240 USA

For more information about this book or another Sams Publishing title, visit our Web site at www.samspublishing.com. Type the ISBN (excluding hyphens) or the title of a book in the Search field to find the page you're looking for.

Introduction

Microsoft's Visual C++ compiler was first released in 1993, more than a decade ago. Over the years there have been many versions; some represented only a small improvement over the previous versions while others were dramatically improved. The release of Visual C++ .NET 2002 as part of Visual Studio .NET 2002 was perhaps the largest change in the tool since the original release. Everything that had been in earlier versions of Visual C++ was still in the 2002 version, but in addition a door had opened into the new world of managed code and the .NET runtime.

Unfortunately for C++ programmers, the full promise of the .NET world didn't pour out of the Visual C++ .NET 2002 box. There were so many things that Visual Basic.NET and C# programmers could do in the managed world that Visual C++ programmers could not. That's because the effort involved in making "It Just Works," to use one of the phrases the developers of Visual C++ applied to some of their successes, made it impossible to get everything else into the released product.

Then along came Visual C++ .NET 2003. I think of this, to borrow a phrase from an article by Stanley Lippman of Microsoft, as the "Still In Love With C++" release of Visual Studio. Features that had been missing from the 2002 release are in this one, which placed C++ programmers on a par with C# and VB programmers. For example, the WinForms designers can generate C++ code now, allowing you to build managed Windows applications with Rapid Application Development techniques—and the same classes and methods from the Base Class Libraries as the other managed languages.

It's also become quite clear, in the time since the .NET runtime was first released, that managed C++ occupies a special place in the pantheon of managed languages. It's the language of choice for integrating the old and the new worlds, and much of this book demonstrates to you how to combine old-style unmanaged code and new-style managed code in the same application. If interoperability is important to you, you're probably going to be working in C++ more than any other language.

Who Should Read This Book

To get the most out of this book, you should already be an experienced C++ programmer. There's no coverage of C++ syntax, and I assume in places that you're already familiar with functions like `strlen()` or `printf()`. More importantly, I assume that you've faced certain types of problems in the past and have a guess about how to tackle them in Visual C++. I encourage you to draw on your experience and place the approaches I show you in the larger context of the other programming you've done.

If you're new to programming, and you don't know any C++ syntax, you're going to find it harder to understand the examples, but also to understand the motivation for them. When you've faced a particular problem before, using a different programming language or a different class library, you'll appreciate the powerful and simple ways to solve the problems that are presented in this book.

How This Book Is Organized

This book comprises 15 chapters. You can read them in any order, but I recommend you read Chapters 1-3 first to lay the groundwork for understanding the sample code that's presented throughout the book. After that, read the chapters that are appropriate for the particular problem you need to tackle.

Chapter 1: C++, Visual C++, and Managed C++: What's the Difference?

Way back when the first release of Visual C++ appeared, the difference between C++ and Visual C++ was clear; one was a language, and the other was a set of tools and libraries that included a compiler, an editor, a debugger, and so on. That is still the distinction today, but as time has gone by Microsoft has added support for a set of keywords (identified with two leading underscores) that are not standard C++ and are not supported by other compiler vendors. The most significant set of extra keywords are formally known as *managed extensions* for C++, and they are what you use to write managed code in C++. This chapter explains just what that means and discusses the role of managed and unmanaged code in modern software development.

Chapter 2: Creating Test Harnesses and Starter Applications

Although you can and will create Windows applications in C++, console applications play a very important role in the work you do. A great deal of the C++ code you will write and use is deployed as class libraries, not as standalone applications. To use these libraries, you can create test harnesses that exercise the methods of the libraries. Test harnesses are also quick ways to play with a particular coding technique to see how it works without getting caught up in a graphical user interface. They're also excellent for automated testing because they can run from the command line or a batch file. In this chapter you see how to create console applications in both managed and unmanaged C++.

Chapter 3: The .NET Base Class Libraries

This chapter introduces you to the libraries that your managed code can draw on, including classes for input and output, string manipulation, working with dates and times, regular expressions, and multithreading. It also explains the important role of namespaces in the Base Class Libraries and how to translate names in the documentation into C++ syntax.

Chapter 4: Building Simple User Interfaces with Windows Forms

This chapter shows you how to create a graphical user interface in managed C++ using the Windows Forms libraries. It's quite different from performing the same task in MFC or other C++ libraries.

Chapter 5: Writing a Class Library in Unmanaged C++

This chapter discusses some of the design thoughts that lead to a layered design, and how a class library can be used to implement one or more layers. You'll also see how to use an unmanaged class library from both managed and unmanaged C++.

Chapter 6: Writing a Class Library in Managed C++

This chapter shows you how to design and create a managed assembly that implements a class library. It distinguishes between managed (garbage-collected) classes and managed code, and shows you how to use managed classes from another managed language, such as C#.

Chapter 7: Building DLLs in Unmanaged C++

In this chapter you see the difference between an unmanaged DLL and a managed assembly, write a DLL in unmanaged C++, and call it from both managed and unmanaged code. You also learn how to write custom marshaling code for maximum convenience to the developers of the managed code that uses the DLL.

Chapter 8: Writing COM Components in C++

This chapter illustrates another technique for packaging unmanaged code: writing COM components. You will see how to write a COM component and how to call it from managed and unmanaged code.

Chapter 9: Using Existing COM Components in C++

When you write a COM component yourself, calling it from more code you write yourself is quite simple. This chapter shows you how to take on a slightly harder task: reusing code you didn't write, such as Word 2003. It leads you through IDL and the Object Viewer to show you how to discover interfaces and methods in a large automation server. You learn how to write both managed and unmanaged code that relies on the power of other applications to save time and effort.

Chapter 10: Writing and Consuming a Web Service

This chapter describes Web Services and the kind of distributed applications they make possible. You will see how to write and use a Web Service from both managed and unmanaged code.

Chapter 11: Writing a Data Layer in Managed C++

The ADO.NET library provides classes that your managed code can use to work with data from a variety of sources. In this chapter, you will learn about the `DataSet` and `DataReader` classes, and the purposes they serve, and learn how to get information in and out of a database. This chapter also shows you how to use a configuration file to store useful information that can be changed at runtime without requiring a recompile of your application.

Chapter 12: Writing a Windows Service

A Windows service is an application that runs unattended and deals with various background tasks. This chapter shows you how to write and test a Windows service, and how to debug one. Because there is no user interface, the service must communicate with the user in some other way, so this chapter demonstrates sending mail and adding an entry to the event log, two techniques that are likely to be useful in other types of applications as well.

Chapter 13: Strengthening Your Managed Applications with Security and Encryption

Security is an important focus for almost every developer today. In this chapter you learn about role-based security in Windows applications, and how you can use Windows account information in your code. You also see how to encrypt and decrypt data in your applications.

Chapter 14: Moving Layers to Different Machines with .NET Remoting

Building a distributed application is made significantly simpler with .NET remoting. Essentially, you write your application as though it was all on one machine, and use configuration files to spread assemblies over different machines. This chapter shows you how to build and test a two-part application built on .NET remoting, and how to add .NET events to a remote application.

Chapter 15: Building Advanced User Interfaces in Managed C++

Whereas Chapter 4 got you started writing Windows Forms applications, and other chapters throughout the book have created simple Windows applications, many developers will need to put more effort into the user interfaces of their applications. In this chapter, you see how to write your own controls, how to draw with GDI+, how to implement drag and drop, and how to internationalize and localize your WinForms applications.

Conventions Used in This Book

This book uses several conventions to help you prioritize and reference the information it contains.

Various typefaces are used to make code and input easily distinguishable from regular text:

- ▶ Program code appears in a special `monospace font`.

- ▶ Placeholders—words or characters used temporarily to represent the real words or characters you type in code—are typeset in _`italic monospace`_.

- ▶ Material that you are instructed to type appears in **`bold monospace`**.

In addition, the following special elements provide information beyond the basic instructions:

HEADLINE SIDEBARS

Sidebars contain special tips, warnings, and extra facts that are related to the text where they are found. They provide a way for the author to communicate with you while preserving the natural flow of information for the concepts you are learning in the normal text. They often emphasize important topics, so you might find them very helpful.

SHOP TALK

SHOP TALK

In most of the chapters, the author uses Shop Talks to share her personal experiences as they relate to the chapter. These elements often contain opinions or preferences; the rest of the book is confined strictly to the facts. The author's opinions or preferences might not always apply to your situation, so keep that in mind when you read a Shop Talk.

Source Code for This Book

The associated source code files described in this book are available on the Sams Web site at `http://www.samspublishing.com`. Enter this book's ISBN (without the hyphens) in the Search box and click Search. When the book's title is displayed, click the title to go to a page where you can download the code.

This is a great time to be a C++ programmer. *Microsoft Visual C++ .NET 2003 Kick Start* is designed to get you using this powerful tool to its full potential. There are things we C++ programmers can do that C# and VB.NET programmers just cannot do. I want you to find a niche for your language skills in your development work, and a way to take advantage of the power of C++ in both the managed and unmanaged worlds. Most importantly, I want you to see how C++ stands alone as the language of choice when you want to bridge those worlds.

I'm very interested in hearing your comments about *Microsoft Visual C++ .NET 2003 Kick Start*. You are welcome to contact me at `kate@gregcons.com`. I also run a Web site for this book at `www.visualc-kickstart.com`. You'll find updates, downloads, and other useful resources there.

C++, Visual C++, and Managed C++: What's the Difference?

Differences Between Visual C++ and C++

C++ is a language, and Visual C++ is a product. The language itself was developed in the early '80s, and C++ compilers have been for sale since about 1985. Visual C++ made its debut in 1993, and has had many major releases since that time. In the late '90s a standard was developed for the C++ language, and the latest release of Visual C++ (in Visual Studio .NET 2003) includes a top-notch C++ compiler that is 98% compliant to that standard, the most compliant version ever.

The Visual C++ Suite of Tools

Of course, Visual C++ is much more than just a compiler. In addition to a compiler, Visual C++ includes

- Two very powerful C++-only class libraries (MFC and ATL).

- An implementation of the Standard Template Library, STL, part of standard C++.

- A debugger that includes a variety of productivity-boosting features to help you understand what your application is doing, and why.

8

CHAPTER 1   C++, Visual C++, and Managed C++: What's the Difference?

- An integrated development environment that enables you to edit, compile, and debug your code all from the same application.

- A suite of wizards and designers that generates code for common application types, or simplifies coding by using dialog boxes like the properties window to automatically modify your code.

- The .NET Framework SDK, which includes another set of class libraries (the .NET Base Class Libraries, ASP.NET, ADO.NET, and Windows Forms) along with command-line compilers and utilities for .NET development.

Visual C++ is available in several editions, all at different prices. The umbrella product, Visual Studio, comes with Visual C++ as well as Visual Basic, Visual C# .NET, and other tools. Visual Studio comes in Professional, Enterprise Developer, and Enterprise Architect versions, each of which contains the three mainstream languages (C++, VB, and C#). Visual C++ .NET Standard Edition comes with only Visual C++—no VB or C# compilers. In addition, there is an Academic edition and evaluation versions are occasionally available.

"I'M A VISUAL C++ PROGRAMMER"— SO WHAT?

For years, if someone told you "I'm a Visual C++ programmer," it meant that person knew C++, had learned the MFC class library (and perhaps also the ATL template library), was familiar with the concepts underlying Windows programming and the Windows API, and knew how to use Visual C++ to write MFC and ATL applications for Windows, or for class libraries and components.

Those skills don't always translate well to the .NET way of building applications and libraries. A Visual C++ .NET programmer building managed applications has more in common with a Visual Basic .NET programmer or a C# programmer than a Visual C++ 6 programmer. To use Visual C++ .NET to build applications for the .NET Framework, you need to understand the concepts behind .NET, and learn an integrated development environment that's quite different from Visual C++ 6. That's what this book is here to help you learn.

This book assumes you're working with the Professional Edition. If a demonstrated feature is from the Enterprise or Enterprise Architect edition, that detail is mentioned.

The first release of Visual C++ that could produce managed code and target the .NET Common Language Runtime was named Visual C++ .NET, and was part of Visual Studio .NET, released in the spring of 2002. Since then, the new release of those products includes the moniker 2003; for example, Visual C++ .NET 2003. The older product has been renamed Visual C++ .NET 2002, part of Visual Studio .NET 2002. The changes between the 2002 and 2003 versions are relatively minor in most of the .NET languages, but they're quite dramatic in Visual C++. This book covers the 2003 product. The architectural concepts of .NET and the description of the class libraries included in the .NET Framework are applicable if you're using the 2002 product, but the menu choices, wizards, code generators, and the like are quite different in the 2003 release.

The Managed Extensions to C++

It's long been a convention among C++ compiler developers that any identifier that starts with an underscore belongs to the compiler. Don't start your variable or function names with an underscore, and you'll never accidentally overwrite something the compiler was using. A similar convention is to use double underscores at the start of identifiers and keywords that are *compiler-specific* (implemented by one compiler vendor but not by others). This reminds developers who use these features that the work they are doing would not compile or run properly if it were built with a different compiler.

Although all compilers have a handful of compiler-specific keywords, these extensions haven't really been important to developers in the past. Millions of lines of code have been written that didn't knowingly use compiler-specific code. (The qualifier knowingly applies because compilers vary dramatically in their standards compliance, and code that compiles and works under one compiler might behave quite differently under another.) Developers have chosen C++ development tools based on criteria like the strength of the class library, or the ease of use of the integrated editor, not the collection of extension keywords offered by the compiler itself.

With the introduction of Visual C++ .NET in 2002, that situation changed. Continuing in Visual C++ .NET 2003, developers use a series of extension keywords (known as the Managed Extensions to C++) to generate code that targets the .NET Framework, also called *managed code*. One of the requirements for the team developing Visual C++ .NET was that existing code must compile and run without error—whether the code now ran in the framework or not. Therefore, the development team could not change the meaning or behavior of any existing keywords. The "escape hatch" of compiler-specific extensions enabled the team to meet this requirement.

In a printed book, it can be hard to spot the double underscores. Can you see the difference between __gc and _gc? Could you see it if they didn't appear side by side? There are a lot more leading double underscores in this book's sample code than leading single underscores, so if you're not sure, it's probably a double underscore.

If you learned C++ with a compiler other than Visual C++, you might be concerned that you have another language to learn—you don't. The keywords, syntax, brace brackets, semi-colons, and other delights of C++ are exactly the same in Visual C++. What's different are the libraries, wizards, and integrated development environment that combine to make you a more productive programmer no matter what kind of application you're creating.

Applications That Run Directly Under Windows

When you develop an application using Visual C++ .NET 2002 or 2003, it will be either a managed or unmanaged application. In either case, it will be built to run on a Windows machine.

10

CHAPTER 1   C++, Visual C++, and Managed C++: What's the Difference?

An unmanaged application runs directly under Windows. Even a console application, which runs in a command prompt, runs under Windows. The compiled executable from Visual C++ cannot be executed on a non-Windows machine, although the code itself might be portable. The source code for a console application can be moved to a non-Windows machine and recompiled with a compiler for that machine. That source code would run, assuming it didn't use any Microsoft-specific libraries such as MFC or ATL, did not attempt to load any DLLs or use any COM components, and avoided compiler-specific extensions. Of course, any kind of Windows application other than a console application is utterly nonportable.

A managed application runs in the .NET runtime. As of mid-2003, no versions of the .NET runtime are generally available for platforms other than Windows. A demonstration/academic research version of a subset of the .NET Framework called *Rotor* runs on at least one flavor of UNIX (FreeBSD) and the Mac. It doesn't include ASP.NET or Web Services, Windows Forms, ADO.NET, or anything Windows-specific such as Registry access. The license agreement prohibits its use for commercial purposes. Another project for implementing the .NET Framework on a non-Windows platform is *Mono*, which targets Linux and other UNIX flavors. The work is partially complete and a completion date has not been announced.

Because Visual C++ is itself a Windows application, it's a good bet that you'll be using it to create Windows applications. That's the assumption throughout this book.

Managed and Unmanaged Code

A compiler that emits unmanaged code compiles your source to machine code, which then just runs under Windows. A compiler that emits managed code does not compile your source to machine code, but rather to Intermediate Language (IL). Managed code runs in the Common Language Runtime, not directly on Windows.

When you build a managed application, your code is compiled to IL in a file called an *assembly*, along with metadata that describes the classes, methods, and attributes (such as security requirements) of the code you've created. This assembly is the one-stop-shopping unit of deployment in the .NET world. You copy it to another server to deploy the assembly there— and often that copying is the only step required in the deployment.

Managed code runs in the Common Language Runtime. The runtime offers a wide variety of services to your running code. In the usual course of events, it first loads and verifies the assembly to make sure the IL is OK. Then, just in time, as methods are called, the runtime arranges for them to be compiled to machine code suitable for the machine the assembly is running on, and caches this machine code to be used the next time the method is called. (This is called Just In Time, or JIT compiling, or often just *jitting*.)

As the assembly runs, the runtime continues to provide services such as security, memory management, threading, and the like. The application is *managed* by the runtime. By contrast, unmanaged code runs under Windows as it always has.

Compilers that emit unmanaged code include

- Visual C++ 6 and earlier

- Visual Basic 6 and earlier

- Any C++ compiler for Windows other than Visual C++ .NET

- Visual C++ .NET 2002 and 2003

Compilers that emit managed code include

- Visual C# .NET 2002 and 2003

- Visual Basic .NET 2002 and 2003

- Other compilers for Visual Studio that meet the Common Language specification

- Visual C++ .NET 2002 and 2003

Notice anything unusual about the two lists? Visual C++ .NET 2002 and 2003 are on both of them—you have a choice of whether you build a managed or an unmanaged application. Visual C++ .NET is the only language provided with Visual Studio .NET that can emit either managed or unmanaged code and can even combine them within a single application.

Advantages of Managed Code

Managed code is, in many ways, a huge improvement over unmanaged code. The services the runtime offers to running code include

- Memory management

- Security

- Threading

- Exceptions

- Interoperability between languages

- Interoperability to and from COM

- Interoperability to old-style DLLs

Interoperability, as provided by the runtime, includes parameter marshalling, type conversions, and even translating COM HRESULTs into exceptions.

One of the astonishing things Visual C++ .NET can do is to take old C++ code, written before the .NET Framework was invented, and compile it to managed code. The classes and objects used in that code will all be unmanaged data, but the code will compile to IL and run in the

12

CHAPTER 1   C++, Visual C++, and Managed C++: What's the Difference?

runtime. If this newly managed code calls methods and functions of unmanaged DLLs or LIBs, no problem! As the C++ Dev Team says, "It Just Works"—and it does.

When you build your application as managed code, you have easy access to all the .NET class libraries, to components written in Visual Basic .NET or C#, and to both managed and unmanaged C++ code. You can leverage all this code for maximum productivity, and enjoy all the latest functionality provided in the libraries.

Advantages of Unmanaged Code

Unmanaged code doesn't run in the runtime, it just runs under Windows. That means the computers on which your application are installed don't need the .NET Framework. During the first few years of .NET, you won't be able to count on every Windows machine having the framework. Starting with Windows Server 2003, every new release of Windows will include the framework, and it's also available as a Windows Update, so everyone who keeps up to date will have it. But there's a large segment of the population who never install Windows Updates or upgrade their operating systems. Code aimed at those users should be unmanaged code, or should be shipped on a CD with an install program that installs the framework automatically.

What if the code you're writing is a library of sorts, designed to be called from older unmanaged code as well as new managed code? You could write it as a .NET object and wrap it so it's exposed as a COM component. That would allow your unmanaged code to access it easily, but at a slight performance cost. Alternatively, you could write it as an unmanaged COM component or an unmanaged DLL, and let the new managed code pay the small performance cost for accessing it. Your decision will probably be based on which of the applications that need to use your code are more performance sensitive. For example, if one application is used by hundreds of clients throughout the day, whereas the other is used by one administrator a few times a week, impose the performance penalty on the administrator's application and ensure the users have the fastest experience possible. That means writing your library as managed if the user application is managed, or unmanaged if the user application is unmanaged. Either way, interoperability will be possible; it's just a matter of deciding who pays the performance penalty.

Performance Considerations

Which is faster, managed or unmanaged code? The answer is a resounding "it depends." In the simplest case—code that doesn't call out to any other code—unmanaged is usually faster. You can test this yourself by writing a simple unmanaged console application, and then writing the same main() as a managed console application. Which version runs faster depends on exactly what the code does. The runtime has more "checks and balances," which can impose some performance penalties, and when you compile to IL you cannot take advantage of certain compiler switches that produced optimized machine code (for example, to take advantage of a particular CPU chip), so you would expect the managed code to always be slower. But once in a while, it's quicker!

Here's an example—an entire application in unmanaged C++:

```
// LegacyArithmetic.cpp : Defines the entry point for the console application.
//

#include "stdafx.h"
#include <iostream>
using namespace std;

#include <atltime.h>

class ArithmeticClass
{
public:
    double Add( double num1,  double num2);
};

double ArithmeticClass::Add(double num1, double num2)
{
    return num1+ num2;
}

int _tmain(void)
{
    ArithmeticClass arith;
    double answer ;

    CTime start = CTime::GetCurrentTime();

    for (long i=0;i<10000000;i++)
        answer = arith.Add(1.1,2.3);

    CTime stop = CTime::GetCurrentTime();
    CTimeSpan span = stop - start;
    cout << "It took " << span.GetTotalSeconds() << " seconds" << endl;
    return 0;
}
```

14

CHAPTER 1 C++, Visual C++, and Managed C++: What's the Difference?

Here's the same application as managed C++:

```cpp
// This is the main project file for VC++ application project
// generated using an Application Wizard.

#include "stdafx.h"

#include <tchar.h>
using namespace System;

class ArithmeticClass
{
public:
        double Add( double num1,  double num2);
};
double ArithmeticClass::Add(double num1, double num2)
{
    return num1+ num2;
}
// This is the entry point for this application
int _tmain(void)
{
    double answer;
    ArithmeticClass arith;
    DateTime start = DateTime::get_Now();

    for (long i=0;i<10000000;i++)
        answer = arith.Add(4.7,3.2);

    DateTime stop = DateTime::get_Now();
    TimeSpan span = stop - start;
    Console::Write("It took " );
    Console::Write(span.TotalSeconds);
    Console::WriteLine(" seconds");
    return 0;
}
```

These applications are presented in their entirety primarily to demonstrate a way of determining how long code takes to run, and partly to show how many times you'll have to repeat a loop to get a measurable time difference. Unless you're writing some computationally expensive code, you might never see a difference between managed and unmanaged C++. However, just as a point of interest, when you run these two applications the managed code runs measurably quicker, every time. The only difference between the two applications is that the unmanaged application uses CTime (from MFC) to time itself and the managed application uses DateTime (from the System namespace) to time itself.

If your code calls out to unmanaged code, going through COM Interop or PInvoke (the only options available to VB and C# programmers) will impose a performance penalty. But calling out to that code using "It Just Works" is as fast as a direct call.

Bottom line? Your decision shouldn't be based on a prejudice about speed. If you can't count on having the framework on the target machine, write your code as unmanaged. If your code will be called from both managed and unmanaged, and the unmanaged calling code is more performance sensitive, write your code as unmanaged. Otherwise, write it as managed. When it's complete, if you have a performance issue, consider compiling portions of it as unmanaged and test to see whether that improves performance.

Managed and Unmanaged Data

When you are writing a unmanaged application, you have only unmanaged data. When you write a managed application in Visual Basic or C#, you will have only managed data. But when you write a managed C++ application, you control whether your data is managed or unmanaged. There are benefits to managed data, but to gain those benefits you have to accept some restrictions.

Unmanaged Data

This term is just a way to describe the way data has always been handled in C++ programming. You can invent a class:

```
class ArithmeticClass
{
public:
    double Add( double num1,  double num2);
};
```

You can create an instance of your class on the stack and use it, like this:

```
ArithmeticClass arith;
arith.Add(2,2);
```

Or you can create an instance on the heap, and use it through a pointer:

```
ArithmeticClass* pArith = new ArithmeticClass();
pArith->Add(2,2);
```

16

CHAPTER 1 C++, Visual C++, and Managed C++: What's the Difference?

When the flow of control leaves the block in which the stack variable was declared, the class' destructor runs and the memory becomes available on the stack again. The heap variable must be explicitly cleared away:

```
delete pArith;
```

And this, of course, is the rub. Memory management is your job in classic C++. What you create with new you must clean up with delete. If you forget, you can suffer a memory leak.

What's more, when you use an unmanaged pointer, you can make all kinds of mistakes that overwrite other memory or otherwise corrupt your application. When your data is unmanaged, it's up to you to manage it. That can be a lot of work, and if you mess up, you might create a subtle bug that's hard to find.

Garbage-Collected Classes

If you create a class as a garbage-collected class, the runtime will manage the memory for you. In exchange, you give up the capability to create an instance on the stack, and you have to follow some rules when designing your class.

You set garbage collection class-by-class, not object-by-object. When you define the class, include the __gc keyword, like this:

```
__gc class Sample
{
private:
    double number;
public:
    Sample( double num): number(num){};
};
```

Having defined your class in this way, you cannot create instances on the stack any more. If you do, this compiler error results:

```
error C3149: 'Sample' : illegal use of managed type 'Sample';
➥did you forget a '*'?
```

Instead, you can only allocate instances of a garbage-collected on the heap, with new. For example

```
Sample* s = new Sample(3.2);
```

When you're finished with this instance, just ignore it. When the pointer goes out of scope, the instance will be eligible for cleanup by the garbage collector. If you do try to delete this instance, you'll get a compiler error:

```
error C3841: illegal delete expression: managed type 'Sample'
➥does not have a destructor defined
```

Just leave the pointer alone and let the runtime manage your memory. It will be cleaned up eventually.

SHOP TALK

DETERMINISTIC DESTRUCTION

One of the hallmarks of a garbage-collected runtime is that you don't know when an object in memory will be cleaned up. If the application uses a lot of memory and is constantly allocating more, anything that's eligible to be cleaned up will be destructed quickly. In an application that doesn't use much memory and runs for a long long time, it might be hours or days before an object is cleaned up.

C++ programmers are used to putting clean-up code in the destructor. They know when the destructor will run: when the object goes out of scope or when they use the delete operator on the pointer. This is called *deterministic destruction*, because programmers know when the destructor will run. But when you use managed data, you have no idea when the destructor will execute, which is called *indeterministic destruction*. In this case, having clean-up code is a bad idea. For example, if the destructor closes a file, it will sit open until the destructor runs—and that might be a really long time.

I spent quite a few nights up late with friends arguing about deterministic destruction. Finally, I came to an opinion. If a managed class holds only memory—things you would normally clean up with delete—don't write a destructor and don't worry about destruction, deterministic or otherwise. If the class holds a non-memory resource (an open file, a database connection, a resource lock of some kind, or anything else that isn't memory and therefore isn't garbage collected), don't use a destructor either—implement the Dispose pattern. The heart of this pattern is a method called Dispose that cleans up the non-memory resource (closes a file, for example). Code that creates instances of your class should call the Dispose method when it's through with the instance. You can write a destructor as a sort of backup plan in case client code forgets to dispose your object.

Making your class a garbage-collected class is not always as simple as adding the __gc keyword to the definition. There are some restrictions about the way you can define your class if you want it to be garbage-collected, and some restrictions on the way you use it, too.

18

CHAPTER 1   C++, Visual C++, and Managed C++: What's the Difference?

Inheritance Restrictions

When you write an unmanaged class, you can inherit from any kind of base class at all, or no base class if you prefer. Garbage-collected classes don't have quite the same freedom. Specifically, a garbage-collected class cannot inherit from an unmanaged class.

Consider this pair of classes:

```
class A
{
protected:
    int a;
};


__gc class Sample: public A
{
public:
    Sample(int x) : a(x) {}
};
```

This looks like perfectly good C++. And it would be, if it weren't for that __gc extension keyword in the definition of Sample. If you type this code and try to compile it, you'll be told

```
error C3253: 'A' : a managed class cannot derive from an unmanaged class
```

To fix the problem, make the base class managed if possible, or leave the derived class unmanaged.

Single Inheritance

Not only must garbage-collected classes inherit only from other garbage-collected classes, but they also can't use multiple inheritance. Consider this variant on the Sample class shown earlier:

```
__gc class A
{
protected:
    int a;
};


__gc class B
{
protected:
    int b;
};
```

```
__gc class Sample: public A, public B
{
public:
    Sample(int x, int y) : a(x), b(y) {}
};
```

Compiling these classes produces this error:

```
error C2890: 'Sample' : managed class can only have one non-interface superclass
```

You can, if you want, inherit from as many managed interfaces as you need to, but you can't use traditional multiple inheritance. Most C++ programmers don't use multiple inheritance. If you're such a programmer, it's no great loss to give it up. If you have working code that uses multiple inheritance, it's best to leave it as unmanaged and access it from new managed code. You'll see how to do that later in this book.

Additional Restrictions on Garbage-Collected Classes

Garbage-collected classes have some other restrictions:

- You cannot use the `friend` keyword to give another class access to the private members of a managed class.

- No member variable of the class can be an instance of an unmanaged class (unless all the member functions of the unmanaged class are static).

- You cannot override operator & or operator new.

- You cannot implement a copy constructor.

At first glance, these might seem restrictive. But remember that the reason you usually write a copy constructor is that your destructor does something destructive, such as freeing memory. A garbage-collected class probably has no destructor at all, and therefore has no need for a specialized copy constructor.

Value Classes

Many programmers feel uncomfortable when they are told they cannot create instances of a garbage-collected class on the stack. There are a number of advantages, in "classic" C++, to creating an object on the stack:

- The object is destructed for you when it goes out of scope.

- The overhead of allocating on the stack is slightly less than allocating on the heap.

- The heap can get fragmented (and therefore you will have a performance hit) if you allocate and free a lot of short-lived objects.

20

CHAPTER 1   C++, Visual C++, and Managed C++: What's the Difference?

In managed C++ (in other words, C++ with Managed Extensions), the garbage collector takes care of destructing the object for you. It can also defragment the heap. The garbage collector introduces overhead of its own, of course, and the allocation cost difference between the stack and the heap remains. So, for certain kinds of objects, it might be a better choice to use a value class rather than a garbage-collected class.

The fundamental types, such as `int`, are referred to as *value types*, because they are allocated on the stack. You can define a simple class of yours to be a value class. You can also do the same for a `struct`. If your class mainly exists to hold a few small member variables, and doesn't have a complicated lifetime, it's a good candidate for a value class.

Here is `Sample` once again as a value class:

```
__value class Sample
{
public:
    int a;
    int b;
    Sample(int x, int y) : a(x),b(y) {}
};
```

To create and use an instance of `Sample`, you must allocate it on the stack, not the heap:

```
Sample s(2,4);
s.Report();
```

These value classes are still managed, but they're not garbage-collected. The restrictions on value classes are

- You cannot use the `friend` keyword to give another class access to the private members of a managed class.

- No member variable of the class can be an instance of an unmanaged class (unless all the member functions of the unmanaged class are static).

- You cannot implement a copy constructor.

- A value class cannot inherit from a garbage-collected class, or another value class, or an unmanaged class. It can inherit from any number of managed interfaces.

- A value class cannot have virtual methods other than those it inherits (and possibly overrides) from `System::ValueType`.

- No class can inherit from a value class.

- A value class cannot be labeled abstract with the `__abstract` keyword.

The best candidates for value classes are small classes whose objects don't exist for long and aren't passed around from method to method (thus creating a lot of references to them in different pieces of code).

Another advantage of value classes is that instances are essentially never uninitialized. When you allocate an instance of Sample on the stack, you can pass parameters to the constructor. But if you do not, the member variables are initialized to zero for you. This is true even if you wrote a constructor that takes arguments, and didn't write a constructor that doesn't take arguments. Look at these two lines of code:

STACK AND HEAP

If you've been reading or hearing about Visual Studio.NET already, you might have heard that structs are value types and classes are reference types, or that structs are on the stack and objects are on the heap. Those statements apply to C#. In C++, you're in charge—you can allocate instances of value types (classes or structs) on the stack and instances of garbage-collected types (classes or structs) on the heap.

```
Sample s2;
s2.Report();
```

When this code runs, it will report

```
a is 0 and b is 0
```

Because the Sample class is managed, the members are initialized automatically.

Pinning and Boxing

The class libraries that come with the .NET Framework are terrific—they provide functionality every application needs. It's natural to use them from your managed C++ applications. One thing you need to know: The methods in these classes are expecting pointers to garbage-collected objects, not the unmanaged data your application might be using. What's more, when you use older libraries, the methods are expecting instances or pointers to instances of unmanaged variables, not instances of managed classes or member variables of those managed instances. When you mix managed and unmanaged data, you need to use two new .NET concepts: boxing and pinning.

Boxing a Fundamental Type

If you try to pass a piece of unmanaged data to a method that is expecting managed data, the compiler will reject your attempt. Consider this fragment of code:

```
int i = 3;
System::Console::Write("i is ");
System::Console::WriteLine(i);
```

22

CHAPTER 1   C++, Visual C++, and Managed C++: What's the Difference?

Simple as it looks, this code won't compile. The error message is

```
error C2665: 'System::Console::WriteLine' : none of the 18 overloads can
➥convert parameter 2 from type 'int'
        could be 'void System::Console::WriteLine
➥(System::String __gc *,System::Object __gc *)'
```

You need to pass a pointer to a garbage-collected object to the WriteLine method. The way you get a pointer to a garbage-collected object is to use the __box extension, like this:

```
System::Console::WriteLine(__box(i));
```

This is referred to as *boxing* the integer, and is a convenient way to use framework methods even from an application that has some unmanaged data.

Pinning a Pointer

Sometimes your problem is the other way around. You have a function, already written, that expects a pointer of some sort. If this is legacy code, it doesn't expect a pointer that can move around; it expects a classic pointer to an unmanaged object. Even a pointer to an integer member variable of a managed object can be moved by the garbage collector when it moves the entire instance of the object.

Consider this simple managed class, another variation on Sample used throughout this chapter:

```
__gc class Sample
{
public:
    int a;
    int b;
    Sample(int x, int y) : a(x), b(y) {}
};
```

You might argue about whether it's a good idea for the member variables a and b to be public, but it makes this code simpler to do so. Consider this simple function, perhaps one that was written in an earlier version of Visual C++:

```
void Equalize(int* a, int* b)
{
    int avg = (*a + *b)/2 ;
    *a = avg;
    *b = avg;
}
```

Say that you want to use this `Equalize()` function on the two member variables of an instance of this `Sample` class:

```
Sample* s = new Sample(2,4);
Equalize(&(s->a),&(s->b));
```

This code won't compile. The error is

```
error C2664: 'Equalize' : cannot convert parameter 1 from 'int __gc *' to 'int *'
        Cannot convert a managed type to an unmanaged type
```

Although they are both pointers, the pointer to a garbage-collected type cannot be converted to a pointer to an unmanaged type. What you can do is *pin* the pointer. This creates another pointer you can pass to the function, and ensures that the garbage collector will not move the instance (in this case, s) for the life of the pinned pointer. Here's how it's done:

```
int __pin* pa = &(s->a);
int __pin* pb = &(s->b);
Equalize(pa,pb);
```

The two new pointers, pa and pb, are pointers to unmanaged types, so they can be passed to `Equalize()`. They point to the location in memory where the member variables of s are kept, and the garbage collector will not move (unpin) the instance, s, until pa and pb go out of scope. You can unpin the instance sooner by deliberately setting pa and pb to 0, a null pointer, like this:

```
pa=0;
pb=0;
```

Boxing unmanaged data into temporary managed instances, and pinning managed data to obtain a pointer to unmanaged data, are both ways to deal with differences between the managed and the unmanaged world. When you remember that you have these extensions available to you, the task of mixing old and new programming techniques and libraries becomes much simpler.

Properties

Managed classes have one other feature you might want to use: properties. You have probably written classes like this:

```
class Employee
{
private:
    int salary; //dollars
```

24

CHAPTER 1 C++, Visual C++, and Managed C++: What's the Difference?

```
   // remaining member variables
public:
   int getSalary() {return salary;}
   void setSalary(int s)
      {salary = s;}
   // remaining public methods
};
```

Even with slightly more complicated code for `setSalary()`, with some kind of error checking, the basic concept is the same—it's a private variable with public `get` and `set` functions. Not every variable is treated like this, of course: A bank balance, for example, shouldn't be settable from outside, but should instead be changed by various business operations such as deposits and withdrawals. But many classes follow this "get and set" paradigm.

The benefit to this, of course, is encapsulation. You are free to add error checking to either the `get` or the `set` method after your system is partially built or in a follow-on phase. You can even change the type of the variable and simply adjust the code to reflect the change. Encapsulation is a great thing, and no wise programmer will give it up.

The downside is the way your code looks when you're using `get` and `set` functions. If you have a pointer to an instance of the `Employee` class, e, and you want to give that employee a $5000.00 raise, here's the code:

```
e->setSalary(e->getSalary() + 5000);
```

That works, but it's not exactly pretty. But in the .NET Framework, you can have your cake and eat it too. You just have to change your definition of `Employee` slightly (the changes are shown in bold):

```
__gc class Employee
{
private:
   int salary; //dollars
   // remaining member variables
public:
   __property int get_Salary()
      {return salary;}
   __property void set_Salary(int s)
      {salary = s;}
   // remaining public methods
};
```

Now the class has a `Salary` property. It's directly tied to the `salary` member variable, but there's no requirement that it should be, and in fact the name of the property cannot be exactly the same as the name of a member variable, which is why in the `Employee` class, the property name (which appears after the get_ and set_ of the function names) is `Salary` and the member variable is `salary`.

To use the property, you write code that treats it like a public member variable:

```
e->Salary = 10000;
e->Salary = e->Salary + 5000;
```

You can use any of the familiar C++ operators with a property:

```
e->Salary += 5000;
```

Yet behind the scenes, your `get` and `set` functions, with all their attendant error checking, are being called. You have all the benefits of encapsulation, yet your code is as easy to read as if all your member variables were public.

In Brief

- Visual C++ is an integrated development environment that includes a compiler, editor, debugger, and other tools.

- Applications written in standard C++ will compile in Visual C++.

- Managed applications written in Visual C++ .NET make extensive use of language extensions, which are keywords starting with double underscores.

- Developers can create garbage-collected classes in Visual C++ if the classes meet a list of restrictions, and save the trouble of managing memory allocated for those classes.

- Developers can create unmanaged classes if that is preferable.

- Managed classes can expose properties that make code simpler to read and to write while retaining the benefits of encapsulation.

Creating Test Harnesses and Starter Applications

Application Types You Can Create with Visual C++

Visual C++ .NET comes with a package of wizards that generate starting code for a wide variety of applications, both managed and unmanaged. A useful way to categorize these applications is by their user interface:

- Console applications run in a command prompt and are text-only, reading from the keyboard and writing to the screen.

- Windows applications are graphical, using the mouse and keyboard and generally using well-known Windows controls such as buttons, text boxes, drop-down boxes, and so on.

- Web applications run on a Web server when a particular URL is loaded, and send HTML to a waiting browser.

- Services are applications that run in the background and respond to requests, but do not have any visual user interface.

- Class libraries are collections of code that can be called by other code.

- Other wizards create project types that are typically used by developers making unusual types of applications by hand or porting applications from another platform.

Table 2.1 categorizes the applications that Visual C++ .NET 2003 will create for you.

TABLE 2.1
Application Types in Visual C++

USER INTERFACE	UNMANAGED	MANAGED
Console	Win32 Console Project	Console Application (.NET)
Windows	MFC Application	Windows Forms Application (.NET)
Web	ATL Server Project, MFC ISPAPI Extension DLL	
Service	ATL Server Web Service	ASP.NET Web Service, Windows Service (.NET)
Class Library	ATL Project, Extended Stored Procedure DLL, MFC ActiveX Control, MFC DLL	Class Library (.NET), Windows Control Library (.NET)
Other	Custom Wizard, Makefile Project, Win32 Project	Empty Project (.NET)

If you took "Intro to C++" at college or were sent on a one-week C++ course, you almost certainly wrote console applications. These applications use the iostream library (cin and cout, for example) to write characters (not graphics) to the screen and read them from the keyboard. They generally can't interact with the mouse. Although this might seem hopelessly out of date, console applications serve a very useful purpose as test harnesses, discussed in the next section. Managed console applications can use the System::Console class (with methods ReadLine, WriteLine, and the like) rather than the iostream library, and they need the .NET Framework installed on the machine where they will run.

The excitement over .NET connected applications, built on Web Services or leveraging the power of ASP.NET, has obscured the very real role of Windows applications in the lives of most computer users. Think about the products you use every day: Word, Excel, even Notepad—they're all Windows applications. They can read from and write to your local hard drive, communicate with local printers, and they are probably the workhorses of your day. Visual C++ .NET 2003 can be used to create Windows applications that require the .NET Framework to run, as you'll see in Chapter 4, "Building Simple User Interfaces with Windows Forms." Alternatively, you can build unmanaged Windows applications that run directly under Windows using the MFC library.

Web applications are accessed through a browser. When the Web server is asked for a specific page or URL, it runs your code to generate the HTML that is returned to the browser. Unmanaged Web applications, which run through ISAPI or through ATL Server, are very high-performance solutions to specific problems. Your code must manually generate any output HTML, so typically the user interface is not visually complex, although of course you can generate any HTML you want. Developers who use VB.NET or C# can create ASP.NET applications for a rich user experience with code that runs on the Web server, but that option is not available to Visual C++ .NET 2003 developers.

Services generally don't have a user interface. They can start when the computer starts—even if no one has logged in—and are controlled from the Services section of Computer Management. They are typically used by other applications or to interact with the operating system. Chapter 12, "Writing a Windows Service," has more details. Web Services are similar to services but, like Web applications, respond to requests directed to a Web server. Unmanaged Web Services can be created with the ATL Server and managed Web Services can be created with ASP.NET. Managed Web services don't require the framework on machines that use the service, but they do require it on the Web server. Learn more about managed Web Services in Chapter 10, "Writing and Consuming a Web Service."

Class libraries are also destined to be called by other applications. Most large applications are separated into layers or *tiers*, and each of these layers is typically implemented as a class library, except for the user interface layer which is a Windows or Web application. As a result, many developers spend more time developing class libraries than any other kind of application. Visual C++ developers can create unmanaged DLLs, unmanaged COM components, and .NET class libraries. Chapter 5, "Writing a Class Library in Unmanaged C++," discusses some of the architectural concepts involved in designing class libraries and the layers of your application for maximum interoperability. Chapter 6, "Writing a Class Library in Managed C++," describes how simple it is to write code that can be used from any .NET language. Chapter 7, "Building DLLs in Unmanaged C++," and Chapter 8, "Writing COM Components In C++," describe two ways of making a unit of code available to both the managed and unmanaged world, while working in unmanaged C++.

What Is a Test Harness?

Because writing class libraries is a big part of any developer's job, it follows that testing class libraries is a big part of your job, too. Testing an application, whether it's a Windows application or a Web application, is relatively straightforward—you run it, and experiment with various paths through the application in terms of which buttons you click, or which fields you fill out or leave blank. But how do you test a class library, or a service, or even a single class that encapsulates an important business process or set of rules?

Console applications are perfect for this kind of testing. They are quick to write, and you don't need a fancy user interface. In fact, it's easy to capture the output of a console application by redirecting it to a file. This enables you to save the results of test after test and compare them. Windows programmers aren't always familiar with the techniques for interacting with users without using controls, but they're quick to learn and definitely useful.

A test harness for working with a single class is the simplest to write. Typically it should perform the following steps:

- Create an instance of the class. If there are several constructors, create several instances.

- Use any `Display()` or `Report()` method of the object to show its contents after creation.

- Exercise each method and property of the class, and display the results of each call or the contents of the object after the call.

- If methods must be called in the right order, have some code that calls them in the right order and also some code that calls them in the wrong order, to confirm that error-checking code works.

- If the methods throw exceptions, set up calls that will fail and surround them with try and catch blocks to prove that the correct exceptions are thrown.

- If you have written a copy constructor or conversion operator for the class, write code that will use them and display the contents of all affected objects to demonstrate successful copying or conversion.

- If the object has a clean-up method such as Dispose(), call it and prove it was called.

- If the object is not garbage-collected, let it go out of scope or delete it to prove that the destructor works correctly.

It's a good idea to have lots of output statements sprinkled throughout this code, so that output might look something like this:

```
Creating account1, default constructor
Account # 123, Balance $0.00
Creating account2, passing 50
Account #124, Balance $50.00
Deposit 100 to account1
Account #124, Balance $100.00
```

This sort of output demonstrates which parts of your code are working and serves as an excellent record of the development process. Generally, all of the values are hard-coded so that you can run the whole thing without having to interact with it, but some people write test harnesses that prompt for values or even for which methods to exercise.

When your test harness is testing a component or a layer, your tests will typically interact either with a single bridging class that provides access to the functionality of the component or layer, or with each of the classes in the component or layer. This can make the harness quite long, but a systematic test of all your functionality is well worth doing, so take the time.

Creating an Unmanaged C++ Application

The best way to test an unmanaged class is with an unmanaged test harness. You'll need to connect the new application with the class you're testing: Either bring copies of both the header file and the implementation file into the test solution, or add the test harness to the solution in which you are building the class. (If you're building a COM component or DLL, your test harness will typically be a separate solution because you will be testing whether your component is properly registered and available from another application.)

This chapter shows you how to make an unmanaged console application that you can use to write C++ programs without needing to know anything about Windows, the Web, or the .NET Framework. Later, when you've written a class, a class library, or a component, you can put your ability to write console application to good use by writing a test harness for your reusable code.

To build a console application that will run on a computer without the .NET Framework installed, follow these steps:

1. Open Visual Studio .NET 2003.

2. On the Start Page, click New Project. If the Start Page isn't visible, choose File, New, Project.

3. Select the Visual C++ Projects folder on the left and Win32 Console Project on the right.

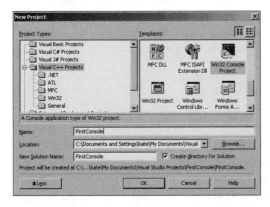

FIGURE 2.1   Creating a Win32 Console Project called FirstConsole.

FIGURE 2.2   The console application runs in a command prompt and writes characters to the screen.

4. Enter FirstConsole as the project name (the dialog box should resemble Figure 2.1) and click OK.

5. Click Finish from the wizard that appears.

The wizard generates the skeleton of an unmanaged C++ application. After the #include statement that was generated, add these lines:

```
#include <iostream>
using namespace std;
```

Before the return statement that was generated, add this line:

```
cout << "Hello from the console" << endl;
```

Build the project by choosing Build, Build Solution. Run it by choosing Debug, Start without Debugging. You should see output like Figure 2.2.

Now that you know how to create, compile, and run a simple console application in unmanaged C++, you can do a tremendous amount of programming. You can define classes, and then write code to create instances of the class and call their methods. You can write and test hundreds of thousands of lines of code in this way, just by adding lines to the `main` function (defined as `_tmain` in Visual C++) that is generated for you when you create a Win32 console project.

These applications don't require the .NET Framework and can't use the functionality of the .NET Base Class Libraries. They can use libraries, such as MFC and ATL, that don't require the framework. They can also use the implementation of the Standard Template Library (STL) that comes with Visual C++. In addition there are hundreds of third-party libraries, most of them free, that manipulate images or equations or molecular simulations while drawing on the power of C++. Your unmanaged C++ code can leverage these libraries to reduce your coding effort dramatically.

Testing an Unmanaged Class with an Unmanaged Test Harness

To illustrate the design of a test harness, this section explains a simple class and some code that will test it. Switch to the solution view in Visual Studio by clicking the Solution tab in the tabbed window at the right or choosing View, Solution Explorer. Right-click the solution name, FirstConsole, and choose Add, Add Class. Select Generic C++ class on the left and click Open.

Writing a Simple Class

Fill in the class name as `Order`. (This class will represent a customer order.) The filenames will be entered for you; click Finish. The definition of the class looks like Listing 2.1, and the implementation appears in Listing 2.2. The implementation of the global operator for sending the object to an `ostream` such as `cout` is included with the actual member functions of the class, because it is a `friend` and has access to the private member variables.

LISTING 2.1   Definition of the Order Class

```
#pragma once

#include <iostream>
using namespace std;

class Order
{
```

LISTING 2.1 Continued

```
private:
    int ordernumber;
    int itemnumber;
    int quantity;
friend ostream& operator<<(ostream& os, const Order& order);

public:
    Order(void);
    Order(int on, int in, int q);
    ~Order(void);
};
```

LISTING 2.2 Implementation of the Order Class

```
#include "StdAfx.h"
#include ".\order.h"

ostream& operator<<(ostream& os, const Order& order)
{
    os << "Order Number " << order.ordernumber << ": " << order.quantity
        << " of item " << order.itemnumber << endl;
    return os;
}

Order::Order(void) : ordernumber(-1), itemnumber(-1), quantity(0)
{
}

Order::Order(int on, int in, int q): ordernumber(on), itemnumber(in), quantity(q)
{
}

Order::~Order(void)
{
}
```

Order is a simple class that holds three variables: It has two constructors and an overload of the << operator that can be used to write the three variables' values. The destructor doesn't do anything, but because the wizard generated it you might as well leave it in case you add members later that need to be cleaned up in a destructor.

Writing a Test Harness

Here is a simple main function that exercises both constructors and the << operator, and confirms that it's okay to allocate an instance on the heap with the new operator and then get rid of it with the delete operator:

```
#include "stdafx.h"
#include "order.h"

int _tmain(int argc, _TCHAR* argv[])
{
    Order blank;
    cout << "Blank Order" << endl;
    cout << blank << endl;

    Order filled(1,345,7);
    cout << "Filled Order" << endl;
    cout << filled << endl;

    Order* p = new Order();
    cout << "Heap Order" << endl;
    cout << *p << endl;
    delete p;

    cout << "Tests complete" << endl;
    return 0;
}
```

The output of this test harness looks like this:

```
Blank Order
Order Number -1: 0 of item -1

Filled Order
Order Number 1: 7 of item 345

Heap Order
Order Number -1: 0 of item -1

Tests complete
Press any key to continue
```

This proves that the constructors perform as they should, that the << operator works, and that the application doesn't blow up or end abnormally when it uses instances of the Order class on either the stack or the heap. That's just what test harnesses are for. Test harnesses you write professionally might be more complex, especially ones that test several classes at once, but they should always be easy to understand and perform one purpose—to test your code and prove it works.

Because FirstConsole is an unmanaged application, you can copy the .EXE file to another Windows machine and it will run there without any problem. The only library it needs is the C runtime, which is installed with Windows. If you created a more complex test harness, you would need to deploy any related COM components or DLLs along with the .EXE file, register them, and perhaps adjust the environment variables such as PATH. Large unmanaged applications can be difficult to deploy. And of course, the executable cannot be copied to a non-Windows machine—it is strictly a Windows application.

Debugging an Unmanaged Console Application

You write a test harness to test your code and prove that it works. What if it doesn't? One of the most powerful tools available to a developer is the debugger, which lets you examine your code and variables while an application executes, so that you can understand why it is doing something you didn't expect.

The debugger is part of Visual Studio, and you can interact with it from the code editor. This makes Visual Studio a very productive development tool. In the code editor, click in the gray margin to the left of this line of code:

```
Order blank;
```

A red dot should appear, as in Figure 2.3, representing a *breakpoint*—a place in the execution of your application where the debugger will pause. Choose Debug, Start, and the application will run until this breakpoint is reached. The yellow arrow in the margin, as in Figure 2.4, indicates the line of code that is about to execute.

The Debug, Step Over menu item (look for a toolbar button and a keyboard shortcut for this command) moves the execution point to the next line of code. Step your way through the code a line at a time. Hover a variable to see its value, and if you like, step into a line of code (such as the construction of an object or the call to the << operator) to watch the called function run. You can switch to the console window where the output of the application appears to watch it being written as you move through the application. When you are debugging, the prompt "press any key to continue" does not appear at the end of the program as it does when you run without debugging.

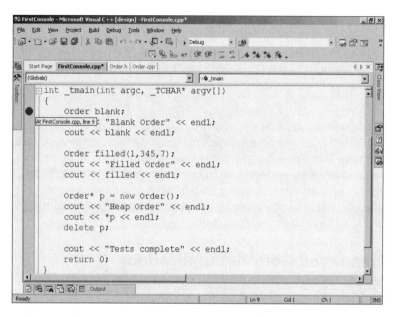

FIGURE 2.3   Click in the margin to set a breakpoint, which appears as a red dot.

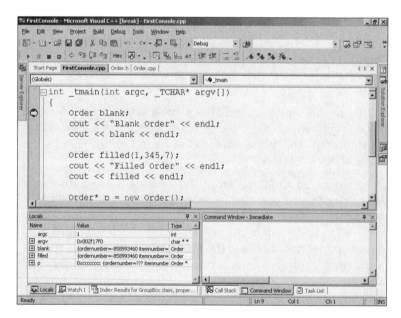

FIGURE 2.4   When the application is running, it will pause at the breakpoint.

Creating a Managed C++ Application

As discussed in Chapter 1, "C++, Visual C++, and Managed C++: What's the Difference?" a managed C++ application is fundamentally different from an unmanaged C++ application. The C++ code compiles not to machine code that can execute directly, but to an *assembly* of Intermediate Language, or IL. The assembly is kept in a file with an extension of .EXE or .DLL, but the content of the file is nothing like a traditional executable or DLL. Instead it holds IL and *metadata*, information about the classes in the assembly. To run the application, you actually ask the runtime to run it for you. The runtime loads the assembly, performing some security checks, and then calls a method in a class that the assembly holds. For console applications like those in this chapter, it calls the main() function, which is disguised as _tmain() in your source because some behind-the-scenes code is taking your character set into account. When any method or function in an assembly is called for the first time, it is compiled *Just-In-Time* (some say it is *jitted*) to machine code. This machine code is cached to be used the next time this method is called. The machine code executes inside the runtime and is watched as it runs.

Managed applications can use the libraries that are provided with the .NET Framework, and can call methods of classes written in other .NET-supported languages without any special keywords or techniques. The runtime handles all the marshalling and conversion that is necessary to call from one language into another. As a result, most programmers are more productive in managed C++ than in unmanaged C++, especially when developing a product that integrates a variety of components. When testing a class written in managed C++, it's best to write your test harness in managed C++, so as not to incur any performance penalties for the transition between managed and unmanaged code.

Even though a managed console application is very different from an unmanaged console application, the process of creating them feels very much the same. Visual Studio takes care of the work behind the scenes for you. Here's what you do:

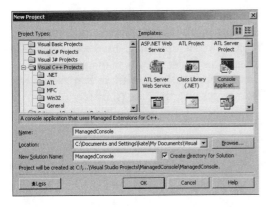

1. Open Visual Studio .NET 2003, if it's not already open.

2. On the Start Page, click New Project. If the Start Page isn't visible, choose File, New, Project.

3. Select the Visual C++ Projects folder on the left and Console Application (.NET) on the right.

4. Enter ManagedConsole as the project name (as shown in Figure 2.5), and click OK.

FIGURE 2.5 Creating a .NET console application called ManagedConsole.

The wizard generates the skeleton of a managed C++ application. Remove the comment that starts TODO and edit the line that was generated for you so that it reads

```
Console::WriteLine(S"Hello from a managed application");
```

Build the project by choosing Build, Build Solution. Run it by choosing Debug, Start without Debugging. You should see output like Figure 2.6.

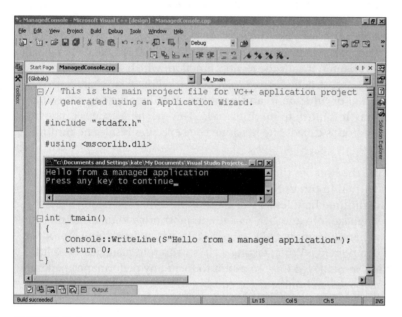

FIGURE 2.6   A console application running on the .NET Framework looks just like an unmanaged console application.

Although this might feel a lot like creating the unmanaged console application from earlier in this chapter, there are some obvious differences. Bring up the solution view and expand the References folder under the ManagedConsole project. In the unmanaged console application, FirstConsole, there were no entries in the References folder. In this managed console application, there are three: System.Data, System, and mscorlib. Each of these entries names an assembly that implements a part of the .NET Framework and the Base Class Libraries. When an assembly is named as a reference, the classes defined in it are available to all of the classes defined in this project.

In addition, the generated code in ManagedConsole.cpp contains this line:

```
#using <mscorlib.dll>
```

This line of code makes the classes in `mscorlib.dll` available to the code in the `main` function. It's redundant, because a reference has already been added to `mscorlib`, but the wizard generates it anyway.

The classes in the Base Class Libraries are divided into namespaces to make them easier to document and understand. For example, the `Console` class is in the `System` namespace. Its full name is therefore `System::Console`. This line of code lets you refer to it, and all the other classes in the `System` namespace, without including the namespace name (`System`):

```
using namespace System;
```

There is really only one line in the `main` function, `_tmain()`:

```
Console::WriteLine(S"Hello from a managed application");
```

The `WriteLine()` member function of the `Console` class takes a managed reference to an instance of the `String` class in the `System` namespace, `System::String`. An ordinary C-style string, as represented by characters in double quotes, is not an instance of a `System::String`. The `S` macro in this line of code converts from a C-style string to a `System::String` reference that can be passed to `Console::WriteLine()`. As you might guess from the name, the method writes text, followed by a line break, to the console screen.

Now that you know how to create, compile, and run a simple console application in managed C++, you can do a tremendous amount of programming for the .NET Framework. You can define classes, and then write code to create instances of the class and call their methods. You can write and test hundreds of thousands of lines of code in this way, just by adding lines to the `main` function (defined as `_tmain` in Visual C++) that is generated when you create a .NET console application with the project wizard.

These applications all require the .NET Framework and leverage the functionality of the .NET Base Class Libraries. They can also use libraries, such as MFC and ATL, that don't require the framework. (Accessing legacy libraries is covered in Chapter 6.) The most common use of a managed console application is to test a managed class, designed as part of a class library and to be used from any .NET-supported language.

Testing a Managed Class with a Managed Test Harness

The managed test harness in this chapter tests the same unmanaged class, `Order`, as the unmanaged test harness did—just to prove that managed code doesn't have to use managed data. In addition, a simple managed class demonstrates how to work with managed data from managed code.

Start by copying (use Windows Explorer) `order.cpp` and `order.h` into the project folder of the `ManagedConsole` project. Then right-click the `ManagedConsole` project in Solution View, and choose, Add, Add Existing Item. A file dialog box appears, displaying the project folder. Select `order.cpp` and `order.h`, and then click Open.

Because the `Order` class overloads the `<<` operator but does not have any other way of displaying its contents, the test harness will have to use `cout` and the `<<` operator rather than `Console::WriteLine()`. There is no problem combining the two ways of writing to the screen. (Although I recommend you use the `endl` or `flush` manipulators liberally when using `cout`, to ensure that none of your output is left in a buffer when `WriteLine()` starts writing to the screen.)

Copy the `main()` function from `FirstConsole` to `ManagedConsole`, and add the `#include` statement at the top that brings in `order.h`. Compile and run the application to make sure everything has been copied correctly.

In Solution view, right-click the `ManagedConsole` project and choose Add, Add Class. Select Generic C++ Class on the right, and click Open. In the Generic C++ Class wizard, name the class `Purchaser` and click Finish.

The class that is generated for you is not garbage collected. In `Purchaser.h`, change this line

```
class Purchaser
```

to this

```
public __gc class Purchaser
```

Note that the `__gc` keyword starts with two underscores. Now `Purchaser` is a garbage-collected class, as discussed in Chapter 1.

REFERENCES TO ASSEMBLIES AND NAMESPACES

If you're working along, don't forget to include any `#using` and `using` statements you see in this sample code. Without them, this code won't compile.

The definition of the class looks like Listing 2.3, and the implementation is in Listing 2.4. Notice that instead of an overload of the `<<` operator, `Purchaser` includes an overload of the `ToString` method, which all managed classes inherit from `Object`. (Even when you don't specify a base class, all managed classes inherit from `Object`, and `Object` declares the `ToString` method.) This makes it simple to pass a `Purchaser` instance to `Console::WriteLine()`, because that method will try converting the instance to a `String` by calling `ToString()`. Notice that the constructors use initializer syntax: This is still C++, so you have all the capabilities and conveniences of the language.

LISTING 2.3   Definition of the Purchaser Class

```
#pragma once
using namespace System;

public __gc class Purchaser
{
private:
    String* name;
    int account;
public:
    Purchaser(void);
    Purchaser(String* n, int a);
    ~Purchaser(void);
    String* ToString();
};
```

LISTING 2.4   Implementation of the Purchaser Class

```
#include "StdAfx.h"
#include ".\purchaser.h"
#using <mscorlib.dll>

Purchaser::Purchaser(void) : name(S""),account(-1)
{
}

Purchaser::Purchaser(String* n, int a) : name(n),account(a)
{
}


Purchaser::~Purchaser(void)
{
}

String* Purchaser::ToString()
{
    return String::Concat(name, " ", account.ToString());
}
```

Adding these lines to the main function exercises the Purchaser and Order classes:

```
Purchaser* blankpurchaser = new Purchaser();
Console::WriteLine(blankpurchaser);


Purchaser* filledpurchaser = new Purchaser(S"Joe Customer", 456);
Console::WriteLine(filledpurchaser);
```

The output from these lines looks like this:

```
 -1
Joe Customer 456
```

Notice that the ToString() method was called by Console::WriteLine().

This simple managed test harness proves that the unmanaged class can be called from managed code, and works just as it did when called from managed code. It also proves that the constructors for the managed class work correctly. Of course, you don't need to delete the instances of Purchaser; the garbage collector will take care of them.

Because ManagedConsole is a managed application, you can copy the .EXE file (the assembly) to any other machine with the .NET Framework installed, and it will run there without any problem. The only libraries it needs are those installed with the framework. If you created a more complex test harness, you would need to deploy any assemblies, but typically they would just be copied into the same folder as the test harness. Large managed applications are much easier to deploy than their unmanaged equivalents. And of course, it can even be possible to the copy an executable to a non-Windows machine—as long as that machine has the .NET Framework. As of this book's writing, the versions of the .NET Framework for non-Windows machines are severely limited, but they do exist and would be able to execute the test harness shown in this chapter on a Mac or UNIX machine without recompiling the C++ source.

In Brief

- Visual C++ .NET 2003 can be used to create both managed and unmanaged applications with user interfaces that range from none at all (services) to simple console interfaces to Windows applications.

- Console applications run in a command prompt and use character-based input and output.

- Although managed and unmanaged console applications use different libraries, they look similar when they run.

- Managed C++ applications can use techniques (such as cout and the << operator) from unmanaged C++ to simplify moving legacy C++ applications to the .NET Framework.

- The debugger in Visual Studio .NET is simple to use for debugging both managed and unmanaged applications.

The .NET Base Class Libraries

Libraries Shared Across Languages

When you write managed C++, you have access to all of the managed code libraries that come with the .NET Framework: the Base Class Libraries, ADO.NET, ASP.NET, and so on. These libraries are modern and powerful. They provide services, such as XML processing, that weren't even thought of when older libraries such as MFC and ATL were first written.

In sharp contrast to the historical capabilities of C++ and Visual Basic, on the .NET Framework these two languages share the same class libraries. Every library class and method that's available from Visual Basic is available from managed C++ and from C#. Every library class and method that's available from C# is available from Visual Basic and Managed C++.

THE C++ ADVANTAGE

C++ can use the same class libraries as C# and VB.NET. Does it work the other way around? No. There are libraries of unmanaged code available from managed C++ that cannot be called from Visual Basic or C#—ATL and MFC are just two examples. However, it's unlikely that a Visual Basic or C# programmer would want to use those libraries, because their functionality is provided elsewhere; the capability to call them from managed C++ helps simplify a port from unmanaged to managed C++.

The advantages of a shared class library are many. They include

- Reduced learning time when moving from one .NET-supported language to another

- A larger body of samples and documentation, because these do not need to be language specific

- Better communication between programmers who work in different .NET-supported languages

SHOP TALK

WORKING IN MULTIPLE LANGUAGES

I have a small consulting firm, and often our clients specify the programming language we are to use for a project. When several projects are on the go at once, I might switch languages several times in the course of a single day, as I help my associates with problems or track down the last few bugs in systems that are almost finished.

Before I starting using the .NET Framework, about once a month I'd suffer a "brain freeze" and for a moment or two forget how to perform some really simple task, like determining whether a string contains a particular character, in the language of the moment. Usually at those times my fingers would start typing the method or operator in randomly chosen other languages or libraries: Perl, Visual Basic, MFC, STL, Java—anything except the one I wanted. Now, with a common set of libraries across languages, I don't have to "context switch" nearly as often—and I avoid those "deer in the headlights" moments.

In the past, just because you knew how to perform a specific task, such as writing some text to a file in Visual C++, didn't mean you knew how to do that same task in Visual Basic. A great tutorial you found on database access in Visual Basic wasn't much help if you wanted to write your database application in Visual C++. Now, as long as you're working in managed C++, the walkthroughs, tutorials, and samples you find for any managed language—and you'll find plenty for Visual Basic and C#—are equally applicable to Visual C++. You'll have to translate the actual language elements, of course, but an explanation of a particular class or a method of that class is valid no matter which .NET supported language you intend to use.

Namespaces in C++

Namespaces are a C++ feature designed to eliminate name conflicts, such as having two classes, each in different libraries, called String. Before namespaces were added to the language, library developers tried to make their names unique by adding letters to them: One developer's string class might be called GCString, whereas another developer might call it TKString, the string class in MFC is called CString, and so on. This approach is ugly and reduces, but doesn't prevent, name conflicts.

With namespaces, classes can have simple names. Name conflicts are much less likely, because in addition to a short or local name, classes have a fully qualified name that includes their namespace. Here's a slightly artificial example (normally namespaces are used in separate libraries, not jumbled together in one piece of code like this) that illustrates how they work:

```
namespace One
{
    class Common
    {
    private:
        int x;
    public:
        Common(int a): x(a) {}
        int getx() {return x;}
    };
    void Do()
    {
        Common c(3);
        Console::WriteLine(__box(c.getx()));
    }
}
namespace Two
{
    class Common
    {
    private:
        double d1, d2;
    public:
        Common(double param1) : d1(param1),d2(param1) {}
        double getd1() {return d1;}
        double getd2() {return d2;}
    };
    void Do()
    {
        Common c(3);
```

```
            String* output = String::Concat(__box(c.getd1()), S" " ,
                __box(c.getd2()));
            Console::WriteLine(output);
        }
    }

int _tmain()
{
    //Common c(3); // ambiguous
    One::Common c1(3);
    Two::Common c2(3);
    //Do(); //ambiguous
    One::Do();
    Two::Do();
    return 0;
}
```

This code defines two namespaces, named One and Two. In each namespace there is a class called Common and a function called Do(). Inside the namespace, there's no problem referring to Common just using its short or local name. The two Do() functions accomplish this without error; each is working with the Common class from its own namespace.

The main function, _tmain(), cannot refer to Common or to Do() using a short name. (The two lines of code commented out in _tmain() cause compiler errors.) It has to use the fully qualified name: the namespace name and the class name, separated by the scope-resolution operator (::).

A using statement allows you to refer to a class with only its short name. It does not cause the compiler or linker to include any files that otherwise wouldn't have been included in your build; it's just a convenience to reduce typing. The example main function can be rewritten as

```
using namespace One;
int _tmain()
{
    Common c1(3);
    Two::Common c2(3);
    Do();
    Two::Do();
    return 0;
}
```

Modern class libraries are each in their own namespace—for example, the templates in the Standard Template Library are in the namespace std. The developers of the .NET Framework built on this concept, dividing the class libraries into namespaces and sub-namespaces. This makes them easier to learn and document.

To use a class in a namespace, you have two choices:

- Call the class by its full name (such as `System::Math`) whenever you're using it:

```
x = System::Math::PI / 4;
System::String* s = new System::String("hello");
```

- Add a using statement at the top of the file, and then call the class by its name within the namespace:

```
using namespace System;
...
x = Math::PI / 4;
String* s = new String("hello");
```

The second choice is a better approach when you're going to be typing class names from the namespace a number of times, because it saves you typing the namespace name repeatedly. I prefer the first choice when I'm only typing a class name once, because the fuller name gives more clues to a maintainer about what the code is doing. This is even more important when you're using classes from more obscure namespaces—everyone uses classes from `System` and is familiar with many of them, but the `System::Web::Security` namespace, for example, might not be so obvious to you or to those who will maintain your code.

Whether you choose to add a using statement to your file or not, you must add a #using directive to the top of your source file. When you create a new .NET project, one of these directives is added for you automatically:

```
#using <mscorlib.dll>
```

This gives you access to all the classes that are directly under the `System` namespace, such as the `System::Math` class used in these examples. The documentation for

PUNCTUATION: USING . OR ::

In most other .NET languages, the punctuation between the namespace name and the class name is a dot (.). For example, in both Visual Basic and C#, a developer would type `System.Math.PI`. But in C++, you use a double colon (`::`), called the scope-resolution operator. In the documentation, if you see a reference to `System.Something`, you just need to change it to `System::Something` in your code. Use the scope-resolution operator between namespace and sub-namespace, namespace and class, or sub-namespace and class.

As always, you use the dot between the name of an object and an ordinary member function, and the scope-resolution operator between the name of the class and a static member function or variable. In the previous examples, `PI` is a static member variable of the `Math` class. In other .NET languages, the punctuation between class or object name and function is always a dot, even when the function is static. This can make the documentation confusing. Most occurrences of . in the documentation should be changed to ::.

IntelliSense, the feature that pops up lists for you to choose from as you type, really helps with this confusion. If you type `"System."` into a file of C++ code, no list appears and the status bar reads

```
IntelliSense: 'Could not resolve type for
➥expression to the left of . or ->'
```

On the other hand, if you type `"System::"`, a list of namespaces and classes appears for you to choose from. Use the lack of feedback from IntelliSense as an indicator that you have typed the wrong thing, and you'll find working from the documentation a lot less confusing.

the classes that are in sub-namespaces of System includes a line like this one, from System::Xml.Document:

```
Assembly: System.XML.dll
```

This is a clue that you need to add this line to your file:

```
#using <System.XML.dll>
```

Don't worry about what seem to be extra dots in the filename, and don't change dots to :: here. If you will be using a particular assembly in every file within a project, you can add a reference to the assembly instead (right-click References in Solution View and choose Add Reference).

The System **Namespace**

You'll use the classes in the System namespace in almost every .NET application. All the data types are represented, for example. Two classes in particular deserve special mention: System::Console and System::String.

The System::Console **Class**

System::Console, called System.Console in the documentation, represents the screen and keyboard in a simple console application. After you add a using statement to your file so you don't have to type System:: every time, the Console class is simple to use. To write a line of text to the screen, you use the static function WriteLine():

```
Console::WriteLine("Calculations in Progress");
```

If you want to write text without a following line break, use the Write() function instead.

To read a line of text from the keyboard, first you should write out a line to prompt the users, and then read the entire line into a System::String object with the static ReadLine() function:

```
Console::WriteLine("Enter a sentence:");
String* sentence = Console::ReadLine();
```

If you want to read in something more complicated than a single string, there really isn't any support for it within the Console class, nor the classes in the System::IO namespace covered later in this chapter. You can read it into a string and then use string member functions to separate it into the pieces you want.

If you want to write formatted output, there's an overload of WriteLine that's reminiscent of printf(), except that you don't have to tell the function the type of each parameter. For example

```
Console::WriteLine("The time is {0} at this moment",
                    System::DateTime::Now.ToShortTimeString() );
```

You can write out a number of parameters at once. Use the placeholders, the things in brace brackets in the format string, to call for the parameter you want. As you can see, the count is zero-based. Here's an example:

```
Console::WriteLine("{0} lives at {1}", name, address);
```

The System::String and System::Stringbuilder Classes

The String class represents a string, such as "Hello" or "Kate Gregory". That's familiar ground for any programmer. But working with .NET strings can be quite strange for an experienced C++ or MFC programmer. They are certainly very far removed from the arrays of characters that you might be used to working with.

If you've ever worked with the MFC class CString, you've probably written code like this:

```
CString message = "Value of x, ";
message += x;
message += "is over limit.";
```

You might guess that the .NET equivalent would be

```
String* message = "Value of x, ";
message += x;
message += "is over limit.";
```

This just gets you a lot of strange compiler errors about illegal pointer arithmetic. The message variable is a pointer to a String instance, so you can't use the + operator. You can't do it in a single line either, like this:

```
String* message = "Value of x, " + x + "is over limit.";
```

The bottom line is that you can't treat .NET strings like C++ or C strings. So how do you build a string from several substrings, or from several pieces in general? If you want to build it so you can write it out, forget building the string, and use formatted output as described in the previous section. Or use the `Format()` method, which is reminiscent of `sprintf()`, and of the `Format()` method of the old MFC class `CString`. But if you need to build a string in little bits and pieces, your best choice is a companion class called `StringBuilder`, from the `System::Text` namespace. You use a string builder like this:

```
String* name = "Kate";
System::Text::StringBuilder* sb = new System::Text::StringBuilder("Hello ");
sb->Append(name);
```

Using a string builder is more efficient than modifying a string as you go, because .NET strings actually can't be modified; instead, a whole new one is created with your changes, and the old one is cleaned up later. `StringBuilder` has all sorts of useful methods like `Append()`, `Insert()`, `Remove()`, and `Replace()` that you can use to work on your string. When it's ready, just pass the string builder object to anything that's expecting a string:

```
Console::WriteLine(sb);
```

The framework gets the built string from the string builder and passes it to the function for you.

The `String` class has its own useful methods too. Consider the problem mentioned earlier— reading something other than a single string from the keyboard. The easiest way for you to tackle the problem is to write code that reads the line of input into a string, and then works with it. Here's a simple example:

```
Console::WriteLine("Enter three integers:");
String* input = Console::ReadLine();
String* numbers[] = input->Split(0);
int a1 = Convert::ToInt32(numbers[0]);
int a2 = Convert::ToInt32(numbers[1]);
int a3 = Convert::ToInt32(numbers[2]);
```

This code uses the `Split()` member function of the `String` class. It splits a `String` into an array of strings based on a separator character. If you pass in a null pointer (0), as in this example, it splits the string based on whitespace such as spaces or tabs, which is perfect for this situation. The `ToInt32()` method of the `Convert` class converts a `String` to an integer.

If you already know how to manipulate strings, you might appreciate a quick "cheat sheet" for the `String` class. Table 3.1 is just such a summary.

TABLE 3.1		
String Functions		
C RUNTIME	**MFC CString**	System::String
strcpy	operator=	operator=
strcat	operator+=	Append
strchr	Find	IndexOf
strcmp	operator == or Compare	Compare
strlen	GetLength()	Length
strtok	n/a	Split
[]	[] or GetAt()	Chars
sprintf	Format	Format
n/a	Left or Right or Mid	Substring

If you've worked with strings in other languages, you'll appreciate System::String functions such as PadLeft(), PadRight(), Remove(), and StartsWith(). If those names aren't familiar to you, check the Visual C++ documentation. You might be able to do what you want with a single function call!

The System::DateTime Structure

The DateTime structure represents a date or a time, or both. It has a number of useful constructors to create instances using a numeric date and time, or a number of ticks (useful when you're working with older C++ code). Here are some examples:

```
DateTime defaultdate;
Console::WriteLine(defaultdate.ToLongDateString());
DateTime Sept28(2003,9,28,14,30,0,0);
Console::Write(Sept28.ToShortDateString());
Console::Write(S" ");
Console::WriteLine(Sept28.ToShortTimeString());
DateTime now = DateTime::Now;
Console::WriteLine(now.ToString());
```

It can be intimidating to remember the parameters to the seven-integer constructor, but it's simple when you realize they go from largest to smallest: year, month, day, hour, minute, second, and millisecond. The millisecond parameter is optional and if you want, you can omit all the time parameters completely.

On September 17, 2003, this code produces the following output:

```
Monday, January 01, 0001
9/28/2003 2:30 PM
9/17/2003 1:17:41 PM
```

It matters that DateTime is a structure, not a class, because it is managed data. Managed classes can only be allocated on the heap with new; managed structures can only be allocated on the stack as in these examples.

To get the individual parts of a date, use these properties:

- Day: The day of the month

- Month: 1 to 12

- Year: Always four digits

- Hour: 0 to 23

- Minute

- Second

- DayOfWeek: 0 means Sunday

- Format: Creates a string based on the time and date, using a format string

The format string passed to Format() is either a single character representing one of a number of "canned" formats, or a custom format string. The most useful canned formats include

- d: A short date, such as 12/19/00

- D: A long date, such as Tuesday, December 19, 2000

- f: A full time and date, such as Tuesday, December 19, 2000 17:49

- g: A general time and date, such as 12/19/00 17:49

- s: A sortable time and date, such as 2000-12-19 17:49:03

- t: A short time, such as 17:49

- T: A long time, such as 17:49:03

If none of the canned formats has what you need, you can make your own by passing in strings such as "MMMM d, yy" for "December 3, 02" or whatever else you desire. You can find all the format strings in the help installed with Visual Studio.

Other Useful Namespaces

There are plenty of other useful classes contained in sub-namespaces of the System namespace. Some are covered elsewhere in this book. Four are covered here because almost every .NET developer is likely to use them: System::IO, System::Text, System::Collections, and System::Threading.

The `System::IO` Namespace

Getting information from users and providing it to them is the sort of task that can be incredibly simple (like reading a string and echoing it back to the users) or far more complex. The most basic operations are in the `Console` class in the `System` namespace. More complicated tasks are in the `System::IO` namespace. This namespace includes 27 classes, as well as some structures and other related utilities. They handle tasks such as

- Reading and writing to a file

- Binary reads and writes (bytes or blocks of bytes)

- Creating, deleting, renaming, or moving files

- Working with directories

This snippet uses the `FileInfo` class to determine whether a file exists, and then deletes it if it does:

```
System::IO::FileInfo* fi = new System::IO::FileInfo("c:\\test.txt");
if (fi->Exists)
    fi->Delete();
```

This snippet writes a string to a file:

```
System::IO::StreamWriter* streamW = new System::IO::StreamWriter("c:\\test.txt");
streamW->Write("Hi there" );
streamW->Close();
```

Be sure to close all files, readers, and writers when you have finished with them. The garbage collector might not finalize the `streamW` instance for a long time, and the file stays open until you explicitly close it or until the instance that opened it is finalized.

WHEN TYPING STRINGS WITH BACKSLASHES

The backslash character (\) in the filename must be "escaped" by placing another backslash before it. Otherwise the combination \t will be read as a tab character. This is standard C++ behavior when typing strings with backslashes.

Check the documentation to learn more about IO classes that you can use in console applications, Windows applications, and class libraries. Keep in mind also that many classes can persist themselves to and from a file, or to and from a stream of XML.

The `System::Text` Namespace

Just as `Console` offers simple input and output abilities, the simplest string work can be tackled with just the `String` class from the `System` namespace. More complicated work involves the System::Text namespace. You've already seen System::Text::StringBuilder. Other classes in this namespace handle conversions between different types of text, such as Unicode and ASCII.

The System::Text::RegularExpressions namespace lets you use regular expressions in string manipulations and elsewhere. Here is a function that determines whether a string passed to it is a valid US ZIP code:

```
using namespace System;
using namespace System::Text::RegularExpressions;
// . . .
String* Check(String* code)
{
    String* error = S"OK";
    Match* m;
    switch (code->get_Length())
    {
    case 5:
        Regex* fivenums;
        fivenums = new Regex("\\d\\d\\d\\d\\d");
        m = fivenums->Match(code);
        if (!m->Success)
            error =  S"Non numeric characters in 5 digit code";
        break;
    case 10:
        Regex* fivedashfour;
        fivedashfour = new Regex("\\d\\d\\d\\d\\d-\\d\\d\\d\\d");
        m = fivedashfour->Match(code);
        if (!m->Success)
            error =   S"Not a valid zip+4 code";
        break;
    default:
        error =  S"invalid length";
    }
    return error;
}
```

The Regex class represents a pattern, such as "five numbers" or "three letters." The Match class represents a possible match between a particular string and a particular pattern. This code checks the string against two patterns representing the two sets of rules for ZIP codes.

The syntax for regular expressions in the .NET class libraries will be familiar to developers who have used regular expression as MFC programmers, or even as UNIX users. In addition to using regular expressions with classes from the System::Text namespace, you can use them in the Find and Replace dialog boxes of the Visual Studio editor, and with ASP.NET validation controls. It's worth learning how they work.

Regular Expression Syntax

A regular expression is some text combined with special characters that represent things that can't be typed, such as "the end of a string" or "any number" or "three capital letters."

When regular expressions are being used, some characters give up their usual meaning and instead stand in for one or more other characters. Regular expressions in Visual C++ are built from ordinary characters mixed in with these special entries, shown in Table 3.2.

Here are some examples of regular expressions:

- `^test$` matches only test alone in a string.

- `doc[1234]` matches doc1, doc2, doc3, or doc4 but not doc5.

- `doc[1-4]` matches the same strings as doc[1234] but requires less typing.

- `doc[^56]` matches doca, doc1, and anything else that starts with doc, except doc5 and doc6.

- `H\~ello` matches Hillo and Hxllo (and lots more) but not Hello. H[^e]llo has the same effect.

- `[xy]z` matches xz and yz.

- `New *York` matches New York, NewYork, and New   York (with several spaces between the words).

- `New +York` matches New York and New   York, but not NewYork.

- `New.*k` matches Newk, Newark, and New York, plus lots more.

- `World$` matches World at the end of a string, but World\$ matches only World$ anywhere in a string.

TABLE 3.2

Regular Expression Entries

ENTRY	MATCHES
^	Start of the string.
$	End of the string.
.	Any single character.
[]	Any one of the characters within the brackets (use – for a range, ^ for "except").
\~	Anything except the character that follows.
*	Zero or more of the next character.
+	One or more of the next character.

TABLE 3.2

Continued

ENTRY	MATCHES
\w	A single letter or number, or an underscore. (These are called *word characters* and are the only characters that can be used in a variable name.)
\s	Whitespace (tabs or spaces).
\d	A single numerical digit.
\	Removes the special meaning from the character that follows.

The `System::Collections` Namespace

Another incredibly common programming task is holding on to a collection of objects. If you have just a few, you can use an array to read three integers in one line of input. In fact, arrays in .NET are actually objects, instances of the `System::Array` class, which have some useful member functions of their own, such as `Copy()`. There are times when you want specific types of collections, though, and the `System::Collections` namespace has plenty of them. The provided collections include

- **Stack.** A collection that stores objects in order. The object stored most recently is the first taken out.

- **Queue.** A collection that stores objects in order. The first stored is the first taken out.

- **Hashtable.** A collection that can be searched far more quickly than other types of collections, but takes up more space.

- **ArrayList.** An array that grows as elements are added to it.

- **SortedList.** A collection of two-part (key and value) items that can be accessed by key or in numerical order.

- **BitArray.** A compact way to store an array of true/false flags.

One rather striking omission here is a linked list. You have to code your own if you need a linked or double-linked list.

The `System::Threading` Namespace

Threading has been a difficult part of Windows programming from the very beginning. It's quite a bit simpler in .NET. The vital classes for threading are in the `System::Threading` namespace. These include classes such as `Mutex`, `Thread`, and `ThreadPool`, which developers with experience in threaded applications will recognize instantly.

A thread is a path of execution through a program. In a multithreaded program, each thread has its own stack and operates independently of other threads running within the same program.

A thread is the smallest unit of execution, much smaller than a process. Generally each running application on your system is a process. If you start the same application twice (for example, Notepad), there are two processes: one for each instance. It is possible for several instances of an application to share a single process: For example, if you choose File, New Window in Internet Explorer, two applications appear on your taskbar, and they share a process. The unfortunate consequence is that if one instance crashes, they all do.

Writing a multithreaded application is simple with classes from the System::Thread namespace. First, you need to think of some work for a new thread to do: some slow calculation that you want to run without slowing the responsiveness of your application. This work will go into a function, and the function will be executed on a new thread.

Your thread proc must be a member function of a garbage-collected class. For example

HOW MANY THREADS?

Any application always has at least one thread, which is the program's primary or main thread. You can start and stop as many additional threads as you need, but the main thread keeps running as long as the application is active.

THE THREAD PROC

For a long time, Windows C++ programmers have called the function the thread *proc* (short for procedure).

```
public __gc class Counter
{
public:
    void Countdown()
    {
        String* threadName = Thread::CurrentThread->Name;
        Console::Write(S"This is the current thread:  ");
        Console::WriteLine(threadName);
        for (int counter = maxCount; counter >= 1; counter--)
        {
            Console::WriteLine(S"{0} is currently on {1}.",threadName,
                            __box(counter));
        }
        Console::WriteLine(S"{0} has finished counting down from {1}.",
                        threadName,
                __box(maxCount));
    }
};
```

The heart of this function is the `for` loop that counts down from `maxCount` to zero. It uses the `Name` property of the thread that is executing the function, because the sample that uses this class calls the function on two different threads. Normally, the function that does the asynchronous work would not communicate with the user; it would be quietly working in the background, doing some long slow work. It might, however, update a progress bar, or an icon that indicates a background task is in progress.

This code calls the `thread` proc on a new thread and also on the application's main thread:

```
Console::Write("Enter a number to count down from:   ");
maxCount = Int16::Parse(Console::ReadLine());
Thread::CurrentThread->Name = "Main Thread";

Counter* counter = new Counter();
ThreadStart* SecondStart = new ThreadStart(counter,Counter::Countdown);
Thread* secondThread = new Thread(SecondStart);
secondThread->Name = "Secondary Thread";
secondThread->Start();

counter->Countdown();
```

This code keeps the number entered by the user in a global variable called `maxCount`. Because `ReadLine` returns a pointer to a `System::String` instance, the static `Parse()` method of `Int16` is used to convert a string to an integer so that it can be stored in `maxCount`.

To execute a particular function on a new thread, you create a `Thread` object and call its `Start()` method. To create a `Thread` object, you need a `ThreadStart` object, and the constructor for `ThreadStart` needs a reference to an instance of a garbage-collected class (`counter` in this example), and a function pointer (just the name of the function without the parentheses) to a member function of that garbage-collected class.

Because this code calls `Countdown` on a new thread and also on the main thread, the output shows the two threads taking turns, as in Figure 3.1.

FIGURE 3.1 A multithreaded application demonstrates how threads take turns doing their work.

In Brief

- The libraries that come with the .NET Framework are large, and cover almost every task programmers are likely to tackle. Using them can save programmers hours or days of work.

- The same class libraries are used in Visual Basic, C#, and managed C++, but managed C++ can also call some unmanaged libraries that Visual Basic and C# cannot access.

- The System namespace holds classes for simple common tasks, and a large number of sub-namespaces for slightly less common (but still important) tasks, including string manipulation, IO, and threading.

Building Simple User Interfaces with Windows Forms

A Managed C++ Windows Forms Application

Applications developed in managed C++ have access to all of the classes that come with the .NET Framework. However, the first release of Visual C++ .NET, now referred to as Visual C++ .NET 2002, did not provide any Rapid Application Development (RAD) support for building Windows Forms applications in managed C++. Developers had to code these applications manually. With the release of Visual C++ .NET 2003 comes wizard and designer support for forms applications.

Whether created with a designer or manually, managed C++ Windows Forms applications run only on machines with the .NET Framework installed. They can use libraries written in any .NET supported language, and thanks to "It Just Works" technology, they can also use unmanaged C++ libraries.

To create a Windows Forms application, choose File, New Project or click New Project on the Start Page. Select Visual C++ projects on the left, and Windows Forms application (.NET) on the right. Name the project SimpleForm, as shown in Figure 4.1.

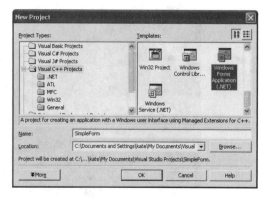

FIGURE 4.1   Visual Studio can create a Windows Forms application in managed C++.

The project wizard creates a blank form for you, and later you'll drag controls onto it. It also generates a file full of code, which will be edited as you add controls and set properties. To see the code, right-click the form in the designer and choose View Code.

When the application runs, the runtime creates an instance of the form class, which is why it must be a garbage-collected class:

```
public __gc class Form1 : public System::
➥Windows::Forms::Form
{
// . . .
};
```

The runtime then calls the InitializeComponent() method of the class. When the form is first created, InitializeComponent() looks like this:

```
void InitializeComponent(void)
{
   this->components = new System::ComponentModel::Container();
   this->Size = System::Drawing::Size(300,300);
   this->Text = S"Form1";
}
```

Switch back to the designer (use the tabs across the top of the editor, or press Ctrl+Tab) and bring up the properties of the form by choosing View, Properties Window. Use the Properties window to change some aspects of the form such as the Text property, the background color, and the like. Use your mouse to resize the form. Without saving your work, switch back to the code view and you will see that the designer has updated the code to reflect your changes. Switch back to the code and edit it (for example, change the size), and then switch to Design view again and you'll see your code changes take effect in the designer.

Although it can be fun to play with your code in this way, for day-to-day work you'll generally ignore this code. Let the designer maintain it, and use the toolbox and the Properties window to work with your form.

Using the Toolbox to Build the User Interface

The toolbox is a tabbed window that usually appears on the left side of the editing screen. If it's not visible, choose View, Toolbox. If necessary, pin it in place by clicking the pin at the top of the window. When it is unpinned it will collapse out of the way while you are working in the main pane of the editor or designer. This can be very convenient, but when it pops out, it can hide the form you are working on. Pinning it moves the form over so that you can see the toolbox and the entire form.

Controls in the Toolbox

FIGURE 4.2
The toolbox contains controls from which you can build your interface.

When you're working with the designer on a Windows Form, the toolbox has a Windows Forms tab, from which you can drag popular Windows controls onto your form. Figure 4.2 shows this tab.

Figure 4.3 shows an application with a selection of Windows controls. This sample uses the following controls:

- **Label**: This one says "Enter a name:". Labels should be used generously to instruct the users about how your application works and to prompt for input. For example, you might put a label with the text *Name* next to a text box where you expect the user to enter a name. Use the Properties window to edit the text of the label.

- **Text box**: By default, the text is initialized to the name of the control, such as textBox1. Use the Properties window to delete the default text.

- **Button**: Forms do not have OK or Cancel buttons by default. You must code the behavior of each button you add.

- **Check box**: Check boxes can be selected or deselected independently and come with a built-in label. This one reads "optional".

- **Radio buttons**: There are three (red, yellow, and green) and they are in a group box (labeled Color). Selecting one automatically deselects all the others in the group.

- **Group box**: If you don't use a group box, all the radio buttons on a form are in the same group. Using a group box makes it possible to have two sets of radio buttons on the same form.

- **Picture box**: Displaying images on a form is very simple with a picture box. Just set the image property to a file on your hard drive.

- **DateTime picker**: When the user clicks the drop-down arrow, a calendar is displayed to simplify choosing a date (see Figure 4.4). Alternatively, the users can edit the date shown. Try pressing the up and down arrows after clicking on the month or day in a DateTime picker.

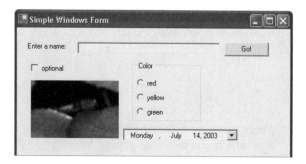

FIGURE 4.3   This chapter's sample application uses a variety of controls.

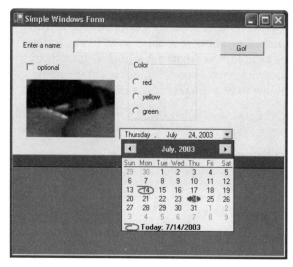

FIGURE 4.4   The DateTime picker can display a calendar so the users can choose a date easily.

- **Data grid:** Used to display tabular information, such as filled from a data source or a file of XML.

CAPITALIZATION CONVENTION

The capitalization of control names generated by the designer in Visual C++ always follows the convention known as *camelCase*: The first letter is lowercase and if there are any other words within the name, they start with an uppercase letter.

Controls have two very important properties: Text and Name. The Name property is the actual name of the variable you will be accessing in code. By default, it's the type of the control with a number on the end, such as textBox1 or dateTimePicker1. The Text property varies in meaning from control to control: For a form it's the caption across the top, for a button it's the text on the button, and so on—but it's always called Text. Only a handful of controls, such as the picture box, don't have a Text property.

If you drag on a control that you don't want on the form, just click it and press Del. If you move or resize a control and don't like the result, choose Edit, Undo or press Ctrl+Z.

Try to re-create the user interface shown in Figure 4.3 in your SimpleForm application. If you're finding it difficult to place and size the controls correctly, read the next section for details on Visual Studio functionality that will help you lay out the controls on the form surface.

The Layout Toolbar

When you're building a form, the layout toolbar (shown in Figure 4.5) is very useful. The buttons on this toolbar are also available on the Format menu, but they require more clicking. Generally, these buttons work only on groups of controls. For example, the Align Left button (or Format, Align, Lefts) moves the selected controls (all but the last one you selected) to the left or right so that the left edges of all the controls line up. The Make Vertical Spacing Equal command moves the selected controls (again, all but the last one) up or down so that they are equally spaced up and down. Each of these commands leaves all the controls selected, so that you can move them around as a group. Take some time to become familiar with this toolbar and you will dramatically reduce the time it takes to create professional-looking forms and dialog boxes.

FIGURE 4.5   The layout toolbar has buttons to simplify aligning and resizing controls.

Anchoring, Docking, and Other Properties of Controls

After you've dragged some controls onto your form, try resizing the form to a larger size. You're likely to be disappointed by the result: just extra background next to and below the existing controls. The same thing happens if the user enlarges the form while the application is running. Experienced MFC programmers know how to resize individual controls when the form resizes, and you can apply those techniques, slightly adapted, to a managed Windows Forms application. It's more likely, though, that you'll use two new properties, Anchor and Dock, to give you the behaviors you want without writing any code.

The Anchor Property

By default, a control is anchored to the left side and top edge of its container—usually the form on which the control has been placed. As the size and position of the container changes, the control always stays the same distance from the left and top of the container. This isn't always the most desirable behavior. A button like the Go! button in the sample application shown in this chapter would be better staying the same distance from the top and the right, and letting the distance from the left edge vary as the form changes size. Arranging this is simple: Select the button by clicking it, and scroll down in the Properties window until you find the Anchor property. Click it, and a drop-down box will appear. Click that and a small window appears in which you can select the sides of the box to which the button will be anchored. Figure 4.6 shows the anchoring changed to top and right. Pressing Enter or clicking another control saves the changes.

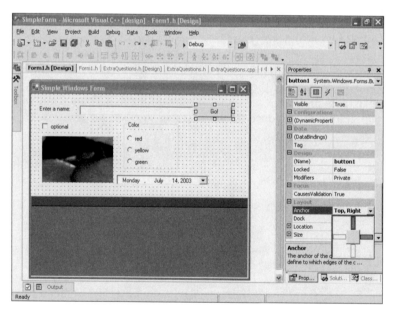

FIGURE 4.6   Many controls should be anchored differently than the top-left default.

When a control is anchored to both the left and right sides, or to both the top and bottom, it changes size when the container changes size, in order to stay the same distance from both sides. Anchoring to both left and right is an excellent choice for a text box, so that it can enlarge when the user enlarges the form.

The Dock Property

The data grid at the bottom of the sample form has been sized to fit the form exactly. You can use the Anchor property to keep it the current distance, zero, from both sides and the bottom, but it's much simpler to use the Dock property. When a control is docked, it moves up right against one edge of the container and it automatically resizes to continue to fill that entire edge. To dock a control, first select it. Then find the Dock property in the Properties window. Click the current value (None) and a drop-down list will appear: Click that and a small window appears, showing the sides to which you can dock the control. If you choose the center, the control will dock to all sides of the container at once—not a good choice if there's anything else on the form. Figure 4.7 shows the Dock property being set to Bottom for the data grid in the sample application.

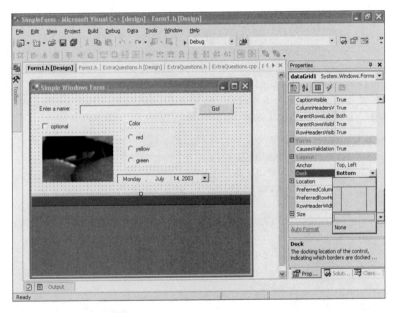

FIGURE 4.7   This chapter's sample application uses a variety of controls.

After the text box has been anchored left, right, and top, the button has been anchored top and right, and the data grid has been docked to the bottom, the sample application responds nicely to resizing requests. Figure 4.8 shows how the controls resize and reposition themselves when the form is enlarged—and I didn't have to write any code to get this behavior.

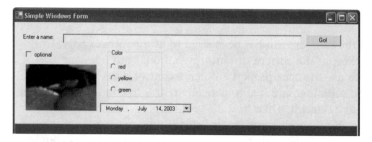

FIGURE 4.8   This chapter's sample application resizes and repositions controls when the form is resized.

Writing Event Handlers

As a user interacts with a Windows Forms application, events are triggered by the user's keyboard and mouse activities. (There are events triggered by other happenings as well, but in this section only user activities are relevant.) For example, when the user clicks the mouse while it is over a button, the button's `Click` event occurs. This is the most important event for a button: It's unusual for you to write code to deal with lesser events like "the mouse has been moved above the button" or "this control has just lost focus" on a button.

When an event occurs over a particular control, the system checks to see if the control has a handler for that event. If it does, the event handler is called. An event handler is a void function that takes a pointer to a `System::Object` and a pointer to a `System::EventArgs`. The `System::Object` is the control over which the event occurred, and the `System::EventArgs` contains more details about the event, such as the mouse coordinates or whether Shift, Ctrl, or Alt were pressed. As often as not, developers ignore both of these arguments: If you're writing a handler for a click on `button1`, you don't need to check the first argument to know this is `button1`, and you don't need to know if someone held Shift while they clicked the button. However, for those handlers that need it, the information is always available.

Adding an Event Handler

There are two ways to add a handler to an event. The simplest is to double-click the control in the designer. This adds a handler to the default event, which varies from control to control. For example, double-clicking the Go button in this sample adds this function to the class:

```
private: System::Void button1_Click(System::Object *  sender,
                                     System::EventArgs *  e)
{
}
```

That's because `Click` is a button's default event. It also adds this line to `InitializeComponent`:

```
this->button1->Click += new System::EventHandler(this, button1_Click);
```

This line ensures the handler is called when the event occurs. Double-clicking the text box in the sample would add this event:

```
private: System::Void textBox1_TextChanged(System::Object *  sender,
                                       System::EventArgs *  e)
{
}
```

It also adds a line to `InitializeComponent` that registers the handler. Table 4.1 lists the default events of the most popular controls.

TABLE 4.1

Controls and Their Default Events

CONTROL	DEFAULT EVENT
Button	Click
TextBox	TextChanged
Label	Click
CheckBox	CheckedChanged
GroupBox	Enter
RadioButton	CheckedChanged
PictureBox	Click
DateTimePicker	ValueChanged
DataGrid	Navigate

Writing the handler is as simple as filling code in to the function. Examples are in the next section.

To add a handler for another event, use the Properties window. Click the control, and then if the Properties window is not displayed, choose View, Properties Window. Look for the lightning bolt at the top of the Properties window (see Figure 4.9) and click it.

At the top of the Properties window is a toolbar with five buttons: Categorized, Alphabetic, Properties, Events, and Property Pages. The first two control the way the properties are organized: By default and when Categorized is pressed, properties are organized into categories

Events button

FIGURE 4.9   The Events button causes the Properties window to display events instead of properties.

such as Appearance and Behavior. When Alphabetic is pressed, properties appear in alphabetical order. By default and when the Properties button is pressed, the Properties window displays properties. But when the Events button is pressed, it displays all the events that can occur for this particular control. (They appear in one long alphabetical list or divided into categories, depending on which of the first two buttons is pressed.) The final button, Property Pages, is enabled only when you are looking at the Properties window with the entire project or solution selected, and provides a quick shortcut to the project properties or solution properties. It's not enabled when a control is selected. Understanding and using this toolbar will make the Properties window a more productive part of the Visual Studio user interface.

For example, if you select the check box on the form in the sample application, the Events button in the Properties window lists all the events that can happen to a check box. Double-clicking to the right of an event adds a handler for that event and opens the editor, scrolled to the function that was just added.

Writing an Event Handler

Many event handlers are a single line long. For example, this pair of handlers is in the sample application for this chapter:

```cpp
private: System::Void checkBox1_MouseEnter(System::Object *  sender,
                                           System::EventArgs *  e)
{
    checkBox1->BackColor = Color::AliceBlue;
}


private: System::Void checkBox1_MouseLeave(System::Object *  sender,
                                           System::EventArgs *  e)
{
    checkBox1->BackColor = BackColor;
}
```

These handlers respond to the mouse entering the area of the check box and to it leaving that area. The MouseEnter handler changes the background color of the check box to AliceBlue and the MouseLeave handler restores it to the same background color as the form as a whole.

When writing an event handler, refer to the controls on the form using the same names, such as checkBox1 or textBox1, that you see in the Name property when working with the form in the designer. If you change the name of a control in the designer, the code in

InitializeComponent() will be edited to use the new name immediately, but other functions, such as your handlers, will not be edited. To simplify your life, make sure you are happy with the names of all the controls on your form before you start to write handlers for their events.

A more complicated event handler can interact with more than just a single control. The handler in Listing 4.1 displays a message box showing the values of the text box, check box, and radio buttons (see Figure 4.10). It also changes the image displayed in the picture box control.

CONTROL NAMES

It's generally a bad idea to accept the names the designer generates for your controls. This chapter uses these default names to make it easier to follow along. But if you have three text boxes on a form, it's a lot easier to use the right one when they're called `firstName`, `lastName`, and `employeeID` than when they're called `textBox1`, `textBox2`, and `textBox3`. Just remember to make these changes as you add the controls, rather than later when you'll have to change a lot of code to reflect the new names.

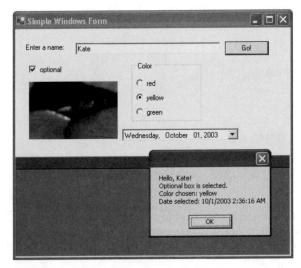

FIGURE 4.10 This chapter's sample application displays a message box demonstrating the values of its controls.

LISTING 4.1 Form1.h—button1_Click()

```
private:
System::Void button1_Click(System::Object *  sender, System::EventArgs *  e)
{
    System::Text::StringBuilder* message = new System::Text::StringBuilder;
    message->Append("Hello, ");
    message->Append(textBox1->Text);
```

LISTING 4.1   Continued

```
    message->Append("!");
    message->Append(Environment::NewLine);
    message->Append("Optional box is ");
    if (!checkBox1->Checked)
        message->Append("not ");
    message->Append("selected.");
    message->Append(Environment::NewLine);
    message->Append("Color chosen: ");
    if (radioButton1->Checked)
        message->Append("red");
    else if (radioButton2->Checked)
        message->Append("yellow");
    else if (radioButton3->Checked)
        message->Append("green");
    else
        message->Append("none");
    message->Append(Environment::NewLine);
    message->Append("Date selected: ");
    message->Append(dateTimePicker1->Value.ToString());
    message->Append(Environment::NewLine);

    MessageBox::Show(message->ToString());
    pictureBox1->Image = Image::FromFile(S"Winter.jpg");
}
```

Some points to note about Listing 4.1:

- The text message to be displayed in the message box is not built by adding strings directly, but instead with an instance of the StringBuilder class. The ToString() method of StringBuilder is used to extract the string that was built and pass it to MessageBox::Show at the end of the routine.

- The Environment::NewLine constant is used to embed new line characters into the message. This is more readable and portable than C-style constants such as \r\n.

- The Text property of the text box holds the characters the user typed before pressing the button.

- The Checked property of the check box returns true if the box is checked and false if it is not.

- There is no property of the group box to tell which radio button has been selected. Instead, use the Checked property of each radio button. By default, none is selected, so be sure your logic considers that possibility.

- The Value property of the DateTime picker returns the date that the user chose as a DateTime structure. You must use the ToString method to convert it to a string that can be passed to the Append method of the StringBuilder.

- The Image property of the picture box accepts an Image pointer. An easy way to get one is to use the static FromFile() method and pass in a filename. For this sample project, a number of image files are in the project folder for you to use.

Using a DataGrid, DataView, and DataFilter

In addition to basic building blocks like labels and text boxes, a simple user interface can also use controls that hold several pieces of information at once. The DataGrid is the most widely-used of these classes; it presents information in a grid format that is easy and intuitive for most users. Two related classes, the DataView and the DataFilter, can be used to add remarkable power to your application, without making your user interface complicated.

The bottom half of the sample application form holds a DataGrid. It's not there just to show how docking works, but also to demonstrate some of the purposes to which you can put this very powerful control. A full treatment of how to get data into a datagrid is in Chapter 11, "Writing a Data Layer in Managed C++," but this chapter includes a very neat shortcut using XML.

SHOP TALK

USING XML IN PROTOTYPES WITHOUT A DATA LAYER

I've used these shortcut techniques to create quick and impressive prototypes without writing a data layer. Keep that in mind as you read how I use a file of XML to fill the DataGrid. It doesn't take long to create the user interface, and to type up a file of XML. The user sees how the application will flow, and can even preview simple query capabilities. Keep this in mind the next time you have to toss something together in less than a day for a big presentation.

Creating XML, Schemas, and Typed Datasets

The DataGrid control displays data in a grid format. In order to do that, it needs some data. In this chapter, you'll use a shortcut to load some static data into the grid so that you can explore the properties of the DataGrid control and get used to working with it.

To get some data for the DataGrid to work with, start by creating a file of XML. You can create an empty one like this: Right-click the project in Solution Explorer and choose Add, Add New Item. On the Add New Item dialog box, choose XML File and name it People. Click

Open. Visual Studio will create an almost-empty file and open it with the editor. You can then type some sample XML. Listing 4.2 shows some XML that will be used in this section to populate the DataGrid. If you type this in yourself, or open the sample application, you'll notice the syntax coloring provided by Visual Studio when you edit XML. Syntax coloring simplifies working with complicated files.

LISTING 4.2   People.xml—Sample Data in XML

```xml
<?xml version="1.0" encoding="utf-8"?>
<members>
    <member>
        <first>Kate</first>
        <last>Gregory</last>
        <phone>705 789 1234</phone>
        <SIN>123 456 789</SIN>
    </member>
    <member>
        <first>Brian</first>
        <last>Gregory</last>
        <phone>705 678 2345</phone>
        <SIN>987 654 321</SIN>
    </member>
    <member>
        <first>Todd</first>
        <last>Green</last>
        <phone>416 345 6789</phone>
        <SIN>123 654 987</SIN>
    </member>
</members>
```

Working with XML is well-supported throughout the .NET Framework. Both Visual Studio and the Base Class Library have a wide variety of tools and methods that are founded on XML. For example, if you right-click in the editor while editing the new file, people.xml, you can choose Create Schema. This will set Visual Studio to work creating an XML schema that matches the sample XML you provided.

After you generate the schema, flip back to the file of XML. You'll notice that Visual Studio edited it to reflect the name and location of the schema. What's more, once a file of XML has an associated schema, you get Intellisense when you edit it. It closes tags as you open them (if you type <member>, it will type </member>) and provides a drop-down menu of the only elements that belong where you are typing, as in Figure 4.11.

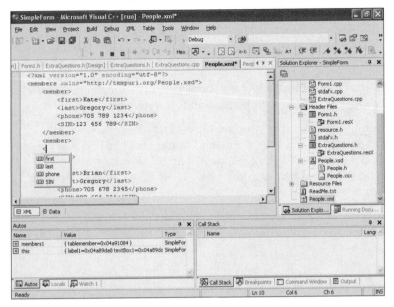

FIGURE 4.11 When a file of XML has a schema, you get Intellisense while editing it in Visual Studio.

Once you have a schema, you can use it to generate a very useful class called a *typed dataset*. This is a class that inherits from the `Dataset` class in the `System::Data` sub-namespace (discussed more fully in Chapter 11) and is typically used to hold the results from a query of the database. By default, Visual Studio .NET 2003 generates a typed dataset whenever you generate a schema, and regenerates the typed dataset every time you save the schema.

What good is a typed dataset? It's the definition of a class. An actual instance of that class can hold data from a database (or elsewhere as you'll see shortly) and can then be used as the data source for a control that knows how to display data. A perfect example of such a control is a DataGrid.

Connecting a DataGrid to a DataSet

Here's how to hook up the DataGrid in the sample application so that it displays the contents of the sample file of XML:

1. Open the form in the designer and make sure the toolbox is visible and pinned.

2. Click the Data tab in the toolbox to display a completely different set of controls.

3. Drag a DataSet onto the form and let go. The Add Dataset wizard will appear.

4. The wizard offers you a choice of typed or untyped dataset, and for a typed dataset, a drop-down list of all those you have defined in the project. Because you only have one typed dataset in this project, click OK to accept the suggestion of using `SimpleForm.members`.

5. The dataset appears in the designer just below the form. That makes it simple to select it so that you can set properties with the Properties window if necessary.

6. Select the DataGrid, and in the Properties window, set the Data Source property to `members1.member`—the member table of the member's DataSet instance that was created when you dragged the DataSet onto the form. Immediately the headings of the DataGrid change to reflect the field names in the table. These field names came from the XML when the data set was generated.

7. Open the code for the form, and edit the constructor so it reads like this:

```
Form1(void)
{
    InitializeComponent();
    members1->ReadXml("people.xml");
}
```

Build and run the project, and you should see something like Figure 4.12: The DataGrid displays the contents of the XML file in an intuitive grid. You can resize the columns with the mouse, click any column heading to sort by the column, and if you resize the application so that it's narrower than the DataGrid, scroll bars will appear automatically. The only thing that's a bit of a cheat here is filling the DataGrid by just reading in XML from a file. Normally, you would use a data layer to provide a DataSet for the grid to display.

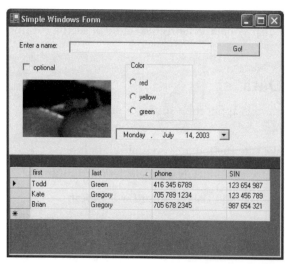

FIGURE 4.12   The DataGrid displays the contents of the XML file with very little coding effort.

Working with a Data View

For simple filtering of records, a DataView is hard to beat. You bring all your results from the database once, and keep them in a data set. Then instead of hooking the data grid directly to the data set, you hook it to a data view, and you hook the data view to the data set. The data view has a Filter property that you can use to control which records the data grid displays—without going back to the database over and over again. This `Filter` property holds an instance of the DataFilter class.

Here's how to change the sample application to use a data view:

1. In the Design view, select the Data tab on the toolbox and drag a DataView into the tray area where `member1` already appears.

2. Select this new non-visual control and use the Properties window to change its `Table` property to `members1.member`. (Click the + next to `members1` to expand it and show the member table.)

3. Select the data grid and use the Properties window to change its Data Source property from `members1.member` to `dataView1`. (These property changes are quick and easy if you use the drop-down lists, which offer you lists of the possible controls in the solution that could serve as a data source.)

4. Drag on a text box and a button just above the data grid (you might have to resize the data grid a little to make room). Remove the default text from the text box, change the button text to Last Name Filter, and then resize the button so that all the text shows. Change the background color of the button to `Control` on the System tab of the color dialog box that appears in the Properties window when you select the `BackColor` property. The revised interface should resemble Figure 4.13.

5. Double-click the button to add and edit a handler for it.

6. Edit the handler to read like this:

```
private: System::Void button2_Click(System::Object *  sender,
                                     System::EventArgs *  e)
{
    String* filter = String::Concat(S"last LIKE '*", textBox2->Text);
    filter = String::Concat(filter,S"*'");

    dataView1->set_RowFilter(filter);
}
```

The text for the filter builds a selection clause around the context of `textBox2`. For example, if `textBox2` held the letter G, the filter string would be `"last LIKE '*G*'"`. This instructs the data view to give the data grid only records for which the column called last contains a G. If you want the text box to mean "the column should start with this string", remove the first * from the filter string.

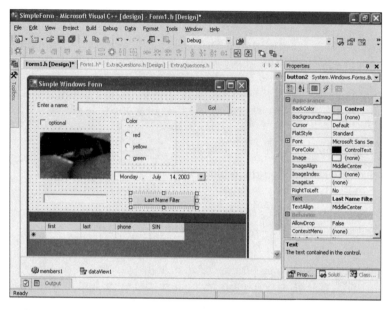

FIGURE 4.13 Add a text box and button to control the data grid's data source.

If you've been coding along, try running the sample application now. You can sort the data grid, restrict it to displaying only certain rows by entering a last name or part of a last name in the text box and clicking the button, and generally get a good feel for the way a real application (one with real database technology behind it) would work. In just a few lines of code, and a little dragging and dropping, you can create very realistic prototypes. You'll be seeing more of data grids and data sets in Chapter 11, but don't think you have to know all about databases to use them: Their power is in their simplicity for the user interface designer.

Creating a Multiple-Form Interface

When you build a Windows Forms application, your first form is given to you to work with, and so is the code to display it. But what if you want to display a second form? For example, you might want to ask the user for several pieces of information at once. To display such a form, you must first write a class that represents the form. Then you must add something to your user interface—a button or a menu item—that the user will choose to bring up the form. The handler for this user interface item must

1. Create an instance of this class.

2. Optionally, set properties of the object that will be used by the form.

3. Call the Show() or ShowModal() method of the object to display the form.

4. Gather information from the form to use as required.

These steps are further described in the sections that follow.

Writing a Form Class

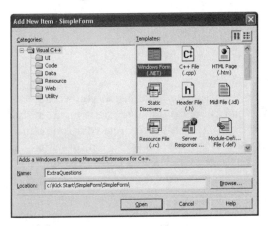

FIGURE 4.14 Adding another Windows Form to the project.

Like the form class that is generated for you when you create a Windows Forms application, the new form class you write to display a form must inherit from System::Windows::Forms::Form. To have such a class generated, right-click the project in Solution Explorer and choose Add, Add New Item. On the Add New Item dialog box, select Windows Form (.NET), as in Figure 4.14.

By entering ExtraQuestions for the form name, you arrange for a form to be created in the file ExtraQuestions.h. Double-clicking ExtraQuestions.h opens the form in the designer. Right-click either ExtraQuestions.h or the form in the designer and choose View Code to see the code that was generated. The class definition looks like this (comments have been removed to save space):

```
public __gc class ExtraQuestions : public System::Windows::Forms::Form
{
public:
    ExtraQuestions(void)
    {
        InitializeComponent();
    }

protected:
    void Dispose(Boolean disposing)
    {
        if (disposing && components)
        {
            components->Dispose();
        }
```

```
        __super::Dispose(disposing);
    }

private:
    System::ComponentModel::Container* components;
    void InitializeComponent(void)
    {
        this->components = new System::ComponentModel::Container();
        this->Size = System::Drawing::Size(300,300);
        this->Text = S"ExtraQuestions";
    }
};
```

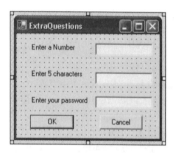

FIGURE 4.15   The new form has three text boxes and two buttons.

FIGURE 4.16   The password character replaces the text a user types with the character of the programmer's choice.

To build the form, use the visual designer just as you would when building the primary application, dragging items from the toolbox onto the form surface. This will change your code automatically. Figure 4.15 shows the ExtraQuestions form with three labels and text boxes, plus an OK and Cancel button.

Properties of Text Boxes

To limit the number of characters the user can enter into a text box, use the MaxLength property. It defaults to 32,767—a limit most users are unlikely to reach. If you change it, characters typed after the length has been reached are simply ignored. No error message is shown to the users, but an error beep is sounded.

To keep the text box from echoing the characters the user types, type a character in the Passwordchar property. This character will appear instead of each character typed by the user. Figure 4.16 shows the form echoing stars in the third text box while the user types a password.

Displaying a Form

When you display a new form (a dialog box is a special kind of form, with OK and Cancel buttons and no menu), you can display it either as a modal or a modeless form.

Most of the forms you will code will be modal. A modal form is on top of all the other windows in the application: The user must deal with the form or dialog box and then close it before going on to other work. An example of this is the dialog box that appears when the user chooses File, Open in any Windows application.

A modeless form enables the user to click the underlying application and do some other work and then return to the form. An example of this is the dialog box that appears when the user chooses Edit, Find in many Windows applications.

In unmanaged C++, when using MFC, modeless dialog boxes are quite a bit more trouble than modal ones. This is primarily a memory-management issue, so when you're working with garbage-collected form classes in managed C++, modeless forms are not much harder than modal ones, because the framework manages memory for you. You can make your decision based on the way you want your application to behave.

Displaying a Modal Form

To display a modal form, first add a user interface component, such as a button, to the application's main form. Then write the handler for the user interface component: it should create an instance of the form class, and then call that instance's ShowDialog() method. Here's a handler for a button added to the sample application for this chapter:

```
private: System::Void button3_Click(System::Object *  sender,
                              System::EventArgs *  e)
{
   ExtraQuestions* extraquestionsform = new ExtraQuestions();
    extraquestionsform->ShowDialog();
}
```

If you run this application and click the Show Modal Form button to bring up the form as a modal form, you will not be able to click back on the original form or interact with the application other than through the new ExtraQuestions form that

CLASS DECLARATION

Don't forget to #include the header file in which the new form has been declared (ExtraQuestions.h in this example).

is being displayed. You can close the form by clicking the X in the upper-right corner; neither the OK nor the Cancel button will close the form until you write code to make them do so.

ShowDialog() actually returns a value: an instance of the enumeration Windows::Forms::DialogResult. This enumeration has the values Abort, Cancel, Ignore, No, None, OK, Retry, and Yes. When you write code in the form class that sets the DialogResult property of the form, and the form is being displayed as a modal form, ShowDialog hides (but does not destroy) the form and returns the value that you assigned to the DialogResult property.

It's very common to have button handlers assign this property, so as a useful shortcut, buttons have a DialogResult property. If you set this property, when the button is clicked,

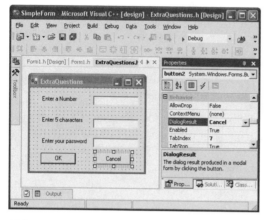

FIGURE 4.17   The DialogResult property can save a lot of coding.

the value you specify will be assigned to the DialogResult property of the form, which will in turn end the ShowDialog() method. This is excellent for a Cancel button (see Figure 4.17), when the only processing you are likely to want is to set this DialogResult property.

While you're using the Properties window with the form open in the designer, there are two interesting properties of the form itself you should examine: Accept Button and Cancel Button. If the user presses Enter, and you have an Accept Button property set, it's as though the user clicked that button. Similarly, if the user presses Escape, and you have a Cancel Button property set, it's as though the user clicked that button instead. This can save you having to code handlers for those keys while giving your users a more convenient and intuitive user interface.

For an OK button, you might want to do some validation before returning a result of OK. In that case you should still write a handler for the OK button. For example, here is the handler for the OK button on the ExtraQuestions form:

```
private: System::Void button1_Click(System::Object *  sender,
                                     System::EventArgs *  e)
{
   try
   {
      System::Decimal number = Convert::ToDecimal(textBox1->Text);
      if (textBox1->Text->CompareTo(number.ToString()) == 0)
      {
         //user typed a number
         DialogResult = OK;
      }
   }
   catch (Exception* e)
      // probably a format exception on the Convert
   {
      MessageBox::Show("First box must hold a number");
   }
}
```

This code attempts to convert the string in textBox1 into a decimal number such as 12.34. If the string is not in a format that can be converted like this, the framework code will throw a FormatException. This code just catches any exception and displays an error message. If there is no exception, the DialogResult is set, which ends the ShowDialog() method and returns control to the calling form.

The calling form, should, of course, do something with the information that the user entered on the form. It can also clean up the form by calling Dispose, although this isn't strictly necessary. The decision hinges on whether the form holds scarce unmanaged resources, such as database connections or open files. If it does, you should clean it up right away. If it doesn't, you might as well leave it around in case the user brings the form up again. It will come up more quickly the second time if it has not been disposed.

Retrieving Information from a Form

The controls you drag onto the form with the toolbox are private members of the form class:

```
public __gc class ExtraQuestions : public System::Windows::Forms::Form
{
// . . .
private: System::Windows::Forms::TextBox *  textBox1;
private: System::Windows::Forms::TextBox *  textBox2;
private: System::Windows::Forms::TextBox *  textBox3;
```

There's no need to keep repeating the private: access modifier like this, but it made the designer simpler to write. Because the text boxes (as well as the labels and buttons) are private, you can't write code in the application's main form to retrieve the text that was entered in the text boxes.

You must therefore write public methods of the form class that return this information. Here are the ones for the ExtraQuestions form:

```
public:
    String* getText1()    {return textBox1->Text;}
    String* getText2()    {return textBox2->Text;}
    String* getText3()    {return textBox3->Text;}
```

Because the first text box is supposed to hold an integer, you could have this first function return an integer instead of a string, and perform the conversion here. It all depends on the use to which you will put this information back in the calling form. You're the programmer—you decide which functions to add and what they return.

Code in the calling form can use these functions after the call to ShowDialog(), like so:

```
ExtraQuestions* extraquestionsform = new ExtraQuestions();
Windows::Forms::DialogResult answer
    =  extraquestionsform->ShowDialog();
if (answer == OK)
{
   System::Text::StringBuilder* sb =
      new System::Text::StringBuilder(S"You entered ");
   sb->Append(extraquestionsform->getText1());
   sb->Append(", ");
   sb->Append(extraquestionsform->getText2());
   sb->Append(", and ");
   sb->Append(extraquestionsform->getText3());

   MessageBox::Show(sb->ToString());
}
else
{
   MessageBox::Show("You cancelled");
}
```

Passing Information to a Form

It's quite common for a form to need information from the calling application, and to use this information to determine the initial values for some of the controls on the form. You achieve this by writing a constructor for the form that takes parameters, and using these parameters to initialize the controls. The only trick (and it's a small one) is to use the parameters after calling InitializeComponent(). I usually just edit the constructor that was generated, adding a parameter to it, like this:

```
public:
ExtraQuestions(String* start2)
{
   InitializeComponent();
   textBox2->Text = start2->Substring(0,5);
}
```

Of course, if you change the only constructor to take a parameter, you'll have to change the code in the calling form to pass a parameter:

```
ExtraQuestions* extraquestionsform = new ExtraQuestions("hello");
```

In this example, I take a substring of the parameter because the second text box has a MaxLength property set to 5, and it would confuse the user to see more than five characters in the text box when the form loads.

You might see examples elsewhere that catch the OnLoad event, or override the OnLoad() method and put control initialization in there. Usually, they take a parameter in the constructor and save it in a member variable, and then use it in the OnLoad code. For almost all cases, there's no need to do that. Most forms become visible (are loaded) as soon as they are constructed. Putting your initialization code entirely in the constructor is more efficient and makes your forms load more quickly.

Displaying a Modeless Form

To display a modeless form, you can use the same form class as for the modal form; the difference comes down to whether you call ShowDialog() or just Show(). Here's the handler for the Show Modeless Form button in the sample application:

```
private: System::Void button4_Click
➡(System::Object * sender,
➡System::EventArgs * e)
{
    ExtraQuestions* extraquestionsform =
➡new ExtraQuestions("hello");
    extraquestionsform->Show();
}
```

This code passes a string to the form constructor because this particular form class takes a string. Many form classes take no parameters in their constructors. The Show() method does not return a value. You have to write your application so that it doesn't matter whether the second form is being displayed or not, which can be more complicated than working with modal forms.

USING A BUSINESS LOGIC LAYER OR DATA LAYER

The sample application in this chapter has been very shallow. It is not a layered application. Under normal circumstances you will be creating applications in layers or tiers. One layer might handle interacting with the user, and pass numbers or strings along to another layer, which would apply business rules, or go into the database, or connect with another system elsewhere on the Internet. The point of layered and tiered developing is that, as the UI developer, you don't care. You pass along your numbers and strings and you get back answers, which your code displays to the user.

Many C++ programmers are not in the habit of writing user interfaces. They're used to writing class libraries, back ends, data layers, and other computationally intensive parts of applications. With the advent of Windows Forms for C++ in the .NET Framework, it's just as quick and easy for a Visual C++ programmer to develop a forms-based user interface as it is for a Visual Basic developer.

Chapter 5, "Writing a Class Library in Unmanaged C++," explores the concepts of layers and tiers in more detail. You'll see how to write a class library in unmanaged C++ (or use a class library that you already have) and call the methods of that library from unmanaged C++ or from managed C++ (perhaps a WinForms application like the one in this chapter). Chapter 6, "Writing a Class Library in Managed C++," explores similar territory but using managed code. Chapter 7, "Building DLLs in Unmanaged C++," Chapter 8, "Writing COM Components in C++," and Chapter 9, "Using Existing COM Components in C++," cover the various ways that different kinds of code can interoperate. In all these cases, if your user interface is written in managed C++, you can use either the simple test harness (console applications) of Chapter 2, "Creating Test Harnesses and Starter Applications," or the more complex WinForms user interfaces of this chapter to build your user interface.

In Brief

- To work with the Windows Forms library, create a Windows Forms project in Visual Studio, and then use the visual designers to create the application's main form.

- The Properties window enables you to control almost every aspect of each control's appearance and behavior, and dramatically reduces the amount of code you must type.

- Controls such as the data grid offer rich and intuitive behavior with little or no coding.

- You can create new forms of your own by inheriting from `System::Windows::Forms::Form`. Create an instance of the form class and call `ShowDialog()` or `Show()`.

Writing a Class Library in Unmanaged C++

The Role of a Class Library in a Layered Application

A class library is a collection of classes. Unlike an application, it can't be executed—either in a console prompt or as a Windows application—it can only provide services, on request, to other applications.

Why would a project include a class library, a collection of classes? After all, you can just put all your classes in your application. For small projects, you might not need a class library, but large projects benefit from the organization that it offers. If you have performed a full object-oriented design on a complex system, you can have hundreds or thousands of classes. The same concepts of encapsulation and abstraction that you used to gather 5 or 10 functions (methods) and variables (attributes) into classes should drive you to gather 10 or 20 classes into a class library.

TERMINOLOGY

When you're reading about design and architecture that involves class libraries, you are likely to come across words like module, package, subsystem, layer or tier. These words have precise meanings to certain people—unfortunately five different people can have five completely different very precise meanings for the same word. In this chapter I'm going to use them loosely to mean a group of related classes.

Often it's intuitive, even obvious, that certain corners of your design will be a module or a layer. Perhaps you have a number of classes that deal with a particular piece of hardware, or that communicate with another server over the network, or that interact with the database. When you gather these into a single layer, you encapsulate everything about the hardware or the other server or the database and you insulate the rest of the system from that detail.

One of the really obvious layers in your application is the user interface. By gathering all the classes that ask questions of the user or that handle events from the user into one layer, and refusing to have any user interface code in the other classes in your system, you gain a number of benefits:

- If you ever change your user interface, for example by replacing a logo or color scheme because of a corporate change, the number of classes to change will be smaller than if every class in the system was part of the user interface.

- In a team environment, you can assign the developer who is best at user interface design to the user interface layer rather than asking every developer to work on part of the user interface.

- All the other layers can be used to support another application with a different interface (a service, a console application, a Windows application, a Web service, and so on) without any changes.

If you split your application into multiple modules or subsystems, almost invariably one will be the user interface and all the others will be class libraries.

SHOP TALK

LAYERS IN REAL LIFE

One of the first remote projects I undertook showed me how dramatic the results of layering could be. We were developing software that simulated a chemical plant or oil refinery. Many of the developers, including me, were high-level chemical engineers, not user interface experts or graphic artists. I was working on classes in the business layer that simulated the behavior of a pump, a pipe segment, or other pieces of a chemical plant. My classes had no user interface component: They had methods that the user interface classes could call to pass along requests or information from the user.

SHOP TALK

As I worked on my code, I linked with a C++ .LIB file that held the compiled version of the user interface. From time to time the client would send me a new version of this .LIB file. One day I recompiled and—presto!—the console application I had been testing had become a Windows application. All of my code worked just the same even though a dramatic appearance change had happened throughout the application. Separating your code into layers gives you flexibility, portability, and durability.

The process of developing a layered application becomes simpler when you look for certain "obvious" or popular layers. These include

- User interface layer—the parts of the application that report information to the user and accept requests and input from the user.

- Data layer—everything that interacts with the database.

- Communications layers—any sets of classes that communicate with the hardware or another system.

- Business logic—any sets of classes that enforce line-of-business rules, such as authorizing purchases, determining prices, tracking absences, calculating marks, and the like. Complex systems can have several modules within the business layer.

No matter what purpose your layer serves, if it can't be executed, it's a class library.

Creating a Class Library

The simplest way to write a class library to be called from an application is to make a second project within the solution that already contains the application. A library like this is designed to be used by a single application. It's quite simple to write other applications that can also use it.

Writing a class library should always start with design. In order to keep the code simple and concentrate on the connections between the calling application and the class library, the design in this sample library is simple. The library does arithmetic. There is a class called `Arithmetic`, with methods such as `Add()`, `Subtract()`, `Multiply()`, and `Divide()`. These methods each take two `double` parameters and return `double` results.

Future versions of this library might add more classes to it, such as a class that represents complex numbers, or matrices, or fractions represented as a numerator and a denominator instead of as a floating-point number. A class library with only one class in it can serve as a useful illustration, even if it's not really a very useful library.

The user interface for the sample class library in this chapter could be a Windows application or a console application. Just for simplicity, this chapter builds a console application to demonstrate how to use a class library.

To create the sample application, follow these steps:

1. In Visual Studio, choose File, New, Blank solution and name the solution AllInOne.

2. In Solution Explorer, right-click the solution and choose Add, New Project.

3. Select a C++ Win32 project and name it Math Library. On the Win32 Application wizard, change the Application Settings to a static library. Accept all the other defaults.

4. In Solution Explorer, right-click the solution and choose Add, New Project.

5. Select a C++ Win32 Console application and name it Harness. Accept all the defaults on the wizard.

6. Right-click the MathLibrary project in Solution Explorer and choose Add, Add Class. Select Generic C++ Class and click Open.

7. On the Generic C++ Class wizard, fill in Arithmetic for the class name. The other boxes are filled in for you. Click Finish.

At this point you have two projects in a solution, and the MathLibrary project has a header file, Arithmetic.h and an implementation file, Arithmetic.cpp. Listing 5.1 shows the simple definition of this class, and Listing 5.2 shows the implementation. The constructor and destructor were generated by the wizard.

LISTING 5.1   Arithmetic.h—Class Definition

```
#pragma once

class Arithmetic
{
public:
    Arithmetic(void);
    ~Arithmetic(void);
    double Add(double num1, double num2);
    double Subtract(double num1, double num2);
    double Multiply(double num1, double num2);
    double Divide(double num1, double num2);
};
```

LISTING 5.2 Arithmetic.cpp—Class Implementation

```cpp
#include "StdAfx.h"
#include ".\arithmetic.h"

Arithmetic::Arithmetic(void)
{
}

Arithmetic::~Arithmetic(void)
{
}

double Arithmetic::Add(double num1, double num2)
{
    return num1 + num2;
}

double Arithmetic:: Subtract(double num1, double num2)
{
    return num1 - num2;
}

double Arithmetic::Multiply(double num1, double num2)
{
    return num1 * num2;
}

double Arithmetic::Divide(double num1, double num2)
{
    return num1 / num2;
}
```

The code for the test harness calls these member functions. To write code that calls these functions, you need to ensure that the compiler knows where to find the definition of the class and the linker knows where to find the compiled code for the implementation.

The harness file must include the header file for the Arithmetic class. You might simply add this line:

```cpp
#include "arithmetic.h"
```

This won't work: arithmetic.h and harness.cpp are in different folders. Each is in a project folder beneath the solution folder. You could provide the full path to the header file:

```
#include "../MathLibrary/arithmetic.h"
```

This will work, but it's not very maintainable—if you ever rearrange the folders, you might have to change hundreds of include statements throughout a large project. It's better to arrange with Visual Studio to look in the MathLibrary folder whenever it's looking for header files that you've included. Here's how:

1. In Solution Explorer, right-click the Harness project and choose Properties.

2. Under Configuration Properties on the left, expand the C/C++ folder. Click General. Click next to Additional Include Directories on the left (see Figure 5.1) and type the relative path to the MathLibrary folder:

   ```
   ../MathLibrary
   ```

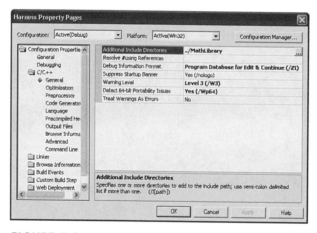

FIGURE 5.1   Adding another directory to those that are searched for include (.H) files.

3. Click OK. Now the compiler knows how to find the arithmetic.h file.

4. In Solution Explorer, right-click the Harness project and choose Properties.

5. Under Configuration Properties on the left, expand the Linker folder. Click Input. Click next to Additional Dependencies on the left (see Figure 5.2) and type the relative path to the Debug build of the MathLibrary folder:

   ```
   ../MathLibrary/Debug/MathLibrary.lib
   ```

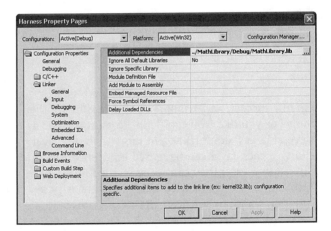

FIGURE 5.2 Adding another library to those that are linked together to form your executable file.

6. Click OK. Now the linker will be able to find MathLibrary.lib, which holds the compiled code for the methods of the Arithmetic class.

All that remains is to write some test code that exercises a few of the Arithmetic member functions. That looks like this:

```
#include "stdafx.h"
#include "arithmetic.h"
#include <iostream>
using namespace std;

int _tmain(int argc, _TCHAR* argv[])
{
    Arithmetic a;
    cout << "1.2 + 3.2 = " << a.Add(1.2, 3.2) << endl;
    cout << "2.1 * 3 = "<< a.Multiply(2.1, 3) << endl;
    cin.get();

    return 0;
}
```

Build the entire solution (choose Build, Build Solution) and you're almost ready to test. When a solution holds more than one project, one is the startup project, the one that runs when you press F5. The name of that project is bold in Solution Explorer. By default, the project you create first (MathLibrary in this case) is the startup project. Right-click the

Harness project in Solution Explorer and choose Set As Startup Project. Now run the test harness by pressing F5. You should see something like this:

```
1.2 + 3.2 = 4.4
2.1 * 3 = 6.3
```

There you have it—a simple class library in one project, and a simple test harness in another. In reality, your class library can be as complex as you like. You can define as many classes as you like. If your overall architecture has several layers, don't try to put more than one layer into each .LIB file. You'll have more flexibility if each layer can be reused independently. And think twice about splitting a layer across two .LIB files. If they can really be used independently, perhaps they represent two layers. And if they can't be used independently, why set other developers up for trouble by implying that they can be? It's better to keep logical units, such as a layer or module, intact.

Because your library was statically linked (from a .LIB file) into your application, when you distribute the application, you only need to distribute the .EXE file. All the code from the library that your application uses has been copied into the .EXE file. This can make .EXE files large, which is one of the appeals of DLL programming, but it makes distribution simple— there is only one file to distribute. You can test this by copying Harness.exe to any other folder on your hard drive, and then double-clicking it to run it. It will run perfectly.

Calling the Library from Other Applications

Because the MathLibrary project created a static library, a .LIB file, you can use it from other applications that are outside the AllInOne solution. Typically you deploy a library like this as the .LIB file and the associated header file (or files). In order to create the sample applications in this section, you should copy the .LIB and .H files from the AllInOne folder to another location, to more closely resemble the circumstances under which you would use a real class library.

Creating a Release Version of the Library

The instructions so far in this chapter created a debug version (also called a Debug build) of the library, and a debug version of the test harness to go with it. For distribution to other developers, it's better to create a release version. This has many advantages, including

- Release builds are smaller, because they don't contain debugging symbols. Even in this tiny application, it makes a difference: The debug library is 10KB and the release library is only 6KB.

- Release builds are faster, because the optimizer is turned off in Debug builds and some blocks of code are not included by the compiler in Debug builds.

■ Release builds only use Release builds of other libraries; and because license agreements often forbid redistributing debug versions of libraries, a Release build might be the only build you can distribute anyway.

These are the most significant differences between the default Debug build and the default Release build. Once you are experienced working with different kinds of builds, you can use the Properties page for the project to tweak your settings.

To build a release version of MathLibrary.lib, follow these steps:

1. On the toolbar next to the Start button (a blue rightward-pointing arrow) is a drop-down box with Debug selected. Drop it down and select Release.

2. Bring up the properties of the Harness project as before. Expand the C/C++ folder and select General. In the Configuration drop-down box at the top of the dialog box, select Debug.

3. From the Debug settings, select the path to the additional include directory that you added and copy it into the Clipboard.

4. In the Configuration drop-down box, select All Configurations. Paste the path into the Additional Include Directories property. Now both Debug and Release builds will find the header file in the same location.

5. Expand the Linker folder and choose Input. Again switch to the Debug configuration (if you're prompted to save the changes you have made so far, choose Yes), and copy the Additional Dependencies path.

6. Switch to the Release configuration, paste in the path, and change `Debug` to `Release` so the path reads as follows:

   `../MathLibrary/Release/MathLibrary.lib`

7. Now the linker uses the Release build of the library when it builds a Release build of the harness, and a Debug build of the library when it builds a Debug build of the harness. Click OK to save your changes.

Build and run the application to be sure you made all your changes correctly.

Calling the Library from an Unmanaged C++ Application

To call the library methods from another application, start by creating an application. The sample in this section is an MFC application just to show that class libraries aren't restricted to console applications. Here's how to create the application and start using methods from the library:

1. Create an MFC application called UseLibrary.

2. On the MFC Application wizard, click Application Type on the left.

3. Select the Dialog Based option. Click Finish to accept all the other defaults.

4. A form appears in the form editor. This is an MFC form, and working with it is similar to working with Windows Forms in Managed C++, as described in Chapter 4, "Building Simple User Interfaces with Windows Forms."

5. Click the static text with a caption that starts *TODO* and press delete to remove it from the form.

6. Drag two edit controls, two static text controls, and a button from the toolbox onto the form.

7. Use the Properties window to change the caption of the first label to +, the caption of the second label to no text, the ID of the second label to IDC_ANSWER, and the caption of the button to =.

FIGURE 5.3
Building a simple MFC dialog-based application that will use the library.

8. Rearrange the controls and resize the form so that it resembles Figure 5.3. (If you lose the label that has no text on it, use the drop-down box at the top of the Properties window to select the IDC_ANSWER control and you will see it highlighted on the form.)

9. Right-click the first edit control and choose Add Variable. On the Add Member Variable wizard, change the Category (on the right) to Value and the Variable type to double. Enter num1 for the name and click Finish.

10. Repeat this process for the second edit control, naming the variable num2.

11. Right-click the IDC_ANSWER static control (you might have to use the Properties window to select it first) and choose Add Variable. This time, leave the variable type and category as the defaults, and simply name the variable answer, and then click Finish.

12. Double-click the = button to add a handler for the click event and open the source code for editing.

At this point, the dialog box has been created, and all the required variables and methods have been added to the associated class. In order to actually code the button handler, the compiler and linker must be told about the library. Copy the header file, Arithmetic.h, and the release version of the library, MathLibrary.lib, to another folder on your computer. In the instructions that follow, that folder is assumed to be C:\MathLibrary.

Just like the Harness project that tested the library, the UseLibrary project has settings that can be changed to ensure the compiler and linker can find the class definition and the executable code. Add the folder C:\MathLibrary to the Additional Include Directories property by right-clicking UseLibrary in Solution Explorer and expanding C/C++ and then selecting General and entering the path. Then expand the Linker folder and select input, and enter the full path to the .LIB file.

When the library was created, it included a reference to the C runtime library (CRT). Microsoft ships many different versions of the CRT with the compiler. The default settings when creating a static library include the single-threaded version of the CRT. This is also the default for console applications, so both Harness and MathLibrary used the same version of the CRT. However the MFC dialog-based application created in this section uses the multi-threaded debug DLL version of the CRT. As a result, all the functions in the CRT are linked in twice—once from the single-threaded version of the CRT and once from the multi-threaded debug version. This causes linker errors such as this:

```
LIBC.lib(malloc.obj) : error LNK2005: _malloc already defined in
➥ msvcrtd.lib(MSVCR71D.dll)
LIBC.lib(crt0dat.obj) : error LNK2005: _exit already defined in
➥msvcrtd.lib(MSVCR71D.dll)
```

The project will not build at this point. There are several approaches to solving this problem, some better than others:

- You could change the library to use the multi-threaded debug DLL version of the CRT. (Bring up the properties for the project, expand C/C++, select Code Generation, and change the Runtime Libraries property.) Unfortunately, this would cause linker errors for your console application.

- You could change the MFC application to use the single-threaded version of the CRT. This doesn't work: MFC requires some constants that are only in the multi-threaded versions.

- You could build two versions of the library, each using a different version of the CRT. This is hard to maintain.

- You could instruct the linker to bring in MathLibrary but to ignore the single-threaded CRT that MathLibrary tries to bring in with it. This is the recommended approach.

To instruct the linker to ignore the single-threaded version of the CRT, bring up the properties for the UseLibrary project. Expand the Linker folder and select Input. Click next to Ignore Specific Library and type **libc.lib**—this is the name of the single-threaded release version of the CRT. Now the project builds successfully—and you don't have to change the library.

CRT LIBRARY NAMES

To find the names of each of the versions of the CRT, search for one of them (such as libc.lib) in the online help.

The file UseLibraryDlg.cpp is where the button click handler has been added. At the top of this file, after the include statements already present, add an include statement:

```
#include "arithmetic.h"
```

The handler for the button click creates an instance of the Arithmetic class and uses it to add the numbers that were entered in the edit controls. Then it converts the answer to a string and uses that as the new caption for the static text control. The code looks like this:

```
void CUseLibraryDlg::OnBnClickedButton1()
{
    UpdateData(true);
    Arithmetic a;
    double ans = a.Add(num1,num2);
    CString answerstring;
    answerstring.Format("%g",ans);
    answer.SetWindowText(answerstring);
}
```

The call to UpdateData() copies the entries from the actual controls on the dialog box to the member variables you mapped to them with the Add Variable wizard.

Now you have seen how to use a simple class library from an unmanaged C++ console application and an unmanaged C++ MFC dialog-based application. There is no difference in technique when the library is in the same solution as the calling code or in a different solution: You still need to inform the compiler and the linker of the location of the library's header and .LIB files. When you are using the library from an application that uses the multi-threaded version of the CRT, you need to instruct the linker not to bring the single-threaded version in with the library.

Calling the Library from a Managed C++ Application

Using the library from another unmanaged C++ application was straightforward. Using it from a managed C++ application is also straightforward, even though it combines managed and unmanaged code in one application.

Start by creating a managed C++ console application called ManagedUseLibrary. Update the Additional Include Directories, Additional Dependencies, and Ignore Specific Libraries properties just as for the MFC dialog-based application. Here is the code for the main function:

```
#include "stdafx.h"
#using <mscorlib.dll>
using namespace System;
```

```
#include "arithmetic.h"

int _tmain()
{
    Arithmetic a;
    Console::Write(S"1.2 + 3.2 = ");
    Console::WriteLine(__box(a.Add(1.2, 3.2)));
    Console::Write(S"2.1 * 3 = ");
    Console::WriteLine(__box(a.Multiply(2.1, 3)));
    Console::ReadLine();
    return 0;
}
```

It's as simple as that to use an unmanaged class library from a managed application. The C++ team at Microsoft call this "It Just Works"—and it does! You'll also see It Just Works referred to as IJW.

BOXING UNMANAGED DATA

The use of the __box extension to convert unmanaged data (such as a double) to managed data was first discussed in Chapter 1, "C++, Visual C++, and Managed C++: What's the Difference?"

Calling the Library from Other Managed Languages

If you've been reading about the Common Language Runtime and how all the managed languages use the same class libraries and share the same capabilities, you might well assume that the library created in this chapter can be used from Visual Basic .NET and Visual C# as easily as from managed C++. However, that's not the case. All the languages share the same libraries, and produce code that is easily compatible. Code written in managed C++ can be used in a Visual Basic .NET application without any difficulty at all. Managed C++ code can use code written in C# as simply as though it were written in C++. But—and this is a huge advantage of C++—the other languages cannot access unmanaged code using It Just Works. There are several techniques for calling unmanaged C++ code from Visual Basic .NET or C#:

- Write a wrapper class in managed C++ that uses IJW to call into the library. This should be the simplest method, but it has a few pitfalls. Chapter 6, "Writing a Class Library in Managed C++," guides you through them.

- Convert the unmanaged code into a Dynamic Link Library (DLL) and access it through PInvoke. Chapter 7, "Building DLLs in Unmanaged C++," explains how this is done.

- Convert the unmanaged code into a COM component and access it through COM Interop. Chapter 8, "Writing COM Components in C++," covers this technique.

Advantages and Disadvantages of Writing an Unmanaged Class Library

If you're writing a class library from scratch today, you might wonder whether you should write it in unmanaged C++. Well, that depends on what languages will be using it. If you plan to use the library extensively from Visual Basic .NET or C#, it's far better to write the library in managed C++ and take advantage of the language interoperability on the .NET Framework. If you plan to use the library mainly from existing unmanaged C++ applications, writing it in unmanaged C++ makes sense. You can use IJW to access it from managed C++.

In general, unmanaged C++ is faster than managed C++. If you're writing a library where performance is very important, and the calculations are weighty enough that other languages might be slow, unmanaged C++ is the way to go. It's also more portable, allowing you to use the same code base to maintain a library for several different operating systems. Managed C++, Visual Basic .NET, and C# class libraries can be used only on systems where the .NET Framework has been installed. Unmanaged C++ libraries will work on a larger population of systems.

Of course, the .NET Framework was invented for a reason. It brings simple interoperability, memory management, and consistent Rapid Application Development techniques to programmers in a variety of managed languages. When you look at the advantages of managed C++ over unmanaged C++, you might well choose to write in managed code. On every count except code execution speed, managed C++ is preferable. So if you're not counting CPU cycles, and you don't need to support any operating systems other than fairly recent versions of Windows, a managed class library is a better choice. The next chapter shows you how that's done.

In Brief

- Unmanaged class libraries compile to a static link library (a .LIB file).

- Both managed and unmanaged C++ applications can use .LIB files after changing linker settings to add an additional dependency.

- You might need to instruct the linker in the calling project to ignore the single-threaded C runtime library that is brought in with your library.

- Calling unmanaged C++ code from Visual Basic .NET or C# is more difficult than from managed C++.

Writing a Class Library in Managed C++

Advantages and Disadvantages of a Managed Class Library

The previous chapter discussed the advantages of a layered design, and of putting functionality into a class library, whether that library is shared among several applications or used by only one. If you're building a class library, you need to consider whether it should be written in managed or unmanaged code.

At first glance, unmanaged code seems like the better choice. After all, managed C++ can call unmanaged code through It Just Works (IJW), but unmanaged code can only call managed code through .NET Interop, which is a little slow. And unmanaged code is generally faster than managed code. But the runtime offers services to your running code, including memory management, that will make your class library simpler to write and more reliable when it's running. As well, managed code can be called from any other managed language (such as Visual Basic .NET or C#), which can simplify (and speed up) multi-language application development.

The binary compatibility provided by the .NET runtime is an enormous benefit. When you develop unmanaged code in Visual Basic 5 or unmanaged C++, the applications you create can only interact through COM. This imposes a performance penalty, and the development techniques are anything but simple. You can learn more about COM in

Chapter 8, "Writing COM Components in C++," and Chapter 9, "Using Existing COM Components in C++." When you develop managed code, you write none of the plumbing to enable your applications to interact; they simply interact within the runtime. What's more, the performance is far better than traditional COM applications.

When you write an unmanaged class library, using it from other code requires at least two and perhaps three steps:

- You must tell the C++ compiler what classes and functions are in the library by including a header file (and usually you must set an option to help the compiler find the header file).

- You must tell the C++ linker where to find the compiled code by adding the library file to the dependencies.

- You might need to set linker options to ignore a version of the C runtime library that is brought in with the library you are using.

In contrast, a managed class library is in an assembly, a complete self-describing unit. When you add a reference to an assembly, it takes care of everything for you in a single step, as you'll see in the sample applications later in this chapter.

Building a Managed Class Library

The library in this chapter serves the same purpose as the unmanaged library in the previous chapter: It has one class, named Arithmetic, which has four methods: Add, Subtract, Divide, and Multiply. These methods each take two System::Double parameters and return a System::Double answer.

To create the sample library, start by using Visual Studio .NET 2003 to create a Class Library (.NET) project called ManagedMathLibrary. This creates an implementation file, ManagedMathLibrary.cpp, and a header file, ManagedMathLibrary.h. The compiler doesn't care whether you put the entire implementation into the header file or put the declarations into the header file and the method bodies into the implementation file.

When you work in unmanaged code, you move as much of the code as you can into an implementation file to keep the header small, because all the code that uses the class must include the header file. However, when you work with managed code, the header file is not included: The reference to the assembly provides the compiler with the information it needs. So in managed code, it doesn't matter where you put your method bodies. For simplicity, the sample code in this chapter is in the header file.

The class that is created in the ManagedMathLibrary project is called Class1—change it to Arithmetic in ManagedMathLibrary.h. There's no code to change in

ManagedMathLibrary.cpp. Then you add the methods and their bodies right in the header file. The class ends up looking like this:

```cpp
// ManagedMathLibrary.h

#pragma once

using namespace System;

namespace ManagedMathLibrary
{
   public __gc class Arithmetic
   {
   public:
      System::Double Add(System::Double num1, System::Double num2)
      {
         return num1 + num2;
      }
      System::Double Subtract (System::Double num1, System::Double num2)
      {
         return num1 - num2;
      }
      System::Double Divide(System::Double num1, System::Double num2)
      {
         return num1 / num2;
      }
      System::Double Multiply(System::Double num1, System::Double num2)
      {
         return num1 * num2;
      }
   };
}
```

There is very little difference between this code and the code you would write for the same library in unmanaged code. The differences are as follows:

- The keyword public on the class declaration ensures that in the assembly built for this project, the Arithmetic class will be available for use by classes in other assemblies.

- The keyword __gc on the class declaration makes this class garbage-collected; its memory will be managed by the runtime.

- The method parameters and return types are System::Double.

System::Double is a managed value type, equivalent to the double type in unmanaged C++. Unlike the fundamental type double, System::Double is a structure, with member functions. It inherits from System::Object and its memory is managed by the runtime. As a value type, you can create instances on the stack; you don't need to use pointer semantics to work with your instances. As you can see in the code for these member functions, operator overloads for the basic arithmetic operations have already been defined for this type. You can think of it as being just like double, but under the hood it's very different.

Using the Class Library from Managed Code

If a class library is being developed for a particular application, it's easy enough to have the application and the library in the same solution. A shared class library will be called by applications that are not in the same solution as the library. The difference between the two scenarios is less than you might think.

Using the Library from Code in the Same Solution

To test the managed class library, the simplest approach is to add another project to the solution, this one containing a test harness. Simply right-click the solution and choose Add, Add Project. Select a Console Application (.NET) and name it ManagedHarness. A source file is generated for the console application.

Before you can enter code that uses the library, you have to arrange for the compiler to know about the classes and methods inside it. Rather than including a header file as in unmanaged C++, you add a reference to the assembly. Right-click the ManagedHarness project in Solution Explorer and choose Add Reference. Because the assembly is in another project inside the same solution as the class library, you use the Projects tab on the Add Reference dialog box.

Once the reference is added, you can use the Arithmetic class like any other managed class. Because it's a garbage-collected class, you must create instances on the managed heap with new and work with them through pointers. Here's the test code in the console harness:

```
// This is the main project file for VC++ application project
// generated using an Application Wizard.

#include "stdafx.h"

#using <mscorlib.dll>

using namespace System;

int _tmain()
{
```

```
ManagedMathLibrary::Arithmetic* a = new ManagedMathLibrary::Arithmetic();
Console::Write("2.3 + 4.5 is ");
Console::WriteLine(a->Add(2.3, 4.5));
Console::ReadLine();
return 0;
}
```

Notice that there is no need to include ManagedArithmetic.h, or to add an additional linker dependency. Adding the reference takes care of everything. Also, because this version of Add returns a `System::Double` structure, you don't need to use __box around the answer before passing it to `Console::WriteLine`.

Creating a Release Version of the Library

The instructions so far in this chapter created a debug version (also called a debug build) of the library, and a debug version of the test harness to go with it. For distribution to other developers, it's better to create a release version. This has many advantages, including

- Release builds are smaller, because they don't contain debugging symbols. Even in this tiny application, it makes a difference: The debug library is 7KB, whereas the release library is only 6KB.

- Release builds are faster, because the optimizer is turned off in debug builds and some blocks of code are not included by the compiler in debug builds.

- Release builds only use release builds of other libraries; and because license agreements often forbid redistributing debug versions of libraries, a release build might be the only build you can distribute anyway.

These differences are between the default debug build and the default release build. There are a few other differences too, but they are out of the scope of this chapter. What's more, you can change the definition of these builds—even enabling debugging symbols in a release build!—but that too is out of scope.

To build a release version of MathLibrary.lib, just look on the toolbar next to the Start button (a blue right-pointing arrow) for a drop-down box with Debug selected. Click it and select Release. Build the application to create the Release version.

Using the Library from Code in a Different Solution

Working on the .NET runtime makes deploying libraries far simpler than it was with unmanaged code. To demonstrate this, consider a Windows application that uses the sample managed class library. To create a new solution with an application that uses the class library, follow these steps:

1. In Visual Studio .NET 2003, create a new Windows Forms Application (.NET) called WinTest.

2. Details on creating a managed Windows Forms application are in Chapter 4, "Building Simple User Interfaces with Windows Forms." If you need to understand the steps presented here, review that chapter as a reference.

3. Drag two text box controls, two label controls, and a button from the toolbox onto the form.

4. Use the Properties window to change the text property of the first label to +, the text of the second label to no text, the name of the second label to Answer, and the caption of the button to = (equals sign). Change the text property of the text boxes to no text.

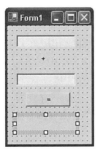

5. Rearrange the controls and resize the form so that it resembles Figure 6.1.

6. Double-click the = button to add a handler for the click event and open the source code for editing.

FIGURE 6.1
Building a simple Windows Forms application that will use the managed library.

Before you can code the button handler, you need to add a reference to the managed library. To more accurately simulate a deployment, copy the release version (it's in the Release folder under the project) of ManagedMathLibrary.dll to another folder on your computer. In the instructions that follow, that folder is assumed to be C:\MathLibrary.

To add the reference, right-click the project in Solution Explorer and choose Add Reference. On the .NET tab, click the Browse button and browse to C:\MathLibrary, select ManagedMathLibrary.dll, and click Open. Click OK on the Add Reference dialog box to complete adding the reference.

At this point, the class inside the managed library is available to your code, using the full name of ManagedMathLibrary::Arithmetic. Here is the code for the button click handler:

```
private:
System::Void button1_Click(System::Object *  sender, System::EventArgs *  e)
{
    ManagedMathLibrary::Arithmetic* a = new ManagedMathLibrary::Arithmetic();
    System::Double ans = a->Add(Double::Parse(textBox1->Text),
                                Double::Parse(textBox2->Text));
    Answer->Text = ans.ToString();
}
```

Enter this code into the button click handler, and then build and run the Windows application. Enter numbers into the text boxes, and click the = button to see the sum of the two numbers.

This simple library accomplishes the same tasks as the unmanaged library shown in the previous chapter, and the two sample applications (a console application in the same solution and a Windows application in a different solution from the library) also accomplish the same tasks. Yet when you compare the effort to implement the managed solutions to the effort to implement the unmanaged solutions, it becomes very clear what the runtime has to offer. Deployment is much simpler in the managed case, and the Windows Forms application is developed far more rapidly than the MFC Dialog application. This simplicity is what motivates developers to move to managed code.

Calling the Library from Another Managed Language

Because the Arithmetic class in this sample is a garbage-collected (managed) class, it can be used by any managed language. It's just a matter of adding the reference (by browsing to the file that holds the assembly) and using the class. Here's how to do it in a C# console application:

1. In Visual Studio, create a C# console application named CSUseLibrary.

2. Add a reference to ManagedMathLibrary.dll (use the .NET tab and browse to C:\MAthLibrary, and then select the file).

3. Enter the code for the test harness.

Some suitable testing code in C# follows:

```
using System;

namespace CSUseLibrary
{
    /// <summary>
    /// Summary description for Class1.
    /// </summary>
    class Class1
    {
        /// <summary>
        /// The main entry point for the application.
        /// </summary>
        [STAThread]
        static void Main(string[] args)
        {
```

```
        ManagedMathLibrary.Arithmetic a = new ManagedMathLibrary.Arithmetic();
        Console.Write("4.1 + 5.9 is ");
        Console.WriteLine(a.Add(4.1, 5.9));
        Console.ReadLine();
    }
  }
}
```

Some things to notice about C# in contrast to Managed C++:

- The Main() function has a different signature than the _tmain() of a C++ console appli-cation. Because the code is generated, you don't need to remember the signature (or the attribute on the method), but you do need to remember that the C# Main() does not return a value.

- C# uses . to separate a class name from a static method name, whereas C++ uses ::.

- C# uses references to access managed data, and reaches members with the . operator, whereas C++ uses pointers and the -> operator.

This code compiles and runs with no further work on your part: Adding the reference takes care of everything. Binary compatibility, even across languages, is simple on the .NET runtime. It's just as simple from Visual Basic, assuming you're comfortable with the syntax.

Managed and Unmanaged Data in a Managed Library

The Arithmetic class is a managed class; it was defined with the _gc keyword as follows:

```
public __gc class Arithmetic
{
// . . .
};
```

When you create instances of this class, they must be created on the managed heap:

```
ManagedMathLibrary::Arithmetic* a = new ManagedMathLibrary::Arithmetic();
```

When you're finished with them, you don't clean them up with the delete operator. You don't do anything; the garbage collector will clean up the memory for you later.

The __gc keyword is an addition to the C++ language. You can write managed code that declares unmanaged classes. Just omit the __gc keyword, like this:

```
class Simple
{
private:
    int x;
public:
    Simple(int xx): x(xx){};
    int getx() {return x;}
};
```

When you're writing managed C++, you can use unmanaged classes such as `Simple`, creating instances either on the heap or the stack.

```
Simple s(3);
Console::WriteLine(__box(s.getx()));
Simple* ps = new Simple(4);
Console::WriteLine(__box(ps->getx()));
```

However, you must remember to clean up any instances you create on the heap, or your program will suffer a memory leak. Just use the `delete` operator, like this:

```
delete ps;
```

Visibility

C++ programmers are used to controlling the visibility of member variables and functions with the `public`, `private`, and `protected` keywords. In a managed class, the `public` keyword can also be applied to a class.

The `Arithmetic` class was declared with the `__gc` keyword, but also with the `public` keyword. Without the `public` modifier, the class would not be available to managed code outside the assembly, such as the `ManagedHarness` console application and the `CSUseLibrary` C# console application. You can use the unmanaged class `Simple` from outside the assembly only if it is defined entirely in its .h file, and you include that file in the code that will use the class. This results in the class being recompiled into that assembly. If parts of the `Simple` code are in the .cpp file, you won't be able to use the class from another assembly.

When you design a managed class library, you will plan for one or more garbage-collected classes—managed data in your managed code. You can choose whether to expose these classes to managed code outside the assembly with the `public` keyword. You may also write some unmanaged classes, none of which will be accessible outside the assembly.

Accessing Legacy Libraries Such as the STL

One example of unmanaged data that can be very useful in a C++ application is a template instance. The Standard Template Library gathers together numerous template classes and functions, such as collection classes (linked lists, queues, and so on) and common operations (sorting, finding, and the like). Using the STL from your C++ applications requires no special work, whether you're working in managed or unmanaged C++.

What's more, the C++ compiler in Visual C++ .NET 2003 is over 98% compliant with the ANSI C++ standard. This astonishing level of compatibility opens up a world of libraries to Visual C++ developers. A number of template-based libraries exist that have tremendous power and can save you days or weeks of programming effort, including

- Boost (www.boost.org) is a community-supported outgrowth of the STL. The libraries within Boost handle collections, mathematics, and memory management.

- Blitz (www.oonumerics.org/blitz) is a class library for scientific computing with an emphasis on high-speed code.

- Loki (www.moderncppdesign.com) is a library of generic components that implement design patterns.

These libraries make intensive use of templates and of advanced template features. Parts of these libraries would not build on earlier versions of Visual C++. When you write managed code for the .NET runtime in Visual C++, these libraries are available to save time and effort.

It Just Works (IJW) Interoperability and the Mixed DLL Problem

The previous chapter, "Writing a Class Library in Unmanaged C++," showed how to write an unmanaged class and, among other things, call it from managed code. The capability of managed C++ code to call into unmanaged code contained in a .LIB file is part of the appeal of managed C++ as a language to use on the .NET runtime. Visual Basic and C# don't have this capability.

This means that you can use not only your own unmanaged libraries, but all the unmanaged libraries that already exist: MFC, ATL, STL, libraries you bought from a vendor, and so on. Working in managed C++ opens up a world of interoperability.

When you write a managed console application that uses IJW to call unmanaged code, you create what's known as a mixed EXE—an assembly that contains both intermediate language and native code. Mixed EXEs are simple to create and they work flawlessly. When you create a mixed DLL, you usually need to go to a little trouble to make sure it works just as flawlessly. Otherwise you might run into what's known as the loader-lock bug.

The Loader-Lock Bug

The issue is not mixing native code and intermediate language, but rather a seemingly trivial issue: initializing statics. When you write an unmanaged DLL, global variables and static member variables are initialized in a function called DllMain, which is generated for you when you create the project. If you are using any libraries, DllMain would normally call out to these libraries to initialize them.

At first glance, you can do the same thing in a managed library, with a few lines of managed code in DllMain, using IJW to call the unmanaged libraries. However, because of the architecture of the .NET loader in versions 1.0 and 1.1 of the .NET Framework, it's very important not to call any managed code from DllMain. If you write a DllMain with managed code in it, the .NET loader has to be called from DllMain to load and run the managed code, and under certain circumstances your machine could lock or hang unexpectedly. Code with this issue can run normally until the system is at very high load, and then lock up at a critical time. It's also more likely to happen if your assembly has a strong name—that is, after you've deployed it onto customer computers. (This is called the loader-lock bug and will be fixed in a future version of the Framework.)

Starting in version 1.1 of the .NET Framework, all managed-code DLLs are generated with an option called /NOENTRY, which suppresses the generation of a DllMain function. This prevents the loader-lock issue from hurting you, but leaves you the task of initializing the libraries you will use. Your own unmanaged libraries might not need initializing, but ATL, MFC, the C runtime (CRT), and other popular libraries do have statics that must be initialized before the libraries are used. You must write code to initialize these libraries, and what's more, you must expose this code in methods that users of your libraries must call.

A Sample Mixed DLL that Needs Library Initialization

To demonstrate the issue of library initialization, here is a changed version of the Add() method in the managed Arithmetic class that uses the C runtime library:

```
System::Double Add(System::Double num1, System::Double num2)
{
    cout << endl << "I am in Add" << endl;
    return num1 + num2;
}
```

To tell the compiler about cout and endl, you add these statements:

```
#include <iostream>
using namespace std;
```

To tell the linker about cout and endl, you add msvcrt.lib as an additional dependency. You do this by accessing the Properties page for the ManagedMathLibrary project, expanding

Linker, selecting Input, and adding msvcrt.lib (for a release build; use msvcrtd.lib for a debug build) to the entries already there, as in Figure 6.2. Microsoft recommends also removing nochkclr.obj, because that additional dependency is for managed-only DLLs that want to emit verifiable code.

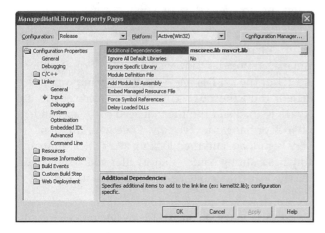

FIGURE 6.2   Adding the C runtime library to your linker dependencies.

If you build the project at this point, you'll get a rather strange set of linker warnings:

```
ManagedMathLibrary.cpp
Linking...
msvcrt.lib(checkclr.obj) : warning LNK4210: .CRT section exists; there may be
➥ unhandled static initializers or terminators
msvcrt.lib(secchk.obj) : warning LNK4210: .CRT section exists; there may be
➥ unhandled static initializers or terminators
libcpmt.lib(xlock.obj) : warning LNK4210: .CRT section exists; there may be
➥ unhandled static initializers or terminators
libcpmt.lib(cout.obj) : warning LNK4210: .CRT section exists; there may be
➥ unhandled static initializers or terminators
libcpmt.lib(iosptrs.obj) : warning LNK4210: .CRT section exists; there may be
➥ unhandled static initializers or terminators
libcpmt.lib(locale0.obj) : warning LNK4210: .CRT section exists; there may be
➥ unhandled static initializers or terminators
```

Because these are only warnings, and the build succeeds, you might be tempted to just run the harness application. It will run into a NullReferenceException (see Figure 6.3), and if you choose Break, you'll see that execution was in the ostream code.

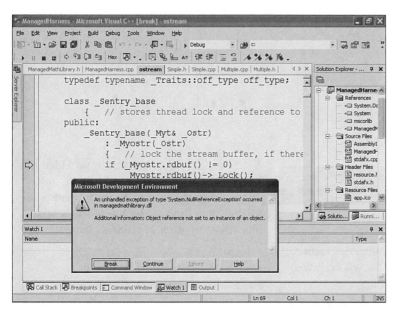

FIGURE 6.3   A NullReferenceException is thrown because the CRT has not been initialized.

This runtime error is just what the linker was warning about. The cout object is an instance of the ostream class, a static instance that is shared by all the code in a process. That static instance is created when the C runtime library is initialized. And when you write a managed DLL, you don't have a DllMain that would quietly initialize the CRT for you.

Initializing the CRT Library

The solution to errors caused by uninitialized libraries is to add a method to the DLL that will initialize the CRT. And, because the CRT should also be cleaned up when your DLL is not going to be used any more, you should also add a method to clean up the CRT. You could make these member functions of the Arithmetic class, but if you need to use the CRT in the Arithmetic constructor, this won't work: The initializer needs to run before the constructor. Also, if your DLL contains several classes, which is normal, you have the problem of deciding which class should hold these administrative methods. A good solution is to create a separate class, and add these methods as static functions:

```
public __gc class DLL
{
public:
    static void Initialize()
```

```
    {
        __crt_dll_initialize();
    }
    static void Cleanup()
    {
        __crt_dll_terminate();
    }
};
```

INITIALIZE IN CONSTRUCTOR? CLEANUP IN DESTRUCTOR?

It's tempting to make these methods the constructor and destructor of the DLL class, but garbage-collected classes don't get deterministic destruction; you don't know when the destructor will be called. These have to stay as regular methods.

How do you know the names of the functions to call? The help for that linker warning, LNK4210, explains the loader-lock bug and library initialization, and provides the names of these functions, along with the related header file.

A new header file, _vcclrit.h, is provided in Visual Studio .NET 2003 and you should include it in the library. It needs windows.h, so add these lines at the top of the source file, after the other include statements:

```
// windows.h is for _vcclrit.h
#include <windows.h>
#include <_vcclrit.h>
```

Rebuild the library and you should see that the linker warnings have disappeared. Unfortunately, the runtime errors will still occur unless you change the calling code (the test harness) to use the new functions:

```
ManagedMathLibrary::DLL::Initialize();
ManagedMathLibrary::Arithmetic* a = new ManagedMathLibrary::Arithmetic();
Console::Write("2.3 + 4.5 is ");
Console::WriteLine(a->Add(2.3, 4.5));
Console::ReadLine();
ManagedMathLibrary::DLL::Cleanup();
```

Now the code not only builds without warnings, it runs without errors, producing this output:

```
2.3 + 4.5 is
I am in Add
6.8
```

Use this technique to initialize any libraries your managed code is using through IJW, and you'll never be bitten by the loader-lock bug.

Mixing Your Own Managed and Unmanaged Code

All of the sample code presented to you in this chapter has been managed code that compiles to intermediate language. Some of it calls unmanaged code in the C runtime library, but the assembly produced in all the sample projects is 100% IL.

When you combine managed and unmanaged code, you must keep in mind that there is a slight performance cost to call unmanaged code from managed code. One way to optimize the performance of your application is to move the boundary between managed and unmanaged code. Consider the system represented in Figure 6.4, with three classes. Class A must be written in managed code (for example, it's a garbage-collected public class that will be exposed to other code running on the runtime) and makes one call into Class B. Class B could be written in managed or unmanaged code. It makes multiple calls to Class C, which is an existing unmanaged class, part of a legacy library.

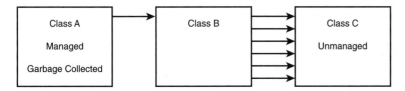

FIGURE 6.4   A class that is called by managed code, and calls unmanaged code, can be written in either.

If Class B is written in managed code, your application will pay the performance cost of calling unmanaged code from managed code hundreds of times each time the application is run, as calls go from Class B to Class C. Alternatively, if Class B is written in unmanaged code, that performance penalty will only be incurred once, when Class A calls Class B. After that, the calls from Class B to Class C will all be unmanaged-to-unmanaged. Clearly, writing Class B in unmanaged code will make your application faster.

Ideally, you could write Class B in unmanaged code using the same tool you use for Class A, and with the two classes in the same project. You can do just that with Visual Studio .NET 2003. In this section, you see how to compile one source file to unmanaged code in a project that builds to managed code.

Using ILDASM to Explore Assemblies

You can examine the contents of an assembly using a tool called ILDASM, intermediate language dissassembler. The easiest way to start ILDASM is from a Visual Studio command

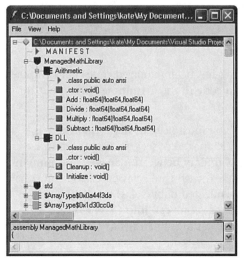

FIGURE 6.5   ILDASM shows the contents of the ManagedMathLibrary assembly.

prompt. Go to Start, Programs, Visual Studio .NET 2003, Visual Studio .NET Tools, and then Visual Studio .NET 2003 command prompt. Type **ildasm** at the prompt to start the tool, and open the release version of ManagedMathLibrary.dll.

Figure 6.5 shows this assembly in ILDASM. The ManagedMathLibrary namespace has been expanded to show the two classes, Arithmetic and DLL, and each class has been expanded to show its methods. Static methods are marked with a yellow S in the pink square before each method name.

If you double-click a method, such as Add() or Subtract(), you can see the intermediate language for the method in a new window. This intermediate language is similar to assembly language. The IL for Subtract is simple:

```
.method public instance float64  Subtract(float64 num1,
                                          float64 num2) cil managed
{
  // Code size       6 (0x6)
  .maxstack  2
  IL_0000:  ldarg.1
  IL_0001:  ldarg.2
  IL_0002:  sub
  IL_0003:  br.s       IL_0005
  IL_0005:  ret
} // end of method Arithmetic::Subtract
```

Even with no assembly language background, you might be able to guess what the numbered lines do:

0000:	Loads argument #1 into a register
0001:	Loads argument #2 into a register
0002:	Subtracts the registers
0003:	Copies the answer into the return value
0005:	Returns

The IL for Add is a little more complex, because it has calls to the << operator, but it is still intermediate language. It makes calls to unmanaged code without being unmanaged code.

A managed class, with the __gc keyword, can only be defined in managed code. A source file that doesn't define any managed classes can be written in either managed or unmanaged code, as you prefer. Consider the Simple class, defined in the same project as Arithmetic. It's not a garbage-collected class and it's not in a namespace. It has a constructor and a getx() method, which have been defined as in-line functions. Here's the class definition again:

```
class Simple
{
private:
   int x;
public:
   Simple(int xx): x(xx){};
   int getx() {return x};
};
```

Because all the member functions of this class have been defined in-line, they don't appear in the disassembly of the intermediate language. They'll be expanded into the code that uses them and compiled in that location. To serve as a demonstration of unmanaged data in managed code, Simple can be changed so that the functions are no longer defined in-line. The header file, Simple.h, becomes

```
class Simple
{
private:
   int x;
public:
   Simple(int xx);
   int getx() ;
};
```

The implementation file, Simple.cpp, becomes

```
#include "StdAfx.h"
#include "simple.h"

#using <mscorlib.dll>
Simple::Simple(int xx): x(xx)
{
}
int Simple::getx()
{
   return x;
}
```

When you build this project, the assembly contains IL for the constructor and the getx()
function. You have to look hard for them among all the other methods from the CRT that
are displayed in the ILDASM tool, but Simple.__ctor and Simple.getx are listed. The IL for
the constructor looks like this:

```
.method public specialname static valuetype Simple*
➥modopt([mscorlib]System.Runtime.CompilerServices.CallConvThiscall)
        Simple.__ctor(valuetype Simple* modopt([Microsoft.VisualC]
➥Microsoft.VisualC.IsConstModifier) modopt([Microsoft.VisualC]
➥Microsoft.VisualC.IsConstModifier) A_0,
                      int32 xx) cil managed
{
  .vtentry 66 : 1
  // Code size       5 (0x5)
  .maxstack  2
  IL_0000:  ldarg.0
  IL_0001:  ldarg.1
  IL_0002:  stind.i4
  IL_0003:  ldarg.0
  IL_0004:  ret
} // end of method 'Global Functions'::Simple.__ctor
```

It basically just stores the argument that was passed to it. The first line is long and strange
because this is a constructor, and specifically a constructor for a value type.

Turning Off /clr for a Single File

Why does Simple compile to intermediate language? Because the compiler was directed to
compile it in that way. The directive is available on the property pages for the project as a
whole, but also for each individual file. You can change the directive to compile to intermediate language for Simple.cpp while the rest of the project remains managed code by following
these steps:

1. Right-click Simple.cpp in solution view and choose Properties. Click the Configuration
   box and choose All Configurations.

2. Expand the C/C++ folder and select General.

3. Click next to Compile As Managed to reveal a drop-down box.

4. Change Assembly Support (/clr) to Not Using Managed Extensions.

5. Still on the property pages, switch to Precompiled Headers under C/C++.

6. Change Create/Use Precompiled Headers from Use Precompiled Header (/Yu) to Not
   Using Precompiled Headers.

7. Still on the property pages, switch to Advanced, and click next to Force #using. Click the . . . that appears, and then clear the Inherit From Project check box. Click OK.

8. Click OK to close the property pages.

9. Remove the #using directive from Simple.cpp because unmanaged code cannot use an assembly.

10. Remove the #include directive that brings in stdafx.h because the precompiled headers in this project are for managed code.

At this point you have changed the Simple.cpp properties so that it does not compile to intermediate language, does not use precompiled headers, and does not automatically bring in all the assemblies used by the project. But because this project has references to other assemblies, there is still work to do. Turning off the Force #using option does not override references. As a result, you must convert references to #using directives. You can do this file-by-file in each source file of the project, but it's more maintainable to use the Force #using property of the project. Here's how to do so:

1. Expand the References node of the ManagedMathLibrary project in Solution Explorer.

2. The references added when the project were created are not always ones that you need. For example, in this project the reference to System.Data is unused. Note which references the project is actually using: System and mscorlib.

3. For each reference the project needs, click it and then switch to the Properties window. Write down the name of the assembly—System.dll, for example.

4. Bring up the Properties page for the ManagedMathLibrary project by right-clicking it and choosing Properties (not by switching to the Properties window).

5. Expand the C/C++ folder and switch to Advanced.

6. Click next to Force #using and enter the assembly names, separated by semicolons. For this sample, enter **system.dll; mscorlib.dll**, as shown in Figure 6.6.

7. Click OK to close the property pages.

8. Click the first reference under ManagedMathLibrary and press Del to delete it. Repeat until all the references have been deleted.

Now build the project. There should be no errors or warnings. All the files in the project except Simple.cpp are using system.dll and mscorlib.dll and compiling to IL. Simple.cpp is not using any assemblies or precompiled headers, and is compiling to native code.

By just declaring a class and function without using them, you leave the opportunity for the optimizer to not bother putting them into the assembly. Add some lines to the Add method in Arithmetic that use Simple, so that it looks like this:

```
System::Double Add(System::Double num1, System::Double num2)
{
    Simple s(2);
    cout << endl << "Simple is " << s.getx() << endl;
    cout << endl << "I am in Add" << endl;
    return num1 + num2;
}
```

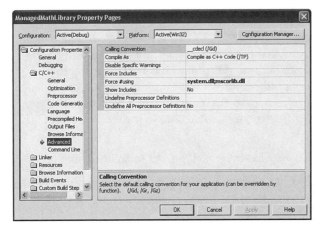

FIGURE 6.6   Use the Force #using property instead of references when some files are compiling to native code.

Build the project, and open the assembly in ILDASM. Find the Simple member functions, and double-click them to examine the code. Instead of the IL that was shown to you when you disassembled the Simple constructor before, you will see something like this:

```
.method public specialname static pinvokeimpl(/* No map */)
        valuetype Simple* modopt([mscorlib]
➥ System.Runtime.CompilerServices.CallConvThiscall)
        Simple.__ctor(valuetype Simple* modopt(
➥ [Microsoft.VisualC]Microsoft.VisualC.IsConstModifier)
➥modopt([Microsoft.VisualC]Microsoft.VisualC.IsConstModifier) A_0,
                    int32 A_1) native unmanaged preservesig
{
    .custom instance void [mscorlib]System.Security.
➥ SuppressUnmanagedCodeSecurityAttribute::.ctor() = ( 01 00 00 00 )
    // Embedded native code
    //   Disassembly of native methods is not supported.
    //   Managed TargetRVA = 0x4c80
} // end of method 'Global Functions'::Simple.__ctor
```

This constructor has compiled to native code, not IL. You have succeeded in creating a class written in unmanaged code within a project that creates managed code. There are several important applications for this technique. One is to create a wrapper for a complex legacy class with a "chatty" interface. Like Class C in Figure 6.4, many legacy classes expose 10 or 20 functions, each setting a single parameter, and then expose another function that actually does something using those parameter values. An unmanaged wrapper class would have one method that takes all the parameters at once, and makes multiple calls to the legacy object, setting all the parameters and then calling the action function. This would reduce the impact of the switch from managed to unmanaged code, because the switch would happen only once instead of tens or hundreds of times. Remember, this capability is unique to Visual C++.

In Brief

- A library written in managed code is simpler to access from other managed code than an unmanaged library.

- A garbage-collected class written in managed C++ is simple to use from other managed languages, such as C#.

- A class library in managed C++ is vulnerable to the loader-lock bug, but you can prevent the bug by eliminating `DllMain` and initializing libraries manually.

- A managed class library can include classes that have been implemented in native code to improve the performance of the library.

Building DLLs in Unmanaged C++

What Is a DLL?

A Dynamic-Link Library, or DLL, is an older technology than the .NET runtime, but it solves a similar set of problems. Code in a DLL can be called from Visual Basic 6 or unmanaged C++, so it provides some degree of binary compatibility. The word *dynamic* in the name refers to the fact that code in a DLL is linked in only while the application is running: If the DLL changes after the application has been compiled, the new version of the code will be used. This is in contrast to a statically linked library like the ones covered in Chapter 5, "Writing a Class Library in Unmanaged C++."

SHOP TALK

DLL HELL

The dynamic nature of a DLL can be a double-edged sword. At first glance it sounds amazing: Any upgrades or improvements to the library are immediately available to all the code that was using it. There's no need to recompile or redeploy those applications. That is very appealing.

But what if what was added to a DLL wasn't exactly an upgrade? What if some functionality you were relying on worked differently in the new version, so differently that your application no longer worked at all? Believe me, it happened, and it happened a lot.

Many times I've had phone calls that went like this: "Hey Kate, we've got something weird happening here. That application you wrote for us has stopped working." "Really? What's changed?" "Nothing really, it was fine last week and now it just hangs up when I try to use the Gizmo dialog box." "Is it like this on all the machines?" "No, that's what's strange, just on mine." "Oh, really? And you haven't installed anything?" "Well, I did install a new version of Internet Explorer, but that couldn't change anything in your application, could it?"

Oh, it certainly could. Internet Explorer installs dozens of DLLs, and quite often working code that was using the old versions of those DLLs just stops working after the install. And I don't mean to single out IE; there are all kinds of applications, from many vendors, that can have this effect. We came to call it *DLL Hell,* and it certainly was unpleasant. It's one of the problems the .NET Global Assembly Cache was designed to solve.

In this chapter, I recommend you copy the DLLs you are using to the executable folder for the client application. That means that any new version installed on the system in some other folder won't affect you. That's no protection against changes in the Windows DLLs, but it can at least keep things under control as far as private DLLs are concerned.

Creating a DLL in unmanaged C++ is straightforward, as you'll see in this chapter. Once created, a DLL can be used from many languages: Visual Basic 6, unmanaged C++, managed C++, and any other managed language. You can't write a DLL in managed C++—a managed C++ class library like those created in Chapter 6, "Writing a Class Library in Managed C++," is kept in a file with a .dll extension, but the internal layout of a DLL is very different from a managed assembly containing a class library.

Creating a DLL

Visual C++ can create two kinds of unmanaged DLL: a Win32 DLL and an MFC DLL. For simplicity, this chapter creates a Win32 DLL. Creating an MFC DLL relies on the same concepts but makes the MFC libraries available to the code within the DLL.

To create a non-MFC DLL, choose File, New, Project, choose Visual C++ projects on the left and Win32 Project on the right, and enter **Legacy** for the project name. Click OK and the Win32 Application Wizard dialog box appears. On the Application Settings tab, choose DLL as the Application Type and select the Export Symbols check box. Click Finish and your project will be created.

Writing DLL Header Files

The functions defined in a DLL are exported for other programs to use. To designate a function or variable as exportable, add the keywords __declspec(dllexport) before the type of the variable or the return type of the function.

Two underscores precede the keyword __declspec.

The DLLs in this chapter are used from several kinds of applications. An unmanaged C++ application that uses the DLL needs a header file that defines the functions. In that header file, the keywords __declspec(dllimport) must precede the type of the variable or the return type of the function.

The DLL header file generated by the wizard uses the preprocessor to enable the same header file to be used both in the DLL itself, which is exporting the functions, and also in the applications that use the DLL, which are importing the functions. Here's how the generated header file looks:

```
#ifdef LEGACY_EXPORTS
#define LEGACY_API __declspec(dllexport)
#else
#define LEGACY_API __declspec(dllimport)
#endif


// This class is exported from the Legacy.dll
class LEGACY_API CLegacy {
public:
    CLegacy(void);
    // TODO: add your methods here.
};


extern LEGACY_API int nLegacy;

LEGACY_API int fnLegacy(void);
```

In the DLL itself, which exports the functions, the properties of the project include a preprocessor definition (see Figure 7.1) that defines the LEGACY_EXPORTS symbol. Because the symbol has been defined, the preprocessor will substitute the export declaration for any instances of LEGACY_API. In any code that uses the DLL, the header would be included without defining the LEGACY_EXPORTS symbol, so the preprocessor will substitute the import declaration for any instances of LEGACY_API.

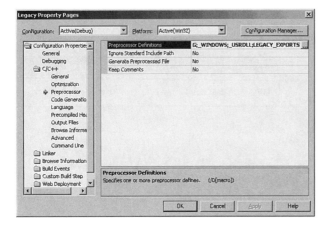

FIGURE 7.1   The project defines the symbol LEGACY_EXPORTS using the project properties, ensuring the DLL functions are declared as exported.

A DLL can export a C++ class with member functions, global functions, or variables. Because member function names are decorated or mangled, they're a little harder to call from managed C++ than global functions. In this chapter, the sample DLL will only export global functions.

Creating the Sample DLL

The sample code generated for you by the wizard includes the definition of a class, a variable, and a global function. Delete these and add two function definitions to the header file, legacy.h:

```
extern "C" {
LEGACY_API bool Log(char* message, SYSTEMTIME* time);
LEGACY_API double Add(double num1, double num2);
}
```

These function declarations are wrapped in the extern "C" specifier so that the export names will be just Log() and Add(). Without that specifier, their names would be more like Log@@YA_NPADPAU_SYSTEMTIME@@@Z() and Add@@YANNN@Z(). The extra symbols are called *decoration* (some old-timers call it *mangling*, and you can probably see why) and are used to differentiate between overloads, which have the same name but take different parameters. The extern "C" convention suppresses this decoration.

The Log function is a sample of the sort of functions you are likely to find in a legacy DLL: It uses a traditional C-style string and a pointer to a structure. The structure represents a time and is defined in winbase.h, which is included in windows.h, which in turn is included in the stdafx.h file generated for this project. As a result, no include statements need to be added to legacy.h to use the structure, which is defined as follows:

```
typedef struct _SYSTEMTIME {
  WORD wYear;
  WORD wMonth;
  WORD wDayOfWeek;
  WORD wDay;
  WORD wHour;
  WORD wMinute;
  WORD wSecond;
  WORD wMilliseconds;
} SYSTEMTIME, *PSYSTEMTIME;
```

The Add() function is simpler than Log() because it works only with fundamental types (double in this case). This makes the marshalling less complicated when Add() is called from managed code later in this chapter.

The two functions need bodies. The implementation belongs in legacy.cpp. Edit it as follows:

- Remove the sample code generated by the wizard.

- Add an include statement for stdio.h after the other include statements.

- Add the bodies of the two functions, as in Listing 7.1.

LISTING 7.1   legacy.cpp   Log() and Add()

```
LEGACY_API bool Log(char* message, SYSTEMTIME* time)
{
   FILE* logfile = fopen("C:\\log.txt","a");
   fprintf(logfile, "%d/%d/%d - %d:%d %s \r\n",
      time->wYear, time->wMonth, time->wDay,
      time->wHour, time->wMinute, message);
   fclose(logfile);
   return true;
}

LEGACY_API double Add(double num1, double num2)
{
   return num1 + num2;
}
```

The Log() function opens a file (the name is hardcoded) in append mode, and then writes a line to the file with the date and time that was passed, pulled apart into the year, month, and so on, and the message that was passed. Then it closes the file.

Build the project and fix any typing errors. Now the DLL is available for use from a variety of applications.

How to Use a DLL from Unmanaged C++

When your application loads a DLL, Windows searches for it, just as it does when you run an executable. First the directory of the application loading the DLL is searched, and then the current directory, and then the system directory (\Windows\System for Windows 95, 98, or XP, \Winnt\System or \Winnt\System32 for Windows NT or 2000), and then the Windows directory, and finally each directory specified in the path.

If you plan to have a DLL shared by many applications, it's a good idea to put it in the System directory (Winnt\System or Windows\System) where it will be found easily. When one application installs an updated version of the DLL, all applications that use it will start to use the new one. If you prefer, you can copy the DLL to the same directory as the executable that uses it. You might end up with several copies of the DLL on your hard drive as a result. Some developers prefer to know that the DLL they are using will never be changed by anyone else, and consider a little wasted drive space a small price to pay for this reassurance. In this chapter, you copy the DLL to the same directory as the executable.

The dumpbin Utility

Visual C++ comes with a utility called *dumpbin* that can show you what's going on inside a DLL. To run it, bring up a Visual Studio .NET 2003 command prompt, and then change directories to the directory containing the DLL. The utility takes several command-line options; the two most useful are /exports and /imports.

To see all the methods exported from the legacy DLL, change to the appropriate directory, and then enter this command:

```
dumpbin /exports  legacy.dll
```

You should see output like this:

```
Microsoft (R) COFF/PE Dumper Version 7.10.3077
Copyright (C) Microsoft Corporation.  All rights reserved.
Dump of file legacy.dll
File Type: DLL
  Section contains the following exports for Legacy.dll
    00000000 characteristics
```

```
3F2DDC3E time date stamp Mon Aug 04 00:08:30 2003
    0.00 version
       1 ordinal base
       2 number of functions
       2 number of names
 ordinal hint RVA       name
       1    0 00013479 Add
       2    1 000134EC Log
Summary
    4000 .data
    1000 .idata
    5000 .rdata
    3000 .reloc
   25000 .text
   12000 .textbss
```

You can also uses the /imports option to see how many methods from other libraries this simple library uses. Try it; it's a real eye-opener!

Implicit Linking to a DLL

When you build a DLL in Visual C++, a companion .lib file is generated for you as well. This file is called the *import library*; it contains the definitions of all the functions in the DLL, but not the code. Working from unmanaged C++, you don't have to write any code that finds or loads the DLL. You just link with the import library as though it were a static library. This is called implicit linking of the DLL. It's the simplest approach to use.

To test the DLL, start by creating an unmanaged console application (the details are in Chapter 2, "Creating Test Harnesses and Starter Applications") called UseLegacy. Copy legacy.h from the Legacy project folder to the UseLegacyDLL project folder, and copy both legacy.dll and legacy.lib from the Debug folder under Legacy to UseLegacyDLL.

Edit the UseLegacyDLL.cpp file so that it reads as follows:

```cpp
// UseLegacyDLL.cpp : Defines the entry point for the console application.
//

#include "stdafx.h"
#include "windows.h"
#include "legacy.h"
#include <iostream>
using namespace std;

int _tmain(int argc, _TCHAR* argv[])
{
```

```
    cout << "1 + 2 is " << Add(1,2) << endl;
    SYSTEMTIME st;
    GetLocalTime(&st);
    Log("Testing", &st);
    cout << "log succeeded" << endl;
    return 0;
}
```

This code includes windows.h to get the declaration of SYSTEMTIME, and includes legacy.h to get the declarations of Add() and Log(). Because it writes to the screen with cout, it includes iostream and uses the std namespace. The main function exercises Add(), and then gets the local time and passes it to Log(). GetLocalTime() takes a pointer to a SYSTEMTIME structure, which it changes. It's defined in winbase.h, so you don't need any extra preparation to be able to use it.

Use the property pages for the project to add legacy.lib to the linker dependencies. (Right-click the project in Solution Explorer, choose Properties, Expand the Linker section, select Input, and add legacy.lib to Additional Dependencies.) Build and run the project without debugging: You should see output like this:

```
1 + 2 is 3
log succeeded
Press any key to continue
```

Take a look in the root of your C drive for the file log.txt and open it in Notepad. You should see log messages (one for each time you ran the application) that look like this:

```
2003/8/4 - 11:14 Testing
2003/8/4 - 11:19 Testing
2003/8/4 - 11:35 Testing
```

It's as simple as that to use an unmanaged DLL from an unmanaged application. You can apply these concepts to create a DLL for any of the kinds of unmanaged class libraries discussed in Chapter 5.

Explicit Linking to a DLL

Although implicit linking is the simplest approach, and works well for the sample in this chapter, it's not always the right approach. Explicit linking is needed when one of these situations apply:

- You must minimize the memory used by your application.

- The application must start up as quickly as possible.

- You want to use one of two DLLs (with different filenames) holding functions with the same names, and want to choose which DLL to load while the application is running.

Explicit linking works well in this situation because your application loads each DLL explicitly just before calling a function from it. The benefits are maximized when the functions in the DLL aren't always called each time the application runs. With implicit linking, all the DLLs are found and loaded just as the application starts running. That can make the application slow to start up, and increase the memory it uses. With explicit linking, a DLL that is never used is never loaded, and it's possible that fewer DLLs are in memory at any particular time.

Most developers have no need to write the extra code to link the DLL explicitly. If you do, here are the steps:

- Before your first call to a function from the DLL, call LoadLibrary() to find and load the DLL.

- Replace all calls to the DLL with two lines: one that gets a function pointer by calling GetProcAddress() and one that uses the function pointer.

- When you have finished calling functions from the DLL, call FreeLibrary() to unload it.

You can try this with the DLL for this chapter by creating a Win32 console application called UseLegacyEx. Build the new project to create a Debug folder, and then copy legacy.dll from the Legacy Debug folder into the UseLegacyEx Debug folder. Do not copy the import library, legacy.lib, or the header file, legacy.h.

Edit the UseLegacyEx.cpp file so that it looks like this:

```
// UseLegacyEx.cpp : Defines the entry point for the console application.
//

#include "stdafx.h"
#include "windows.h"
#include <iostream>
using namespace std;

int _tmain(int argc, _TCHAR* argv[])
{
    typedef bool (*FPLog)(char*, SYSTEMTIME*);
    typedef double (*FPAdd)(double, double);
    HINSTANCE hDLL;
    FPAdd fpadd;
    FPLog fplog;

    hDLL = LoadLibrary("legacy.dll");
```

```
fpadd = (FPAdd)GetProcAddress(hDLL, "Add");
cout << "1 + 2 is " << fpadd(1,2) << endl;

SYSTEMTIME st;
GetLocalTime(&st);
fplog = (FPLog)GetProcAddress(hDLL, "Log");
fplog("Testing", &st);
cout << "log succeeded" << endl;

FreeLibrary(hDLL);
return 0;
}
```

ERROR CHECKING

The code that links the DLL explicitly is more complicated than the code that links it implicitly. It should,
however, be more complicated still. Error checking
has been omitted so the flow is easy to see.

The call to LoadLibrary() should be followed by an
if block that tests hDLL is not a null pointer: Only if
hDLL is not null should the rest of the code execute.
If it is null, the user should probably be informed of
the problem.

Each call to GetProcAddress() should be followed by
an if block that tests the function pointer is not null;
if it is null, FreeLibrary() should be called and the
rest of the code should not execute.

You could consider using exceptions to make your
error-handling less intrusive. Whether you use if
checks or exceptions, remember to implement error
checking and handling in your own DLL-loading
applications.

This code includes windows.h for the declaration of SYSTEMTIME, and iostream for cout.
It also uses the std namespace. Notice that it
does not include legacy.h or declare Add()
and Log().

Working with function pointers is a lot
simpler if you use a typedef. That's especially
true in this case, because GetProcAddress
returns a generic pointer that must be cast to
the correct kind of function pointer. You will
need one typedef for each signature (parameter types and return type) in your DLL.
Because Add() and Log() have different
signatures, they each need a typedef.

After setting up the typedefs and declaring a
DLL handle and the function pointers, this
code calls LoadLibary() to actually load the
DLL, and saves the return value;
GetProcAddress() and FreeLibrary() will
need it.

Each call to GetProcAddress() needs the DLL handle and the name of the function. Because
name decoration was turned off in the Legacy DLL, you can pass undecorated names such as
Add and Log. Once the function pointer is pointing to a function inside the DLL, you call it
just as though the function pointer was a function, passing the parameters that are destined
for Add() or Log(). Once all the functions have been called, FreeLibrary() unloads the DLL,
reducing the memory used by the application.

The extra work involved in linking a DLL explicitly is not enormous. Nonetheless, you should always start by writing code that links the DLL implicitly, and then test to see whether there are performance issues that explicit loading would improve. Only if it's necessary should you take on this extra work.

How to Use an Unmanaged DLL from Managed C++

The import library that's created for a DLL simplifies using that DLL from unmanaged C++, because you don't have to use LoadLibrary() and GetProcAddress() to make the calls. It can also simplify using the same DLL from managed C++. Not all DLLs can be accessed through the import library from managed C++, but many can.

Using the Import Library

Here's how to create a managed C++ application that uses the legacy DLL through the import library:

1. Create a managed console application called UseDLLManaged.

2. Copy the include file for the DLL, legacy.h, to the project folder.

3. Copy legacy.dll and legacy.lib from the Debug folder under the Legacy project to UseDLLManaged.

4. Add legacy.lib to the linker dependencies as described earlier in this chapter.

At this point you are ready to add code to the application that uses the DLL. Here is the managed equivalent of the unmanaged test harness from earlier in this chapter:

```
// This is the main project file for VC++ application project
// generated using an Application Wizard.

#include "stdafx.h"
#include "windows.h"
#include "legacy.h"

#using <mscorlib.dll>

using namespace System;

int _tmain()
{
```

```
    System::Console::Write(S"1 + 2 is ");
    System::Console::WriteLine(__box( Add(1,2)));
    SYSTEMTIME st;
    GetLocalTime(&st);
    Log("Testing from Managed Code", &st);
    System::Console::WriteLine(S"log succeeded");
    return 0;
}
```

This code runs and works beautifully. Managed C++ is quite happy to deal with old header files like windows.h, to create structures on the stack and pass their address to the DLL, and so on. The string created in managed code can be passed to the old unmanaged code without incident. This is It Just Works (IJW) in action again, and most developers are pleasantly surprised every time they come up against it.

However, this code is using a classic C-style string, a pointer-to-char. Your new managed code is far more likely to be using a String pointer that points to memory on the managed heap. For example, the contents of a WinForm text box or other UI components are represented as a managed string pointer, not char*. Here is a version of the console application that tries to work with a String*:

```
System::Console::Write(S"1 + 2 is ");
System::Console::WriteLine(__box( Add(1,2)));
SYSTEMTIME st;
GetLocalTime(&st);
String* s = new String("Testing with a heap string");
Log(s, &st);
System::Console::WriteLine(S"log succeeded");
return 0;
```

This code will not compile. The Log() function doesn't take a String*, it takes a char*. You can make a char* from a String* like this:

```
String* s = new String("Testing with a heap string");
char* pChar = (char*)Marshal::StringToHGlobalAnsi(s).ToPointer();
Log(pChar, &st);
```

This works, but it's a little awkward. What would be much simpler is if you could declare a version of Log() that takes a String*, have the framework convert the String* to a char*, and then call the Log() code from your DLL. You can do just that with PInvoke, discussed in the next section.

Using `PInvoke` to Control Marshaling

When you make a call from managed to unmanaged code, all the parameters you want to send to the unmanaged code are gathered up, rearranged into the right order, possibly copied or converted, possibly pinned to ensure they don't move during the call, and so on. This is called marshaling, and it's supposed to make you think about the beginning of a parade when someone prods and pushes to get all the floats lined up in order before they head out. When you call a legacy library by adding the .lib file to the linker dependencies, you get the default marshaling. If the function only takes and returns so-called blittable types, this is fine. Blittable types have an identical memory representation in managed and unmanaged code. C++ fundamental types such as int are blittable types. Strings are not.

The `Add()` function, which takes and returns doubles, doesn't need any special marshaling. If all the functions in legacy.dll worked well with default marshaling, the IJW techniques of the previous chapter would be all you needed. As you've seen, `Log()` doesn't exactly need special marshaling, it can be used as-is, but the programmer must convert the managed type (such as `String*`) to the unmanaged type (such as `char*`) before each call. The DLL will be much more useful if you can arrange these conversions to be done as part of the marshaling step.

Create another managed console application called `UseDLLPInvoke`. Copy legacy.dll from the Debug folder under Legacy to the UseDLLPInvoke project folder. Do not copy legacy.h or legacy.lib.

Rather than `#include` legacy.h, this code defines the functions and adds attributes to those definitions that govern the marshaling. Before the `main()` function in UseDLLPInvoke.cpp, add these lines:

```
extern "C" {
[DllImport("legacy", CharSet=CharSet::Ansi)]
bool Log(String* message, SYSTEMTIME* time);
[DllImport("legacy")]
double Add(double num1, double num2);
}
```

There are several differences between these definitions of `Log()` and `Add()` and the definitions in legacy.h, as follows:

- The `LEGACY_API` macro has been removed.

- Each function has a `DllImport` attribute naming the DLL (without the .dll extension) as the first parameter.

- The `DllImport` attribute on `Log()` further specifies that managed strings passed to this function are to be marshaled to ANSI strings before being passed to the function in the DLL.

The DllImport attribute is in the InteropServices namespace, so add this line before those function definitions:

```
using namespace System::Runtime::InteropServices;
```

This code won't compile yet, because SYSTEMTIME has not been defined. Rather than including all of windows.h, it's a better idea to just copy in the definition of SYSTEMTIME from winbase.h. That definition, however, uses the typedef WORD. It must be replaced with short in the managed definition. The completed definition looks like this:

```
typedef struct _SYSTEMTIME {
    short wYear;
    short wMonth;
    short wDayOfWeek;
    short wDay;
    short wHour;
    short wMinute;
    short wSecond;
    short wMilliseconds;
} SYSTEMTIME;
```

FINDING DEFINITIONS OF LEGACY TYPES

To find the definition of SYSTEMTIME so that you can copy it, open one of the projects that includes windows.h (Legacy or UseLegacyDLL), right-click SYSTEMTIME in the code, and then choose Go To Definition. You can then copy the definition into the Clipboard and paste it into UseDLLPInvoke.cpp.

To find the definition of WORD, right-click it in the definition of SYSTEMTIME in winbase.h and choose Go To Definition. You'll find it's just a typedef for unsigned short (defined in windef.h). Because unsigned types are not Common Language Specification compliant, use a short to stand in for a WORD.

At this point the project should build without errors, although the main() does nothing yet. The next issue to overcome is getting a SYSTEMTIME that holds the current time. Calling GetLocalTime() is too platform-specific; just as a String* is more likely to be useful (as the text property of a text box perhaps) than a char*, so an instance of a DateTime structure is more likely to be useful (perhaps as the selected date from a date time picker) than a SYSTEMTIME.

In the previous section you saw how to convert a String* to a char*. You can also write a function to convert a DateTime to a SYSTEMTIME. It would look like this:

```
SYSTEMTIME MakeSystemTimeFromDateTime(DateTime dt)
{
    SYSTEMTIME st;
    st.wYear = dt.get_Year();
    st.wMonth = dt.get_Month();
    st.wDayOfWeek = dt.get_DayOfWeek();
```

```
    st.wDay = dt.get_Day();
    st.wHour = dt.get_Hour();
    st.wMinute = dt.get_Minute();
    st.wSecond = dt.get_Second();
    st.wMilliseconds = dt.get_Millisecond();

    return st;
}
```

Type this function into UseDLLPInvoke.cpp before the `main()` function. Then edit the `main()` function so that it reads as follows:

```
int _tmain()
{
    System::Console::Write(S"1 + 2 is ");
    System::Console::WriteLine(__box( Add(1,2)));
    SYSTEMTIME st = MakeSystemTimeFromDateTime(System::DateTime::Now);
    String* s = new String("Testing with a heap string");
    Log(s, &st);
    System::Console::WriteLine(S"log succeeded");
    return 0;
}
```

Build and run the application. It should display that 1 + 2 is 3 and that the log succeeded. When you open log.txt you should see the current date and time, followed by the message from your code.

If a function in a DLL is going to be called repeatedly, it's obviously more convenient to add an attribute to the function definition asking the framework to convert a `String*` to a `char*` than to expect the programmer to do that conversion before every function call. By the same logic, wouldn't it be great if you could just pass a `DateTime` to `Log()` and have the marshaler convert it to a `SYSTEMTIME`? Well, you can. It's not built in the way string conversions are (everybody does string conversions), but it's not terribly hard to do. The next section shows you how.

Writing a Custom Marshaler

The marshaler knows how to convert a `String*` to a `char*` (or to several other popular string types in various languages). All you need to do is ask, by adding to the `DllImport` attribute on the method, like this:

```
[DllImport("legacy", CharSet=CharSet::Ansi)]
bool Log(String* message, SYSTEMTIME* time);
```

When you want to have a conversion performed for you, you write a class that inherits from `System::Runtime::InteropServices::ICustomMarshaler` and override some methods in that class. Then you add an attribute to the function directing the marshaler to use your class (by calling those overridden methods) to perform the necessary conversions. Although you can call your class anything you like, it helps maintainability if you have a naming convention. For example, most of the Microsoft samples name the custom marshaling class with the name of the unmanaged class to which it converts, an underscore, and the words `CustomMarshaler`. Following that convention, the class to convert from a `DateTime` to a `SYSTEMTIME` would be called `SYSTEMTIME_CustomMarshaler`.

The Custom Marshaling Class

The `ICustomMarshaler` interface has eight public methods that must be overridden. This class can be used to marshal from managed to native data (as the example in this chapter uses) or from native to managed, or both. The methods are as follows:

- `Constructor`—If you have no member variables in your implementation, ignore it

- `Destructor`—If you have no member variables in your implementation, ignore it

- `static ICustomMarshaler* GetInstance(String* cookie)`—Used to save marshaler constructing multiple instances

- `IntPtr MarshalManagedToNative(Object* pDateTime)`—For values passed to a DLL

- `void CleanUpNativeData(IntPtr pNativeData)`—Cleans up after `MarshalManagedToNative()` when the call is complete

- `Object* MarshalNativeToManaged(IntPtr pNativeData)`—For values returned from a DLL

- `void CleanUpManagedData(Object* ManagedObj)`—Cleans up after `MarshalNativeToManaged` when the call is complete

- `int GetNativeDataSize()`—For values returned from a DLL

You must implement all these methods (except the constructor and destructor) in order to implement the interface. In the sample presented in this chapter, the marshaling is one way: The code will convert a `DateTime` to a `SYSTEMTIME`. If you want to use this class to convert a `SYSTEMTIME` to a `DateTime`, you would have to implement all the functions in this interface with meaningful bodies. In the interest of space, this chapter only implements the methods needed for converting a `DateTime` to a `SYSTEMTIME` and fools the compiler with stub bodies for the rest of the methods. As well, it implements only the conversion of a single object. Some custom marshalers can handle arrays of objects as well as single objects.

Type this class into UseDLLPInvoke.cpp, before the declarations of `Log()` and `Add()` but after the declaration of `SYSTEMTIME`:

```
__gc public class SYSTEMTIME_CustomMarshaler : public ICustomMarshaler
{
public:
    static ICustomMarshaler* GetInstance(String* cookie);
    IntPtr MarshalManagedToNative(Object* pDateTime);
    void CleanUpNativeData(IntPtr pNativeData);
    Object* MarshalNativeToManaged(IntPtr pNativeData){return 0;};
    void CleanUpManagedData(Object* ManagedObj){};
    int GetNativeDataSize(){return 0;};
private:
    //singleton pattern
    static SYSTEMTIME_CustomMarshaler* marshaler = 0;
};
```

The three methods in boldface must be implemented. Code and discussion for each follows.

GetInstance()

GetInstance() is the simplest of the three methods to implement: You could return a new instance every time it was called, but why waste time and memory doing that when this marshaler has no member variables or anything else to differentiate one instance from another? This code uses the Singleton pattern to provide one single instance that anyone can use by calling the GetInstance() method. It relies on a static pointer (shared between all instances, and created even when no instances are created). The first time anyone calls GetInstance(), the pointer will still be NULL. An instance is created and the pointer is saved; from now on all calls will get the existing pointer. Here's the code for GetInstance:

```
ICustomMarshaler* SYSTEMTIME_CustomMarshaler::GetInstance(String* cookie)
{
    if (!marshaler)
        marshaler = new SYSTEMTIME_CustomMarshaler();
    return marshaler;
}
```

Enter this code immediately after the class definition.

MarshalManagedToNative()

The MarshalManagedToNative()method takes an Object pointer and allocates some memory for the native equivalent, and then copies data from the Object to the native structure or class. This signature cannot be changed, so the DateTime structure that is to be passed to Log() will have to be boxed, converting it to an Object*, so that this function can unbox it and perform the conversion.

Here is the code for MarshalManagedToNative:

```
IntPtr SYSTEMTIME_CustomMarshaler::MarshalManagedToNative(Object* pDateTime)
{
    int size = sizeof(SYSTEMTIME)+sizeof(int);
    IntPtr ptrBlock = (Marshal::AllocCoTaskMem(size)).ToPointer();
    int offset = ptrBlock.ToInt32()+sizeof(int);
    IntPtr ptrST(offset);
    int __nogc * pi = (int __nogc *)ptrBlock.ToPointer();
    *pi = 1;
    SYSTEMTIME* pst = static_cast<SYSTEMTIME*>(ptrST.ToPointer());
    __box DateTime* bdt = static_cast<__box DateTime*>(pDateTime);
    DateTime dt = *bdt;
    *pst = MakeSystemTimeFromDateTime(dt);
    return ptrST;
}
```

This code uses two kinds of pointers—the traditional C-style pointer, such as int* or Object*, and a managed type called IntPtr, which functions just like a pointer, although the C++ compiler doesn't recognize it as one. This function creates a SYSTEMTIME structure in a special area of memory that can be shared by the managed and unmanaged code. Memory is allocated there using AllocCoTaskMem().

The first two lines allocate enough memory for a SYSTEMTIME plus an extra int, which will go before the SYSTEMTIME structure to tell the marshaler how many objects are being passed. Then a second IntPtr object is created that "points" to the start of the structure, after that first integer. The integer is set to 1 because only one SYSTEMTIME is being created.

Now the casting and unboxing happens. First ptrST is put through a static cast to a SYSTEMTIME pointer; later code will use that pointer to set the elements of the structure. Then the Object* that was passed to this function is put through a static cast to a boxed DateTime. This is safe because you know that a boxed DateTime will be passed to Log(). To unbox the DateTime, just declare another DateTime structure and use the dereferencing operator, *.

The second-last line of code takes care of copying all the elements of the DateTime structure into the SYSTEMTIME structure by using the helper function, MakeSystemTimeFromDateTime(), first presented in the previous section. Finally the function returns the IntPtr that "points" to the start of the structure itself. The marshaler will look before this address for the count of the number of objects.

Enter the code for MarshalManagedToNative() after the code for GetInstance().

CleanUpNativeData()

The third function to be overridden is CleanUpNativeData(). It must call FreeCoTaskMem() to reverse the allocation that was performed in MarshalManagedToNative(). Here's the code:

```
void SYSTEMTIME_CustomMarshaler::CleanUpNativeData(IntPtr pNativeData)
{
   SYSTEMTIME * pST = static_cast<SYSTEMTIME*>(pNativeData.ToPointer());
   int offset = pNativeData.ToInt32()-sizeof(int);
   IntPtr pBlock(offset);
   Marshal::FreeCoTaskMem(pBlock);
}
```

This function is handed a pointer to the start of the structure and it needs to "back up" to the beginning of the memory that was allocated, so it subtracts the size of an integer from the pointer it was handed. It then creates an `IntPtr` pointer, and passes it to `FreeCoTaskMem()`.

Enter the code for `CleanUpNativeData()` after the code for `MarshalManagedToNative()`, and build the project to be sure you haven't made any typing errors.

Changing the DllImport Attribute and the Calling Code
Having written a custom marshaling class, you must ask the marshaler to use it. You do this by adding an attribute on the parameter to the `Log()` method. Change the definition of `Log()` to read like this:

```
[DllImport("legacy", CharSet=CharSet::Ansi)]
bool Log(String* message,
         [In,MarshalAs(UnmanagedType::CustomMarshaler,
         MarshalTypeRef=__typeof(SYSTEMTIME_CustomMarshaler))]
         __box DateTime* time);
```

The type of time has changed from `SYSTEMTIME*` to `__box DateTime*`, which will make it much simpler to call from managed code. The `MarshalAs` and `MarshalTypeRef` attributes tell the marshaler to use `SYSTEMTIME_CustomMarshaler` to marshal this parameter.

Now the code that calls the functions in the DLL can be written using data types that are more common in a managed C++ application. Edit the `main()` function to read as follows:

```
int _tmain()
{
    System::Console::Write(S"1 + 2 is ");
    System::Console::WriteLine(__box( Add(1,2)));
    String* s = new String("Testing with a heap string");
    Log(s, __box(System::DateTime::Now));
    System::Console::WriteLine(S"log succeeded");
    return 0;
}
```

Build and run the code, and examine the log.txt file in the root of the C: drive. You should see the current date and time, along with the new message from the main() function. You have successfully written a custom marshaler for PInvoke so that managed code can pass new managed objects to legacy DLL code, rather than having to work directly with legacy structures and classes.

How to Use an Unmanaged DLL from C#

C# code does not have the luxury of IJW. The only way to access code in an unmanaged DLL from C# is using PInvoke. To demonstrate how it's done, create a C# console application called CSUseLegacyDLL.

Although you could set up the custom marshaling in C#, it would be quite a lot of work. Instead, the C# example will pass a SYSTEMTIME to Log(), and use the MakeSystemTimeFromDateTime() helper method. Listing 7.2 shows the code for the C# console application. There are several very significant differences from the equivalent C++ code in the "Using PInvoke to Control Marshaling" section. These include

- In C++, the default visibility for elements of a structure is public. In C# it is not, and you must specify public for each element as you declare it.

- The syntax for declaring a struct is simpler and does not require (or allow) a typedef.

- Global functions are not allowed; all functions must be members of a class, so MakeSystemTimeFromDateTime() is in the Class1 class. Make it a static method so it can be called without creating an instance of Class1.

- C++ calls accessor methods of the DateTime class such as get_Year() directly. C# uses property syntax, for example dt.Year.

- C# requires a cast when putting int values into short variables, because a C# int is always longer than a short.

- The imported methods must be static extern members of a class; add them to Class1.

- The DllImport attribute in C++ specifies the DLL name without the .dll extension; in C# you must provide the extension.

- The methods as declared in C++ took pointers: a char* and a SYSTEMTIME*. In C#, pointers do not exist. When working with a heap-allocated garbage-collected object such as a String, what C# considers a reference is equivalent to a C++ pointer. When working with a stack-allocated structure such as SYSTEMTIME, pass the structure by reference (use the ref keyword both in the definition of the function and in the calling code) to produce something equivalent to a C++ pointer.

- C# uses . to separate a class name, such as Console, from the name of a static method, such as WriteLine().

- C# does not use the S macro to convert quoted strings to String objects; all quoted strings are C# String objects.

- The C# Main() function does not return a value.

- The sample code here uses a different message string to help you spot messages in log.txt from variations on this application; it's "Testing with a C# string" in this version.

LISTING 7.2   Class1.cs   CSUseLegacyDLL

```
using System;
using  System.Runtime.InteropServices;

namespace CSUseLegacyDLL
{
    struct SYSTEMTIME
    {
        public short wYear;
        public short wMonth;
        public short wDayOfWeek;
        public short wDay;
        public short wHour;
        public short wMinute;
        public short wSecond;
        public short wMilliseconds;
    }

    /// <summary>
    /// Summary description for Class1.
    /// </summary>
    class Class1
    {
        static SYSTEMTIME MakeSystemTimeFromDateTime(DateTime dt)
        {
            SYSTEMTIME st;
            st.wYear = (short) dt.Year;
            st.wMonth = (short) dt.Month;
            st.wDayOfWeek = (short) dt.DayOfWeek;
            st.wDay = (short) dt.Day;
            st.wHour = (short) dt.Hour;
            st.wMinute = (short) dt.Minute;
            st.wSecond = (short) dt.Second;
```

LISTING 7.2   Continued

```
        st.wMilliseconds = (short) dt.Millisecond;

        return st;
    }

    [DllImport("legacy.dll", CharSet=CharSet.Ansi)]
    static extern bool Log(String message, ref SYSTEMTIME time);

    [DllImport("legacy.dll")]
    static extern double Add(double num1, double num2);

    /// <summary>
    /// The main entry point for the application.
    /// </summary>
    [STAThread]
    static void Main(string[] args)
    {
        System.Console.Write("1 + 2 is ");
        System.Console.WriteLine( Add(1,2));
        String s = "Testing with a C# string";
        SYSTEMTIME st = MakeSystemTimeFromDateTime(DateTime.Now);
        Log(s, ref st);
        System.Console.WriteLine("log succeeded");
    }
  }
}
```

After entering the C# code, build the project. Copy legacy.dll into the bin/Debug folder under the CSUseLegacyDLL project folder. Run the application and you should see the usual output. Open log.txt and you should see the current date and time, along with the C# version of the text message. The legacy DLL is available to developers in any managed language.

What about the custom marshaling approach? It's quite a bit harder in C# than in C++. A better plan is to create a managed library in C++ that exposes a Log() method, and to have that method use PInvoke and custom marshaling to get to the legacy DLL. That code is out of the scope of this chapter, but would make an interesting exploration for anyone wanting to push a little deeper than usual into legacy DLL interop issues.

In Brief

- DLLs are portable units of code that can be used by applications written in many languages. When a DLL changes, the changed version is used by the client applications without those applications being recompiled or redeployed.

- Managed C++ applications can use an unmanaged DLL through It Just Works interop or by using `PInvoke`.

- Using `PInvoke` provides excellent control over marshaling; you can write code to convert managed types to unmanaged types automatically.

- C# and VB.NET applications can access the DLL only through `PInvoke`.

Writing COM Components in C++

8

COM Components and Their Place in Software Development

COM is a binary standard for Windows objects. That means that objects can execute the executable code (in a DLL or EXE) that describes another object. Even if two objects were written in different languages, they can interact using the COM standard.

How do they interact? Through an *interface*. A COM interface is a collection of functions, or really just function names. It's a C++ class with no data, only pure virtual functions. Your objects provide code for the functions. Other programs get to your code by calling these functions. All COM objects must have an interface named IUnknown (and most have many more, all with names that start with I, the prefix for interfaces).

The IUnknown interface has only one purpose: finding other interfaces. It has a function called QueryInterface() that takes an interface ID and returns a pointer to that interface for this object. All the other interfaces inherit from IUnknown, so they have a QueryInterface() too, and you have to write the code—or you would if there was no ATL. Three functions are declared in IUnknown: QueryInterface(), AddRef(), and Release(). The latter two functions keep track of which applications are using an interface. All interfaces inherit all three functions and the developer of the interface must implement them.

EXE VERSUS DLL IN COM PROGRAMMING

Because the code in a DLL executes in the same process as the calling code, it's the fastest way for applications to communicate. When two separate applications communicate through COM, function calls from one application to another must be marshaled: COM gathers up all the parameters and invokes the function itself. A stand-alone server (EXE) is therefore slower than an in-process server (DLL).

COM provides services to programmers. For example, you don't need to locate a component to execute a function within it. If the component is properly registered, COM can find it and load it for you. COM also handles any marshaling or other preparation that is required for you to call a COM component's functions. (If the component is in-process, as an ActiveX control is, the client speaks directly to the component without having to go through the runtime.)

Applications and libraries that run in the .NET runtime also provide binary compatibility, marshaling, and component discovery and loading. In fact, the .NET runtime is a replacement for COM. As you'll see in this chapter, new managed code (in any language) can call unmanaged code if that unmanaged code defines a COM component. What's more, unmanaged code can call into managed code by treating the .NET component as though it were a COM component. However, this interoperability has a small performance penalty, so you might choose to do new development as a COM component to speed access to that component from unmanaged code, while still permitting access from managed code.

Using ATL to Create an Unmanaged COM Component

Working in COM can be intimidating when you first start, but parts of it move quickly from intimidating to boring. For example, every COM component must implement IUnknown. That's not hard after you have done it once—in fact, the code for IUnknown is the same in every COM component. So each project can start with a copy-and-paste session in which you bring over all the code that will be identical in this project. Yuck!

Both the intimidation and the boredom can be lessened dramatically with a library of some kind. Library code can provide the starting point or backbone for your project. If you don't know how to write that code, the library provides a reassuring starting point. If you know how to write the code and have written it many times before, the library spares you the pain of copying it from an old project into a new one.

This was the motivation behind ATL, the Active Template Library. It provides implementations for "stock" interfaces and makes it simple to build small, lightweight, fast COM components and controls. As you can probably tell from the name, it's a library of templates, but even if you're not an experienced template user, you'll find ATL quite straightforward.

A Sample ATL Component

ATL components should be simple and small. Typically they encapsulate business rules as part of a multi-tiered design. For demonstration purposes, a simple validation rule will do, such as for the format of a phone number. The component will have one method, ValidatePhoneNumber(), that takes a string as an input parameter and gives back two output parameters: an error code and an error message.

To create the component, you first create a project, and then add a component to it. Open Visual Studio and choose File, New, Project. Select Visual C++ projects and then ATL Project, and name the project PhoneFormat.

The ATL Project Wizard includes only one tab other than the Overview. By default, it creates the component as a DLL, so the component will be in-process with its client, for fastest possible execution. Click Finish to create the project.

The next step is to add a component to the project. Right-click the PhoneFormat project in Class View and choose Add, Add Class. Expand the Visual C++ node and select ATL underneath it. Select ATL Simple Object and click Open. On the ATL Simple Object Wizard's Names tab, enter a short name of PhoneNumber. All the other boxes will fill themselves in as you type. Click Finish to create the object.

The wizard gave this object a simple interface called IPhoneNumber. You need to add a method, ValidatePhoneNumber(), to the interface. Expand CPhoneNumber in the Class View and then expand Bases and Interfaces underneath that. Right-click IPhoneNumber and choose Add, Add Method.

The Add Method Wizard appears. Fill in the method name, ValidatePhoneNumber. Then add the parameters one at a time. First, add the input string—select the In check box, choose a type of BSTR (the string type for COM programming), and a name of Number. Click Add. Next, add the

OUT AND RETVAL PARAMETERS

Until you have chosen a type that is a pointer, such as BSTR* or BYTE*, the Out and Retval check boxes cannot be selected.

first output parameter—choose a type of BYTE*, select the Out check box, enter a name of pError, and click Add. For the last parameter, choose a type of BSTR*, select the Out check box, enter a name of pErrorString, and click Add. The completed dialog box should resemble Figure 8.1. Click Finish.

In the Class View, find ValidatePhoneNumber underneath CPhoneNumber and double-click it to edit the code. There are lots of ways you can validate that a string is in a certain format. Because this is an ATL project, it makes sense to use the ATL regular expressions class, CAtlRegExp. Here's an implementation of the ValidatePhoneNumber() method:

```
#include <atlrx.h>

// CPhoneNumber

STDMETHODIMP CPhoneNumber::ValidatePhoneNumber(BSTR Number, BYTE* pError,
                                               BSTR* pErrorString)
{
  USES_CONVERSION;
  CAtlRegExp<> regexp;
  CAtlREMatchContext<> Context; //companion for match

  char* number = W2A(Number);
  regexp.Parse( "\\([0-9][0-9][0-9]\\) [0-9][0-9][0-9]-[0-9][0-9][0-9][0-9]" );
  if (regexp.Match( number , &Context ))
  {
      *pError = 0;
      *pErrorString = SysAllocString(L"OK");

  }
  else
  {
      *pError = 1;
      *pErrorString = SysAllocString(L"Bad Format");
  }

    return S_OK;
}
```

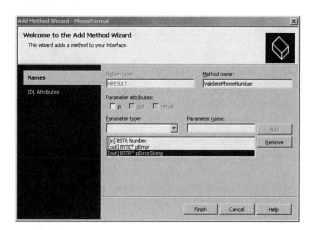

FIGURE 8.1   Adding the method and its three parameters.

Most of what's going on here is pretty obvious, but the way COM handles strings is not obvious at all. This function takes a BSTR—a binary string. The Match() function takes a C-style string: a char*. To convert between them, you can use the W2A macro. The macro USES_CONVERSION that you see at the top of the function defines it. A BSTR always uses wide characters, whereas an ordinary char* string uses ASCII characters—hence the macro name, W2A for wide-to-ASCII.

This code returns the two output parameters by de-referencing the pointers passed into the function. The error code is simple: This function is given a BYTE* and you can simply de-reference it, writing *pError=0 or *pError=1 as appropriate. The BSTR* is more difficult: You can't simply assign a literal string to the BSTR. The function SysAllocString takes care of allocating the memory in which the string is to be held while it is returned to the calling program. The L macro converts an ordinary quoted string to wide characters.

COM components indicate success or failure by returning specific values. The return type of all COM methods in C++ is HRESULT. Returning the predefined S_OK value means that there is no error; the component was able to determine whether the phone number is valid or not. If, for example, the component needed to look up information in a database to perform the validation, when the database could not be reached the component could return a failure value, which is any value other than zero. Several such values are predefined, including E_INVALIDARG and E_FAIL, in winerror.h.

Enter this code into the implementation file and build the project. Don't forget to add the #include statement so that the ATL Regular Expressions header is used. Now the component is complete.

Using a COM Component from Unmanaged C++

COM objects such as the phone number validator don't have a user interface. Putting together a quick application with a very simple user interface serves as a good way to test it. For this component, a dialog-based application with a text box for entering phone numbers will work well. The application creates an instance of the COM component you built with ATL, and uses it to validate the number that is entered. There are just a few steps to building the test project:

- Create an empty project
- Create a dialog box
- Connect the fields on the dialog box to variables
- Connect the button on the dialog box to a function
- Code the function
- Adjust the structure of the application and add COM support

Creating an Empty Project

Close the PhoneFormat solution and create a new MFC Application called PhoneTest. On the Application Type tab of the MFC Application Wizard, select Dialog Based. The other defaults are all okay for this application, so click Finish. This will create a project, and a starter dialog box with the ID IDD_PHONETEST_DIALOG.

Creating a Dialog Box

In the Resource View, double-click IDD_PHONETEST_DIALOG to edit the main dialog box of the application. Delete the static label with the TODO instruction. Click the OK button and use the Properties window to change the ID of the button to IDC_VALIDATE and the caption to Validate. Change the caption on the Cancel button to Close, but leave its ID unchanged.

Add an Edit Control and change its ID to IDC_NUMBER. Put a static label before it, captioned *Number to Validate:*.

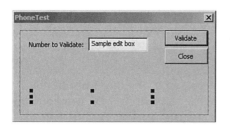

FIGURE 8.2 Building a simple MFC dialog box to exercise the *ValidatePhoneNumber()* method.

Add two more static controls, one with the ID IDC_ERROR and the other with the ID IDC_MESSAGE, between the edit box and the two buttons. Change the caption of each of these to an empty string, and lengthen IDC_MESSAGE so that it can accommodate an error message.

Click in the background of the dialog box (away from all the controls) to select the dialog box itself, and then drag the bottom of the dialog box upward to make a smaller dialog box. The completed dialog box should resemble Figure 8.2.

Connecting the Fields on the Dialog Box to Variables

Right-click the edit box, IDC_NUMBER, and choose Add Variable. This brings up the Add Member Variable Wizard. Leave the Control Variable check box selected, and from the drop-down box at the far right, choose Value rather than the default Control. This changes the Variable Type to CString. Enter **Number** for the Variable Name and click Finish. If you switch to the Class View and expand CPhoneTestDlg, you can see the new member variable.

In the same way, connect the static label called IDC_ERROR to a member variable called Error and connect IDC_MESSAGE to Message. If you have trouble clicking the static controls because they don't have a caption, use the drop-down box at the top of the Properties window to select them. Just drop it down and select the appropriate ID; you'll see the control selected on the dialog box. Then you can right-click it to add the variable.

Connecting the Button on the Dialog Box to a Function

Click the Validate button on the dialog box. At the top of the Properties window is a toolbar. Find the Event button (it looks like a lightning strike) and click it. Click to the right of BN_CLICKED; a drop-down box appears. Drop it down and choose the only entry, <Add> OnBnClickedValidate. The function name appears in the Class View underneath CPhoneTestDlg and you are switched to editing the function.

Coding the Function

When the button is clicked, the test code calls the ValidatePhoneNumber() method of the IPhoneNumber interface, as implemented in the CPhoneNumber class developed earlier in this chapter. Your coding effort will be substantially less if you use the #import directive. The #import directive enables you to treat a COM component as though it were an ordinary C++ object.

FINDING PHONEFORMAT.DLL

If you get any errors when you compile that refer to the #import line, make sure the path to PhoneFormat.dll is correct for your machine. (The .. in this line ensures that as long as the PhoneFormat and PhoneTest project folders are both under the same folder, this line will work.) Don't move the DLL; change the #import directive if necessary.

Open the source code for CPhoneTestDlg, and scroll to the top of the file. After the #include statements that are already there, add this line:

```
#import "..\PhoneFormat\Debug\PhoneFormat.dll" no_namespace
```

Edit OnBnClickedValidate() so that it looks like this:

```
void CPhoneTestDlg::OnBnClickedValidate()
{
    USES_CONVERSION;
    UpdateData();
    _bstr_t number = Number;
    unsigned char errorcode = 0;
    BSTR errormessage;
    try
    {
        IPhoneNumberPtr phone("PhoneFormat.PhoneNumber");
        phone->ValidatePhoneNumber(number, &errorcode, &errormessage);
        Error.Format("%u", errorcode);
        Message = W2A(errormessage);
    }
    catch (_com_error e)
    {
```

```
        Error.Format("%u", 99);
        Message = e.ErrorMessage();
    }
    UpdateData(false);
}
```

This function, like ValidatePhoneNumber(), uses the USES_CONVERSION macro to bring in some simple conversion macros. The call to UpdateData() moves the value the user typed in the edit box into the member variable, Number. Because ValidatePhoneNumber() takes a BSTR, this code creates a _bstr_t variable to pass in. The _bstr_t type encapsulates a BSTR with easy-to-use constructors that call SysAllocString for you, if required.

The actual COM call is wrapped in a try block in case anything goes wrong, such as the COM component being unavailable. Thanks to the #import directive, creating an instance of the COM component and calling its methods looks just like creating an ordinary C++ object. If you were wondering how to decide what string to pass into the IPhoneNumberPtr, it's the progid (short for program ID) of the COM component—the name of the project, a dot, and the name of the class you added into the project—PhoneFormat.PhoneNumber, in this case. In cases where you don't write the COM component you are using, expect to be told the progid.

CSTRING'S FORMAT() METHOD

If you haven't seen the Format() method of the CString class before, it's an easy way to convert a number to a string. The %u for the first parameter indicates that you want the number treated as a simple unsigned number.

After the call to ValidatePhoneNumber(), this code sets the member variables associated with the two static controls, and then calls UpdateData(false) to send the new values to the dialog box.

Build the project at this point to make sure you don't have any errors, but it's not quite ready to run.

Adjusting the Structure of the Application and Adding COM Support

In the Class View, expand CPhoneTestApp and double-click OnInitInstance to edit it. Most dialog-based applications respond differently when the dialog box is dismissed with OK than when it is dismissed with Cancel. This one does not need to, so the code can be quite a bit simpler. Find and remove these lines:

```
INT_PTR nResponse = dlg.DoModal();
if (nResponse == IDOK)
{
    // TODO: Place code here to handle when the dialog is
    //  dismissed with OK
}
```

```
else if (nResponse == IDCANCEL)
{
    // TODO: Place code here to handle when the dialog is
    //  dismissed with Cancel
}
```

In their place, add this single line:

```
dlg.DoModal();
```

(Because you changed the ID of the Validate button from IDOK to IDC_VALIDATE, clicking it doesn't dismiss the dialog box.) To activate COM support for this application, add this line at the very beginning of InitInstance():

```
::CoInitialize(NULL);
```

To clean up your COM work before returning from InitInstance(), add this line after the call to DoModal() and before the return statement:

```
    ::CoUninitialize();
```

Now, build the project again. It's ready to run. Enter a good phone number, such as (800) 555-1212 and click Validate: You see an error code of 0 and a message of OK. Validate a bad phone number, and you see an error code of 1 and a message of Bad format. Click Close, and the application ends.

Debugging a COM Application

If your COM component doesn't behave as you expect, you need to debug it. There's really nothing special about the process in this case, even though some of the code is not in the solution you have open. Here's how to step from OnBnClickedValidate() into ValidatePhoneNumber():

1. Put a breakpoint on the line in OnBnClickedValidate() that calls ValidatePhoneNumber().

2. Start the application by choosing Debug, Start Debugging. When the dialog box appears, enter a phone number.

3. Control stops when it reaches your breakpoint. Click the Step Into button on the Debug toolbar, or press F11.

4. The debugger first steps into a bstr_t copy constructor that is making a copy of number. Press Shift+F11 or click Step Out to leave this constructor.

5. Step into the function call once again and notice that control is inside the overload of operator `->` for the smart COM pointer that the `#import` directive created. Step out of this function also.

6. Step into the call for a third time and notice that the smart COM pointer's code for `ValidatePhoneNumber()` is actually calling a function called `raw_ValidatePhoneNumber()`. Step over (F10) once, and then Step into the call to `raw_ValidatePhoneNumber()`.

7. You'll find yourself in the code for another operator overload. Step out.

8. Step in one more time and—presto! You're in the code you wrote for `ValidatePhoneNumber()`. Now that you're here, try setting a breakpoint. That saves you having to step in and out so much on the way to the relevant code.

After you have set a breakpoint in the COM component from inside your test solution, you should find it pretty simple to watch the component at work and understand any errors. Even if you stop debugging and start up again, your breakpoint will still be in place.

Using a COM Component from Managed C++

Managed code can use a COM component just as though it was a .NET object. It does so through a special piece of code called a Runtime-Callable Wrapper, or RCW. This wrapper (also called an *interop assembly*) accepts .NET calls through the runtime, and inside it holds all it needs to know about your COM component. When the calls come in, the wrapper calls methods of the COM component to handle them. It marshals parameters if need be, and translates error `HRESULT` values from the COM component into .NET exceptions. You don't need to do any work to get all this translated for you.

How do you get a Runtime-Callable Wrapper? There are two ways, and they're both very easy: either someone gives you one, or Visual Studio can generate it for you. The vendor that supplied your COM component may ship a Runtime-Callable Wrapper with it. In this case the interop assembly is known as a Primary Interop Assembly, or PIA. Primary refers to the fact that it was written by the supplier of the COM component, and therefore may take advantage of the internal mechanisms of the COM Component. Many of the Microsoft COM components, including large parts of BizTalk 2002 and Office 2003, ship with PIAs. If nobody gives you an RCW, Visual Studio can make one for you, and that's the approach used in this chapter.

To test using a COM component from managed code, create a C++ WinForms application called `ManagedPhoneTest`. Drag controls onto the form and edit their properties, as follows:

1. A textbox. Name it `Number` and change the `Text` property to no text.

2. A label. Name it `Error` and change the `Text` property to no text.

3. Another label. Name it `Message` and change the `Text` property to no text.

4. A button. Name it `ValidateButton` and change its `Text` to `Validate`.

5. Another button. Name it `CloseButton` and change its `Text` to `Close`.

Double-click the Close button and add this line of code to the handler that is generated for you:

```
Close();
```

Before you can code the handler for the Validate button, your code needs a reference to the Runtime-Callable Wrapper for the COM component. Assuming you are still using the same computer as you used to develop that component, you don't need to copy it anywhere or do anything to be ready to use it. It's registered on your machine, and COM will use the Registry to find it. To generate the RCW and add a reference to it, right-click the References node in Solution Explorer and choose Add Reference. On the Add Reference dialog box, select the COM tab. After a small delay, all the COM components on your system are listed. Scroll down to PhoneFormat 1.0 Type Library, highlight it, click Select and then OK.

Double-click the Validate button on the dialog box and then enter this code for the handler:

```
try
{
    Interop::PhoneFormat::CPhoneNumberClass* pf =
            new Interop::PhoneFormat::CPhoneNumberClass();
    String* errormessage;
    unsigned char errorcode;
    pf->ValidatePhoneNumber(Number->Text, &errorcode, &errormessage);
    Error->Text = errorcode.ToString();
    Message->Text = errormessage;
}
catch (Exception* e)
{
    Error->Text = "99";
    Message->Text = e->Message;
}
```

How do you know what class to create? If you double-click `PhoneFormat` under the References node in Solution Explorer, the Object Browser opens to show you the contents of the reference assembly. Expand `Interop.PhoneFormat` and you'll see a namespace (identified with brace brackets) called `Interop.PhoneFormat`. Expand that namespace and you'll see a class called `CPhoneNumber` and an interface called `IPhoneNumber`.

Click on `CPhoneNumber` in the object browser, and you'll see the Associated COM Class is `Interop.PhoneFormat.CPhoneNumberClass`, and it has one method, `ValidatePhoneNumber()`. Writing the line of code is just a matter of replacing the dots (which VB and C# use) with `::` for C++.

Run the application and test with some good and bad phone numbers as before. Everything should work smoothly.

Now compare the amount of code you had to write to use this COM component from a WinForms application to the amount of code required to use it from an MFC application, even with the `#import` macro simplifying the MFC application considerably from what it otherwise would have been. Building applications on the .NET Framework is fast and simple, and those applications have full access to all the COM components you've already built.

Exposing a Managed Class Library as a COM Component

The principles of COM Interop work in both directions: Just as new managed code can access a COM component through a Runtime-Callable Wrapper, so unmanaged code can access a .NET component through a COM-Callable Wrapper, or CCW. However, it can't access any and all .NET code—there are conditions the .NET object must meet to be exposed as a COM component:

- The library must contain at least one interface, and a class that implements that interface.

- You must generate a type library from the library that COM can use.

- You should put the library into the Global Assembly Cache, which imposes some more requirements on you, most notably that the library have a strong name.

- Information to enable COM to find the component must be added to the Registry.

In this section, you learn how to modify a library so that it meets all of these conditions. The library in question is the sample from Chapter 6, "Writing a Class Library in Managed C++." You can make a copy or work with your original; the changes required here won't affect how managed applications interact with the managed library.

Adding Interfaces to the Library

The `ManagedMathLibrary` namespace contains two classes: `DLL`, which exposes static methods to initialize the C runtime libraries, and `Arithmetic`, which has the familiar `Add()`, `Subtract()`, `Multiply()`, and `Divide()` methods. The corresponding interfaces could have any names, but `IDll` and `IArithmetic` are logical choices.

To ManagedMathLibrary.h, add the two interface definitions, each just before the corresponding class. Make sure they are inside the namespace definition. Each interface definition just lists the methods that are already in the class. Add these lines to define `IDll`:

```
public __gc __interface IDll
{
     void Initialize();
     void Cleanup();
};
```

THE __INTERFACE KEYWORD

The __interface keyword defines a .NET interface. This is a class containing only public, pure virtual methods. Don't forget the semicolon after the closing brace, just as for a class declaration.

Because an interface cannot contain any static methods, change the DLL member functions, removing the `static` keyword. The calling code will need to create an instance of the class in order to initialize the libraries. Edit the companion test harness, `ManagedHarness`, accordingly. Find this line:

```
ManagedMathLibrary::DLL::Initialize();
```

Replace it with these:

```
ManagedMathLibrary::DLL* dll = new ManagedMathLibrary::DLL();
dll->Initialize();
```

Find this line:

```
ManagedMathLibrary::DLL::Cleanup();
```

Replace it with this line:

```
dll->Cleanup();
```

Add these lines to define `IArithmetic`:

```
public __gc __interface IArithmetic
{
     System::Double Add(System::Double num1, System::Double num2);
     System::Double Subtract(System::Double num1, System::Double num2);
     System::Double Divide(System::Double num1, System::Double num2);
     System::Double Multiply(System::Double num1, System::Double num2);
};
```

Change each of the class declarations to indicate that it implements the corresponding interface:

```
public __gc class DLL: public IDll
public __gc class Arithmetic : public IArithmetic
```

There's no need to make any changes to the implementation of the class or the methods—the interfaces only list methods that were already implemented in the classes anyway.

Generating a Type Library

A type library is a file that holds all the information the COM runtime needs about a particular COM component: the interfaces and their methods, the parameters and return types, and so on. A generic COM-Callable Wrapper, mscoree.dll, and this type library are the keys to making the .NET component available to COM.

Build the revised library, and then open a Visual Studio .NET 2003 command prompt and change directories to the location of your freshly built library. Enter this command:

```
tlbexp ManagedMathLibrary.dll
```

A file called ManagedMathLibrary.tlb appears in the directory. Keep the command prompt open; there are more command-line utilities involved in meeting all the conditions for .NET Interop.

Adding the Library to the GAC

One of the appeals of COM was the universality of a component: As long as a Registry entry existed to tell the COM runtime where the component was, the programmer using the component didn't need to know where it was, or make a copy in a local directory. The .NET equivalent is the Global Assembly Cache, or GAC. Although it is possible to access a .NET component from a COM application without putting the .NET component in the GAC, it's not recommended. Not only does it make deploying the combined application more difficult, it can lead to some very strange errors when you make seemingly small changes to your calling application.

Putting an assembly into the GAC is straightforward, but there are some prerequisites: All assemblies in the GAC must have a *strong name*. A strong name pulls together a simple name (such as ManagedMathLibrary) with a version number, localization information, a public key provided by the developer, and a digital signature. Two assemblies may have the same simple name, but be distinguished within the GAC if one of the other components of their strong names are different.

At the same Visual Studio .NET 2003 command prompt you used earlier, change directories up to the project folder and issue this command:

```
sn -k mathlibrary.snk
```

It actually doesn't matter what you name your key file—even what extension you use—but it helps other developers if you use the.snk extension.

Back in Visual Studio, open the file AssemblyInfo.cpp for the ManagedMathLibrary project. At the bottom of the file, you'll find this line:

```
[assembly:AssemblyKeyFileAttribute("")];
```

Edit the line, inserting the name of the key file you created with the sn utility between the quotes. Build the project. If you get an error about Visual Studio being unable to open the key file, try closing Visual Studio and then opening the solution again.

Finally, add the signed assembly to the GAC. Using the command prompt, change directories to the Debug or Release folder (whichever you just built) and issue this command:

```
gacutil -i managedmathlibrary.dll
```

To check that you have successfully added the assembly to the GAC, browse to the Assembly folder under C:\Windows or C:\Winnt (depending on your Windows version) and you will see the GAC itself. Make sure that ManagedMathLibrary is in the GAC.

Creating Registry Entries

The final step in making this .NET component available to COM is adding an entry to the Registry that points to the generic CCW, mscoree.dll. In the same command prompt you've been using all along, enter this command:

```
regasm managedmathlibrary.dll
```

Interestingly, this doesn't record the location of the assembly in the Registry. It points the COM runtime at mscoree, the "execution engine" of the .NET runtime (the original working name was Common Object Runtime, hence the COR in the DLL name) that is used by all .NET assemblies being accessed from COM. The loader looks first in the GAC, and then in the executable path for the application that is using the assembly, and then in a Codebase Registry entry if you used one. By default, regasm doesn't store the codebase information, and because this sample assembly is in the GAC, there's no need to—the assembly is waiting right where the loader will look for it first.

Testing the Component

A console application is the simplest test harness for this component. Create a Win32 Console application called Interop. Copy the generated type library, ManagedMathLibrary.tlb, to the project folder.

Add this code for the `main()` function:

```
int _tmain(int argc, _TCHAR* argv[])
{
    ::CoInitialize(NULL);
    ManagedMathLibrary::IDllPtr dll("ManagedMathLibrary.DLL");
    dll->Initialize();
    ManagedMathLibrary::IArithmeticPtr a("ManagedMathLibrary.Arithmetic");
    cout << "2.3 + 4.5 is " <<  a->Add(2.3, 4.5) << endl;
    dll->Cleanup();
    ::CoUninitialize();
    return 0;
}
```

This code initializes COM with `CoInitialize()`, and later cleans it up with `CoUninitialize()`. It uses the `Initialize()` and `Cleanup()` methods provided by the .NET component to ensure that the CRT is initialized and cleaned up. Between the initialization and the cleanup, it uses the `Add()` method of the `Arithmetic` class. The code is made much simpler by using smart pointers that are generated by a `#import` statement, like the COM client shown earlier in this chapter, `PhoneTest`.

The `#import` statement in this client cannot import a DLL; instead it imports the type library, managedmathlibrary.tlb, generated by the `tlbexp` utility. There is a small problem importing this particular library, and it's worth exploring here in case you meet a similar situation in libraries of your own.

Add these lines to the top of the file so that the code that writes to `cout` will compile:

```
#include <iostream>
using namespace std;
```

Add this line after those, but before the start of the `main()` function:

```
#import "ManagedMathLibrary.tlb"
```

Build the project, and you'll see a really strange error:

```
fatal error C1196: 'allocator<void>' : identifier found in type library
➥'ManagedMathLibrary.tlb' is not a valid C++ identifier
```

This error is strange for two reasons: First, a template declaration is a valid C++ identifier, and second, what is a template declaration doing in your type library? The second one is easiest to answer. The `tlbexp` utility exports all the types defined in the .NET assembly. That assembly, written in managed C++, used IJW to access methods of the CRT, and included the `<iostream>` header. That header in turn included other headers, and all sorts of typedefs, structs, and classes were defined within the assembly. The `tlbexp` utility exported them all. You can confirm this in a command prompt by re-issuing the `tlbexp` command with the verbose option:

```
tlbexp ManagedMathLibrary.dll /verbose
```

This produces output like this:

```
Microsoft (R) .NET Framework Assembly to Type Library Converter 1.1.4322.573
Copyright (C) Microsoft Corporation 1998-2002.  All rights reserved.
Type bad_exception exported.
Type bad_alloc exported.
Type _iobuf exported.
Type _Scalar_ptr_iterator_tag exported.
Type allocator<void> exported.
Type basic_string<char,std::char_traits<char>,std::allocator<char> > exported.
Type logic_error exported.
Type domain_error exported.
Type invalid_argument exported.
Type length_error exported.
Type out_of_range exported.
Type runtime_error exported.
Type overflow_error exported.
Type underflow_error exported.
Type range_error exported.
Type _DebugHeapString exported.
Type _Timevec exported.
Type _Locinfo exported.
Type _Collvec exported.
Type _Ctypevec exported.
Type _Cvtvec exported.
Type locale exported.
Type id exported.
Type _Lockit exported.
Type facet exported.
Type _Locimp exported.
Type codecvt_base exported.
Type codecvt<unsigned short,char,int> exported.
```

```
Type ctype_base exported.
Type ctype<char> exported.
Type ctype<unsigned short> exported.
Type ios_base exported.
Type failure exported.
Type _Iosarray exported.
Type _Fnarray exported.
Type basic_ostream<unsigned short,std::char_traits<unsigned short> > exported.
Type sentry exported.
Type basic_ostream<char,std::char_traits<char> > exported.
Type basic_istream<unsigned short,std::char_traits<unsigned short> > exported.
Type sentry exported.
Type basic_istream<char,std::char_traits<char> > exported.
Type sentry exported.
Type _GUID exported.
Type tagPROPVARIANT exported.
Type tagVARIANT exported.
```
Type IDll exported.
Type DLL exported.
Type IArithmetic exported.
Type Arithmetic exported.
Type Simple exported.
```
Type allocator<char> exported.
Type _DebugHeapAllocator<char> exported.
Type basic_string<char,std::char_traits<char>,std::_DebugHeapAllocator<char> >
➡ exported.
Type basic_ios<unsigned short,std::char_traits<unsigned short> > exported.
Type basic_streambuf<unsigned short,std::char_traits<unsigned short> > exported
Type fpos<int> exported.
Type ostreambuf_iterator<char,std::char_traits<char> > exported.
Type sentry exported.
Type num_put<char,std::ostreambuf_iterator<char,std::char_traits<char> > >
➡ exported.
Type basic_ios<char,std::char_traits<char> > exported.
Type _Sentry_base exported.
Type _Sentry_base exported.
Type basic_streambuf<char,std::char_traits<char> > exported.
Type _String_val<char,std::allocator<char> > exported.
Type _String_val<char,std::_DebugHeapAllocator<char> > exported.
Type _Sentry_base exported.
Type numpunct<char> exported.
Type _Sentry_base exported.
```

```
Type bad_cast exported.
Type lconv exported.
Type exception exported.
Type _s__CatchableTypeArray exported.
Type $_s__CatchableTypeArray$_extraBytes_8 exported.
Type _s__CatchableType exported.
Type _TypeDescriptor exported.
Type $_TypeDescriptor$_extraBytes_16 exported.
Type $_TypeDescriptor$_extraBytes_15 exported.
Type _s__ThrowInfo exported.
Type _Mutex exported.
Type _String_base exported.
Type _IMAGE_DOS_HEADER exported.
Type _DebugHeapTag_t exported.
```
Type Multiple exported.
```
Assembly exported to C:\ManagedMathLibrary\Debug\ManagedMathLibrary.tlb
```

Of all these types, only the ones displayed in bold are actually public types defined by your own code. The rest come from headers that were included to make your code work. This would be harmless if none of them were templated types. The presence of these templated types causes problems when you bring in the type library with #import.

The solution is to use the exclude attribute on the #import directive. This is a little tedious, but it solves the problem. When the build fails, it complains about allocator<void>, so change the import directive to read like this:

```
#import "ManagedMathLibrary.tlb"  exclude("allocator<void>")
```

Build again and you'll get the same error message about a different type. Keep adding entries to the comma-separated list inside the parentheses (use the \ character to spread your #import directive over several lines) until the compiler errors stop. The final statement should resemble this one:

```
#import "ManagedMathLibrary.tlb"  exclude("allocator<void>", \
    "basic_string<char,std::char_traits<char>,std::allocator<char> >", \
    "codecvt<unsigned short,char,int>", \
    "ctype<char>", \
    "ctype<unsigned short>", \
    "basic_ostream<unsigned short,std::char_traits<unsigned short> >", \
    "basic_ostream<char,std::char_traits<char> >", \
    "basic_istream<unsigned short,std::char_traits<unsigned short> >", \
    "basic_istream<char,std::char_traits<char> >", \
    "allocator<char>", \
    "_DebugHeapAllocator<char>", \
```

```
"basic_string<char,std::char_traits<char>,std::_DebugHeapAllocator<char> >", \
  "basic_ios<unsigned short,std::char_traits<unsigned short> >", \
  "basic_streambuf<unsigned short,std::char_traits<unsigned short> >", \
  "fpos<int>", \
  "basic_ios<char,std::char_traits<char> >", \
  "basic_streambuf<char,std::char_traits<char> >", \
  "_String_val<char,std::allocator<char> >", \
  "_String_val<char,std::_DebugHeapAllocator<char> >", \
  "ostreambuf_iterator<char,std::char_traits<char> >", \
  "num_put<char,std::ostreambuf_iterator<char,std::char_traits<char> > >", \
  "numpunct<char>")
```

You can speed things up by using the type names from the `tlbexp verbose` report, if you want. When you build a different project using these techniques, you might need to exclude different templated types, depending on the headers included by the managed project.

The project should now build without errors (ignore any warnings about duplicate types) and run successfully. You are likely to have to go through this same procedure whenever you use a CCW to access a .NET component that uses unmanaged code (such as the CRT). It's tedious, but you only have to do it once.

In Brief

- COM is a long-established programming technique that was designed to meet many of the same needs as the .NET runtime.

- Although .NET components are the preferred technology for new development, you might need to create or support COM components for existing applications.

- ATL makes creating COM components relatively simple, and the `#import` directive creates smart pointers to help you use those components.

- To use a COM component from managed code, create a Runtime-Callable Wrapper by adding a reference on the COM tab.

- To use a .NET component from COM code, export the type library, sign the assembly, add it to the GAC, and register the assembly, and then use the `#import` directive in your COM code.

- Mixed assemblies that use the C runtime libraries need special treatment when importing the `typelib` generated from the assembly.

Using Existing COM Components in C++

Automation Concepts

An Automation server is an application that makes some of its functionality available through COM. However, most Automation servers are quite different from other kinds of COM components, especially ActiveX controls and the small COM components that were covered in Chapter 8, "Writing COM Components in C++." Those components exist primarily to offer services to applications. They have no user interface, or they have an interface designed to be part of a larger whole.

Automation servers are generally large and complicated applications: Visual Studio .NET 2003 is an automation server and so are all the applications in the Office family. Their primary purpose is to be used interactively by a user, but some (often most) of the functionality is also available through macros or other applications that can then automate the use of the application.

The sample applications in this chapter are written as console applications to make them as simple as possible, and use Word 2003 as the automation server. You should be able to apply these concepts to other automation servers and leverage other people's code wherever possible. The Office applications are marvelous opportunities to save work, because Office is installed on almost every computer that runs Windows.

In this chapter, you will see two ways to spell-check some text, and even to get spelling suggestions from Word for the misspelled words. Users ask for this sort of functionality in their applications, and the effort involved in developing a dictionary and writing all the code to check various forms of the same word is prohibitive for most applications. Letting Word do the work is very appealing, and you'll see shortly, it's simple too.

Using Word as a Spell Checker from Unmanaged C++

Because automation is a COM technology, you can use the #import technique to reduce the amount of code you need to write to access Word and give it instructions. The structure of the console application looks like this:

```
#include "stdafx.h"
// import type library, dll etc
// other include files needed for code to compile

int _tmain(int argc, _TCHAR* argv[])
{
   ::CoInitialize(NULL);
   {
      // create smart pointer
      // use it to access Word functionality
   }
   ::CoUninitialize();
   return 0;
}
```

The brace brackets that start after CoInitialize() and end before CoUninitialize() are there for scoping; they ensure that the smart pointer has gone out of scope (triggering the destructor) before COM is cleaned up.

This simple application just prompts the user for a sentence, pulls it apart with strtok(), and passes it by Word for a spell-check, one word at a time. The general approach looks like this:

```
cout << "Enter a sentence and press enter:" << endl;
char testSentence[1000];
cin.getline(testSentence,999);
char* word = strtok(testSentence,"\t,() ");
while (word != NULL)
{
   _// check this word, offer suggestions if any
   word = strtok(NULL,"\t,() ");
}
```

SHOP TALK

GOOD OLD STRTOK()

Why am I using `strtok()` in this example? It's an old-fashioned C function, after all. The answer is simple: It works, and it doesn't bloat your application. There's a `Tokenize()` function in the ATL version of `CString` that does much the same thing, but you have to bring a lot of other code in to get access to that. Oddly, the STL doesn't offer an equivalent. In managed code, the `Split()` method of the `String` class takes care of things for you. If you're working in unmanaged C++ and need to work with strings, don't forget those old-fashioned C functions: They just might be all you need.

Finding Your Way Around

With the overall structure in place, a few questions leap to mind:

- Which type library or DLL should be named in the #import statement?

- Which `progid` do you pass to the constructor of the smart pointer?

- What are the functions offered by the automation classes associated with Word, what parameters do they take, and where can you find documentation?

The answers to these questions, for Word 2003, are in this section, of course, but you need to be able to answer them for any automation server you plan to use. Automation servers usually come with documentation. It can be quite complicated trying to work out these pieces of information using tools alone, and it's simple if the provider of the application just tells you. For completeness, and to remove any air of mystery or magic, this section shows you where all the information can be found.

To automate Word, you need to use the #import statement to bring in three files:

- MSO.DLL—The Microsoft Office library. This "sets the stage" for defining the types you will actually work with. Omit this #import and the others will cause compiler errors.

- VBE6EXT.olb—The object library for the Visual Basic Editor, which in fact applies to all VBA hosts, including Office. Omit this #import and the others will cause compiler errors.

- MSWORD.OLB—The object library for Word. This defines the smart pointers you will actually be using.

If you have no MSDN library and no Google, you can use the OLE/COM object viewer, which comes with Visual Studio .NET 2003, to discover that these are the files you need. You can bring it up from within Visual Studio on the Tools menu. It shows you all the COM components that are in the Registry, arranged by categories. The first place to look is in the Automation Objects section of this tool.

Unfortunately, not all automation servers are in the Registry. Search your hard drive for files with the extensions .DLL, .TLB, and .OLB with names that remind you of the product you're trying to automate, in folders that also remind you of the product. (Use the Search option on the Start menu.) For example, a file called MSWORD.OLB sounds like a really good fit when you're looking for something related to Microsoft Word. Finding it in `Program Files\ Microsoft Office\OFFICE11` makes the connection even stronger. So you've found the first file you'll need, and for some automation servers it might be the only one you'll need. The next step is to look in it and learn a little more about it.

In the OLE/COM object viewer, choose, File, View Typelib. Browse to the folder where you found the likely file, and open it. The viewer shows pages and pages of information for MSWORD.OLB, and it starts like this:

```
// Generated .IDL file (by the OLE/COM Object Viewer)
//
// typelib filename: MSWORD.OLB

[
  uuid(00020905-0000-0000-C000-000000000046),
  version(8.3),
  helpstring("Microsoft Word 11.0 Object Library"),
  helpfile("VBAWD10.CHM"),
  helpcontext(00000000)
]
library Word
{
    // TLib :       // TLib : Microsoft Visual Basic for Applications
➥Extensibility 5.3 : {0002E157-0000-0000-C000-000000000046}
    importlib("VBE6EXT.OLB");
    // TLib : Microsoft Office 11.0 Object Library :
➥{2DF8D04C-5BFA-101B-BDE5-00AA0044DE52}
    importlib("MSO.DLL");
    // TLib : OLE Automation : {00020430-0000-0000-C000-000000000046}
    importlib("stdole2.tlb");
```

The helpstring in this IDL confirms that this object library is for Word in Office 11 (an internal name for Office 2003). You've found the right object library. The `importlib` statements tell you about other libraries on which this one depends. Write down their names; you're going to need them shortly.

After the `importlib` statements comes a long list of all the interfaces defined in this library, including _Application and _Document. Often when a library has a lot of interfaces, some start with an underscore, perhaps just to get them to the top of alphabetical lists, where they're easy to find. The OLEViewer lists these interfaces in the tree view on the left as well; scroll past all the `typedef enum` entries and you'll find some interfaces. Expand

_Application and you'll find pages of methods; this is a big interface. There are no search commands in the OLE/COM viewer, so try this: Click in the right pane, use Ctrl+A to select all the text and Ctrl+C to copy it. Open a Notepad instance, and paste in all the text. Now you can use Notepad's find capabilities.

If you search for *Spelling*, you'll find a lot of typedefs and options, but more importantly a method called CheckSpelling, with IDL that looks like this:

```
HRESULT CheckSpelling(
    [in] BSTR Word,
    [in, optional] VARIANT* CustomDictionary,
    [in, optional] VARIANT* IgnoreUppercase,
    [in, optional] VARIANT* MainDictionary,
    [in, optional] VARIANT* CustomDictionary2,
    [in, optional] VARIANT* CustomDictionary3,
    [in, optional] VARIANT* CustomDictionary4,
    [in, optional] VARIANT* CustomDictionary5,
    [in, optional] VARIANT* CustomDictionary6,
    [in, optional] VARIANT* CustomDictionary7,
    [in, optional] VARIANT* CustomDictionary8,
    [in, optional] VARIANT* CustomDictionary9,
    [in, optional] VARIANT* CustomDictionary10,
    [out, retval] VARIANT_BOOL* prop);
```

IDL reads a lot like C++: This is a function definition and it includes all the parameters. The square brackets hold attributes of the parameters and are fairly self explanatory. This method takes a lot of optional parameters and one non-optional one. It returns a Boolean value indicating whether the word passed in was spelled correctly.

Scrolling up from that line will reveal that the method is in the _Application interface. You've discovered what you need to know to code against the Word object model through COM.

Accessing the Automation Server

Create a Win32 console application called Word. Add this line, after the #include of stdafx.h:

```
#import "C:\Program Files\Microsoft Office\OFFICE11\msword.olb"
➥rename("ExitWindows","WordExitWindows")
```

Make sure the path you type here corresponds to the folder where you found MSWORD.OLB. The #import directive is qualified here by an attribute. The rename("ExitWindows","WordExitWindows") attribute deals with a conflict that occurs whenever you're automating Office products: This function is declared in more than one place. It doesn't matter what you rename it to, you just want to eliminate the name conflict.

Build this application and you'll get compiler errors. That's why you wrote down the libraries imported by this one, as revealed by the OLE/COM object viewer. Add another #import statement, before the one that imports MSWORD.OLB, importing VBE6EXT.OLB, because it's named first in the IDL. Use Start, Search to find the path to the file. Most developers like to impose a namespace name, like this:

```
#import "C:\Program Files\Common Files\Microsoft Shared\VBA\VBA6\VBE6EXT.olb"
➥rename_namespace("VBE6")
```

Build the project again and you'll get some more errors, so add another #import statement, before the other two, bringing in the next importlib mentioned in the IDL:

```
#import "C:\Program Files\Common Files\Microsoft Shared\OFFICE11\mso.dll"
➥rename_namespace("Office2003")
```

Build one more time and you should have only a handful of warnings about duplicate names. There are two ways to suppress these warnings: either add auto_rename attributes to the #import statements, or suppress the warnings with a pragma. Add this line before the import of MSWORD.OLB:

```
#pragma warning (disable:4278)
```

Now the project will build without errors or warnings, and it's ready to have actual code added to it. Remember this process when you use a #import in a project of your own that uses automation, and no one told you which file to import.

Creating a Smart Pointer and Calling Word Methods

Because you know you're going to use the _Application interface, create an instance of the _ApplicationPtr smart pointer object to simplify accessing the methods. This smart pointer is created for you by the #import statement, which makes a smart pointer for every interface in the type library, with Ptr at the end of the name. The constructor takes a string, comprised of the progid of the object you need to create. To discover the progid, you need to look in the OLE/COM viewer again. One of the first lines in the file defines the library:

```
library Word
```

After all the interfaces are a number of coclass statements (search for them in the IDL you copied into Notepad). The first two look like this:

```
[
    uuid(000209F0-0000-0000-C000-000000000046),
    helpcontext(0x000009b9),
    appobject
]
```

```
coclass Global {
    [default] interface _Global;
};


[
  uuid(000209FF-0000-0000-C000-000000000046),
  helpcontext(0x00000970)
]
coclass Application {
    [default] interface _Application;
    [source] dispinterface ApplicationEvents;
    [source] dispinterface ApplicationEvents2;
    [source] dispinterface ApplicationEvents3;
    [default, source] dispinterface ApplicationEvents4;
};
```

For each coclass, the IDL lists the interfaces it supports. The Application coclass supports the _Application interface (not surprisingly) along with some others. Therefore, the progid to pass to the constructor is Word.Application. Whenever you aren't sure which progid to use, check the IDL for the coclass names. Find the coclass that implements the desired interface, and then build the progid from the library name and the coclass name.

That means the line of code to create the smart pointer is this:

```
Word::ApplicationPtr ap("Word.Application");
```

From here it's just a matter of calling the CheckSpelling method. It takes a BSTR and returns an HRESULT, but it also has a retval parameter called prop that is a VARIANT_BOOL*. Thanks to the smart pointers and other behind-the-scenes code generated by the #import statement, you can think of it as taking an ordinary char* string and returning a bool. You call it like this:

```
bool spellingOK = ap->CheckSpelling("helloo");
```

If the function returns true, Word believes the spelling is okay. If it returns false, Word can't find the word in the dictionary. You might want to get some suggestions, in that case. A little trawling around in the IDL will get you what you need. Use the techniques shown earlier and you'll discover

- A method of the _Application interface called GetSpellingSuggestions() that returns a SpellingSuggestions**

- An interface called SpellingSuggestions, which is what GetSpellingSuggestions returns

- A not-very-exciting list of properties on the SpellingSuggestions interface, except for an Item property, which returns a SpellingSuggestion**

- A SpellingSuggestion interface with a Name property that returns a BSTR

If the word you are checking is in a variable called word, this code will check it and offer suggestions:

```
bool spellingOK = ap->CheckSpelling(word);
if (!spellingOK)
{
    cout << word << " is not recognized by Word. Word suggests:" << endl;
    Word::SpellingSuggestionsPtr sugg;
    sugg = ap->GetSpellingSuggestions(word);
    int suggcount = sugg->GetCount();
    for (int i = 1; i <= suggcount; i++)
    {
        Word::SpellingSuggestionPtr suggestedword = sugg->Item(i);
        if (suggestedword)
        {
            cout << suggestedword->GetName() << endl;
        }
    }
    if (suggcount == 0)
        cout << "No suggestions." << endl;
}
```

At this point, you should not only understand this code, and know what it makes Word do, but know how to walk up to any type library that you believe offers automation and learn what is in it and how to use it, without relying on magic strings discovered by Googling late into the night.

Putting It All Together

There are many steps involved in putting together this automation client. You have seen code snippets that import the automation files, create and use smart pointers, prompt the user for input, and write results back to the screen. Listing 9.1 shows the entire console application.

LISTING 9.1   Word.cpp

```
// Word.cpp : Defines the entry point for the console application.
//

#include "stdafx.h"
#import "C:\Program Files\Common Files\Microsoft Shared\OFFICE11\mso.dll" \
        rename_namespace("Office2003")
#import "C:\Program Files\Common Files\Microsoft Shared\VBA\VBA6\VBE6EXT.olb" \
        rename_namespace("VBE6")
#pragma warning (disable:4278)
#import "C:\Program Files\Microsoft Office\OFFICE11\msword.olb" \
        rename("ExitWindows","WordExitWindows")
#include <iostream>
using namespace std;

#include <string>

int _tmain(int argc, _TCHAR* argv[])
{
    ::CoInitialize(NULL);
    {
        Word::_ApplicationPtr ap("Word.Application");

        //to get suggestions, there must be a document
        if (ap->Documents->Count == 0)
            ap->Documents->Add();

        cout << "Enter a sentence and press enter:" << endl;
        char testSentence[1000];
        cin.getline(testSentence,999);
        char* word = strtok(testSentence,"\t,() ");
        while (word != NULL)
        {
            bool spellingOK = ap->CheckSpelling(word);
            if (!spellingOK)
            {
                cout << word << " is not recognized by Word. Word suggests:"
                        << endl;
                Word::SpellingSuggestionsPtr sugg;
                sugg = ap->GetSpellingSuggestions(word);
                int suggcount = sugg->GetCount();
                for (int i = 1; i <= suggcount; i++)
```

LISTING 9.1   Continued

```
            {
                Word::SpellingSuggestionPtr suggestedword = sugg->Item(i);
                if (suggestedword)
                {
                    cout << suggestedword->GetName() << endl;
                }
            }
            if (suggcount == 0)
                cout << "No suggestions." << endl;
        }
        word = strtok(NULL,"\t,() ");
    }
    _variant_t v =  Word::wdDoNotSaveChanges;

    ap->Quit(&v);
  }
  ::CoUninitialize();
  return 0;
}
```

There are three concepts in this code that were not presented earlier:

- It is an oddity of Word that you don't get spelling suggestions unless there is a document open. This code creates one by using the Add() method of the Documents() property of the application.

- Release versions of this code sometimes blow up if Word is not fully initialized before requests are made of it. (In debug, the time you take to step through code gives Word lots of time to come up.) Therefore, the code to create the smart pointer and to open an empty document are before the prompt for the sentence from the users. Make sure you put the creation of the smart pointer as early as possible in your code.

- The last piece of work before unloading COM is quitting Word. If you don't, there will be a lot of WINWORD.EXE entries left running (use Task Manager to see them), and your system might get bogged down. The Quit() method takes a VARIANT*, and this code uses the helper class _variant_t to create the VARIANT in a single line.

Try running the application (if you run in release [Ctrl+F5], the application will pause and remind you to press any key to continue), and entering a sentence with a mix of correctly and incorrectly spelled words. For example, enter this sentence:

```
Tihs sentence hsa some misteaks
```

You should see this output:

```
Tihs is not recognized by Word. Word suggests:
This
Tins
Ties
Tics
Tips
hsa is not recognized by Word. Word suggests:
has
misteaks is not recognized by Word. Word suggests:
mistakes
misspeaks
misdeals
mistake
mistreats
mistrals
```

There you have it: a simple application that uses the power of Word to check spelling and offer suggestions. Think about other capabilities offered by Office applications—they're almost limitless. Your code can tap into them, just this simply.

Using Word as a Spell Checker from Managed C++

Just as you can add the power of other applications to your unmanaged applications, so too you can add it to managed apps. But instead of #import, type libraries, and progids, you have to learn your way around references, interop assemblies, and the GAC.

Primary Interop Assemblies

The temptation is strong to think you know how to get to Word from managed code; just add a reference on the COM tab, it will make you a Runtime Callable Wrapper (RCW) and away you go. But the last thing you want is to create your own RCW. Word comes with a set of Primary Interop Assemblies, or PIAs. A PIA does what you would expect any RCW to do; it looks like a .NET assembly on the outside, but it doesn't have implementation code. Instead it knows where to find that implementation code in COM, and how to marshal and convert back and forth between the managed and unmanaged worlds. What sets a PIA apart from the kind of RCW you could make yourself by just adding a reference? A PIA

- Is signed by the creator of the PIA

- Is marked with an attribute that indicates it is a PIA

- Usually has better performance and marshaling, because it was hand-written and tweaked by a vendor who knows the COM component very well

Make no mistake about it, if you're going to automate Word from managed code, you want to use the PIAs. When you install Office 2003 on a machine that already has the .NET Framework installed (and therefore already has a GAC), you can install the PIAs into the GAC. Look for the .NET Programmability Support options. If Office 2003 is already installed, you can change your installation as follows:

1. Choose Add/Remove programs from Control Panel.

2. Find Office 2003 and click Change.

3. Choose Add/Remove features and click Next.

4. Make sure the Choose Advanced Customization of Applications check box is selected.

5. In the tree view that appears, expand Microsoft Word for Windows.

6. Click the symbol next to .NET Programmability Support and choose Run from My Computer.

7. It's a good idea to do all the PIAs at once, even if you're only planning a Word project at the moment. Repeat steps 5 and 6 for Microsoft Excel for Windows, and under Office Tools for both Microsoft Forms 2.0 and Microsoft Graph.

8. Click Update. The PIAs will be installed into the GAC.

Open Windows Explorer and browse to your Windows directory (C:\Windows or C:\Winnt) and then to the assembly directory beneath that. This shows you all the assemblies in the GAC. Make sure you see plenty of names that start with Microsoft.Office.Interop.

Creating the Sample Application

Create a managed console application called ManagedWord. Bring up the Add Reference dialog box and switch to the COM tab. Scroll until you find Microsoft Office 11.0 Library. Click Select and then OK. The reference is added, along with several dependent references. However, an RCW is not generated for you. In Solution Explorer, expand the References node and select Microsoft.Office.Interop.Word. Switch to the Properties window and you will see the properties of the reference itself. The Full Path property shows where the assembly is located: You will see a path like this:

```
c:\Windows\assembly\Gac\Microsoft.Office.Interop.Word\
➥11.0.0.0__71e9bce111e9429c\Microsoft.Office.Interop.Word.dll
```

This reminds you that the PIA from the GAC was used, rather than a new RCW generated for you by the `tlbimp` utility.

The code for the `main()` function performs exactly the same tasks as the unmanaged version you've just seen, but because it is accessing Word functionality through a managed interface, there are a few slight differences at these stages:

- When creating the application object

- When passing parameters to the methods

- During string manipulation

- When closing Word

Rather than the smart pointers generated by `#import`, in managed code you create an instance of the coclass, and keep it in a pointer to the interface, like this:

```
Microsoft::Office::Interop::Word::Application* ap =
        new Microsoft::Office::Interop::Word::ApplicationClass();
```

To discover the name of the interface and the coclass, double-click the `Microsoft.Office.Interop.Word` reference in Solution Explorer. This brings up the Object Browser, which serves much the same purpose as the OLE/COM object viewer. You can select an interface from the tree view on the right, and see the details of the functions it holds on the left. When you select an interface, the bottom pane holds details about the interface itself. For example, if you select Application on the left, under the node for the `Microsoft.Office.Interop.Word` namespace, you will see the details shown in Figure 9.1.

The `CheckSpelling()` method is just like the equivalent method in the unmanaged interface, with one important exception: optional parameters. Like many of the methods exposed in the managed interfaces, `CheckSpelling()` expects parameters to be passed by reference. From C++ that means that you must pass an address of (a pointer to) a managed instance. This syntax is hard to reconcile with optional parameters.

The call from unmanaged code was

```
bool spellingOK = ap->CheckSpelling(word);
```

From managed code, all the parameters must be supplied. You can pass along a special value that means you are not supplying the parameter, but you must pass it by reference, like this:

```
Object* missing = System::Reflection::Missing::Value;
bool spellingOK = ap->CheckSpelling(s,&missing,&missing,
                                    &missing,&missing,
                                    &missing,&missing,
                                    &missing,&missing,
                                    &missing,&missing,
                                    &missing,&missing);
```

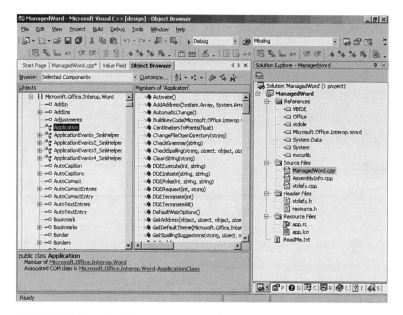

FIGURE 9.1   The Object Browser provides all the information you need about the managed interface.

This is fairly tedious, but it works. Because the Office libraries are so rich in parameters passed by reference, C++ and C# programmers have to do a little more work to use them than Visual Basic programmers. But don't let that stop you!

In the unmanaged version of the spell checker, the strings were just char* pointers and good old C runtime library functions like strtok were the order of the day. In the managed version, it's a little different, although the concepts are the same. The strings are System::String instances, and the Split() method breaks it up according to delimiters you specify. But instead of calling it repeatedly, as with strtok(), you call it once to create an array. The loop is governed not by the return from strtok() but by an enumerator that goes through the array. You call MoveNext() to point the enumerator at the next element of the array, and use the Current property to access the current element.

Finally, the managed version of Quit() is multiply defined, so it's simpler to just close the active window. Because Word exits when the last document is closed, this will ensure you are not left with extra copies of WINWORD.EXE running. To pass the save options constant, you need to create an instance of Object (so you can pass the address to the method, which expects its parameters by reference) and then box the constant into the object, like this:

```
Object* donotsave = __box(
      Microsoft::Office::Interop::Word::WdSaveOptions::wdDoNotSaveChanges);
ap->get_ActiveWindow()->Close(&donotsave,&missing);
```

The Entire Managed Application

The managed version of the spelling checker is in Listing 9.2. Compare it to the unmanaged version.

LISTING 9.2   ManagedWord.cpp

```cpp
// This is the main project file for VC++ application project
// generated using an Application Wizard.

#include "stdafx.h"

#using <mscorlib.dll>

using namespace System;

int _tmain()
{
    Microsoft::Office::Interop::Word::Application* ap =
            new Microsoft::Office::Interop::Word::ApplicationClass();
    Object* missing = System::Reflection::Missing::Value;

    //to get suggestions, there must be a document
    if (ap->Documents->Count == 0)
        ap->Documents->Add(&missing,&missing,&missing,&missing);

    Console::WriteLine("Enter a sentence and press enter:");
    String* testSentence;
    testSentence = Console::ReadLine();

    String* delims = S"\t,() ";
    Char delimiter[] = delims->ToCharArray();
    String* words[] = 0;
    words = testSentence->Split(delimiter);
    System::Collections::IEnumerator* nextword = words->GetEnumerator();
    while (nextword->MoveNext())
    {
        String* s = __try_cast<String*>(nextword->Current);

        bool spellingOK = ap->CheckSpelling(s,&missing,&missing,&missing,
                                            &missing,&missing,&missing,
                                            &missing,&missing,&missing,
                                            &missing,&missing,&missing);
```

LISTING 9.2   Continued

```
   if (!spellingOK)
   {
      Console::WriteLine("{0} is not recognized by Word. Word suggests:",s);
      Microsoft::Office::Interop::Word::SpellingSuggestions* sugg  =
          ap->GetSpellingSuggestions(s,&missing,&missing,&missing,&missing,
                                     &missing,&missing,&missing,&missing,
                                     &missing,&missing,&missing,&missing,
                                     &missing);
      int suggcount = sugg->Count;
      for (int i = 1; i <= suggcount; i++)
      {
         Microsoft::Office::Interop::Word::SpellingSuggestion* suggestedword
                   = sugg->get_Item(i);
         if (suggestedword)
         {
            Console::WriteLine(suggestedword->Name);
         }
      }
      if (suggcount == 0)
         Console::WriteLine("No suggestions.");
   }
}
Object* donotsave = __box(
    Microsoft::Office::Interop::Word::WdSaveOptions::wdDoNotSaveChanges);
ap->get_ActiveWindow()->Close(&donotsave,&missing);

return 0;}
```

The concepts involved in accessing Word are clearly parallel in the managed and unmanaged code; the interface names, method names, and meanings of the parameters are the same. The effort you put into learning your way around a COM interface is immediately applicable to the RCW (or better still, PIA) version of that interface. The skill of learning your way around an unmanaged COM interface using the OLE/COM object viewer is parallel to the skill of learning your way around a managed .NET interface using the Object Browser.

In Brief

- Automation servers are applications (typically large ones such as Word or Visual Studio) that expose some or all of their functionality to applications through interfaces.

- In unmanaged code, use the `#import` directive to simplify access to the COM interfaces exposed by the Automation server.

- The OLE/COM object viewer can be used to find interfaces, methods, parameter lists, and coclasses in a COM type library, object library, or DLL.

- In managed code, add a reference on the COM tab and Visual Studio will automatically use the Primary Interop Assembly, if it is in the GAC.

- The Object Browser can be used to find interfaces, methods, parameter lists, and associated COM classes in an interop assembly.

- The similarities between the managed and unmanaged approaches to using COM automation servers are more numerous than the differences.

Writing and Consuming a Web Service

Web Service Fundamentals

Web Services (sometimes called XML Web Services) are the heart of Microsoft .NET. They represent the ultimate in distributed components—components that you access over the Web, although they might be located anywhere in the world. A Web Service does not have a user interface—it is code for other applications to call. Think of it as similar to a COM component that offers services to other components. One service might have a number of methods that all relate in some way. For example, a doctor's office might offer a Web Service that does the following:

■ Indicates whether a given block of time is available or fully booked

■ Indicates whether a specific doctor is scheduled to be in the office on a specific day

■ Provides the next available block of time, given the requested length of the block

Another Web Service from the same office might, after verifying a user's identity, allow an application to do the following:

■ Book an appointment for the user

■ Confirm an appointment for the user

■ Cancel or reschedule an appointment for the user

Whatever visual aspects you might imagine around these queries and requests come from the application that consumes the Web Service—the Web Service itself does not provide, for example, a clickable calendar. An application designed for a large screen and a high-bandwith connection will have a very different user interface from one designed for a cell phone; both rely on the Web Service for access to the booking system at the doctor's office, but they display that information very differently.

When choosing the methods that you will offer, it's best to avoid a "chatty" model, where the application requests information one piece at a time. Connections over the Internet are likely to be a bottleneck, and because each request and response carries a certain amount of overhead, you'd like as much real information in there as possible. So, for example, if your Web Service offers information about training classes, don't use a method that returns the title, another that returns the price, and a third that returns the length of the course; instead return all this information at once and have the requesting application present it to the user. This is sometimes called a "chunky" interface because it returns large chunks of information at once.

The sample Web Service in this chapter offers two functions: one takes built-in types and the other uses managed types supported by the .NET Framework. Later in the chapter, you'll see the XML that represents this data. The two functions are as follows:

- `Factor(int i, double d)` returns `true` if d multiplied by an integer equals i. For example 1.5 times 2 is 3, so `Factor(3,1.5)` returns `true`. `Factor(4,1.5)` returns `false`.

- `Week(int i)` returns a `DateTime` structure representing the date of Monday of the specified week (1-based) of this year. For example, in 2004, `Week(1)` returns January 5th, 2004.

In reality, these are not great ideas for Web Services. They would work fine as methods of a class you developed along with the rest of your code. Real Web Services access something that the developer doesn't have access to on any other machine: typically that's information, such as the information about which timeslots in the doctor's office are booked. Sometimes Web Services offer access to proprietary code, but usually it's information. These samples have been designed so that you can run them on a single computer, which means that reading a file or otherwise accessing information on the server where the Web Service is running is exactly the same as accessing that information on the client machine. For that reason, the samples just perform simple calculations. What is important here is the techniques for writing the Web Service, an understanding of the way information is passed and returned in a Web Service call, and the techniques for consuming (using) a Web Service.

Writing a Web Service in Managed C++

Not surprisingly, Visual Studio .NET has a wizard to help you create a Web Service. Before you get started, make sure you have IIS running on your development machine. Your Web Service is going to need a Web server to run on. Choose File, New, Project to get started. Choose .NET Projects and then, on the left, select ASP.NET Web Service. Name the project Utilities.

Because a Web Service is implemented on ASP.NET, Visual Studio opens the file in design view. However, because a Web Service doesn't have a user interface, design view isn't very useful. Click the link labeled "click here to switch to code view" and examine the code that was generated for you. Unlike some of the other projects produced by code generators, the Web Service code is split between a header file and an implementation file. With the comments removed for space reasons, the header file looks like this:

```
#pragma once

using namespace System;
using namespace System::Web;
using namespace System::Web::Services;

namespace Utilities
{
    public __gc
        class UtilitiesClass : public System::Web::Services::WebService
    {

    public:
        UtilitiesClass()
        {
            InitializeComponent();
        }
    protected:
        void Dispose(Boolean disposing)
        {
            if (disposing && components)
            {
                components->Dispose();
            }
            __super: :Dispose(disposing);
        }

    private:
        System::ComponentModel::Container * components;
```

```
    void InitializeComponent()
    {
    }

  public:
      [System::Web::Services::WebMethod]
      String __gc* HelloWorld();
   };
}
```

This header declares a class called UtilitiesClass with a constructor, a Dispose() method, and an InitializeComponent() method. These "boilerplate" methods rarely need editing by you. In addition, the class has a public method with a WebMethod attribute, and this method has been implemented in UtilitiesClass.cpp. That file, again with comments removed for space, looks like this:

```
#include "stdafx.h"
#include "UtilitiesClass.h"
#include "Global.asax.h"

namespace Utilities
{
    String __gc* UtilitiesClass::HelloWorld()
    {
      return S"Hello World!";
    }
};
```

The HelloWorld() method is included only as an example. Remove it from both the header and the implementation files. In the header file, add these lines where the declaration of HelloWorld() was:

```
[System::Web::Services::WebMethod]
bool Factor(int i, double d);
[System::Web::Services::WebMethod]
bool Weekend(DateTime d);
```

Each of these methods is decorated with the WebMethod attribute, which is what makes it a Web method. In the implementation file, add these lines where the implementation of HelloWorld() was:

```
bool UtilitiesClass::Factor(int i, double d)
{
    int j = (int)( i / d);
```

```
    return (j*d == i);
}
bool UtilitiesClass::Weekend(DateTime d)
{
    int dow = d.DayOfWeek;
    return (dow == DayOfWeek::Saturday
        || dow == DayOfWeek::Sunday);
}
```

These functions are simple. Factor() divides the double into the integer, and then multiplies the result by the double again. If the result of that is the same as the original integer, the double is a factor. If not, it isn't. The last line of factor can be written more verbosely as

```
if (j*d == i)
    return true;
else
    return false;
```

Condensing this to a single line has no impact on the performance of the application, but makes it simpler to read for experienced C++ programmers. Weekend() uses the DayOfWeek property of the DateTime structure, and compares it to two constants that are defined in the Base Class Library. It returns true if the day of the week is Saturday or Sunday, and false otherwise.

Build the solution and watch your output as the build progresses: You will see messages from the compiler and the linker, but then that familiar output is followed by something like this:

```
Deploying the web files...
Copied file from e:\Utilities\Utilities.asmx to
➥c:\inetpub\wwwroot\Utilities\Utilities.asmx
Copied file from e:\Utilities\Global.asax to
➥c:\inetpub\wwwroot\Utilities\Global.asax
Copied file from e:\Utilities\Web.config to
➥c:\inetpub\wwwroot\Utilities\Web.config
Copied file from e:\Utilities\Debug\Utilities.dll to
➥c:\inetpub\wwwroot\Utilities\bin\Utilities.dll
Copied file from E:\Utilities\Debug\Utilities.pdb to
➥c:\inetpub\wwwroot\Utilities\bin\Utilities.pdb
```

All of the files that are necessary to test and deploy your XML Web Service are copied to a folder where IIS can serve them over the Internet. As you can see, there's a tremendous amount of work being done for you. Not all of it is needed for such a simple service, but when you go to write a real service, you'll be pleased to have such simple deployment.

After the service is built, it should be tested. The deployment process created a folder on the default Web site of the target machine called Utilities, and added a file called Utilities.asmx to that folder. Open a Web browser and type in the URL to the .asmx file (on most machines `http://localhost/Utilities/Utilities.asmx` will work—if you use a proxy server or if localhost doesn't seem to work for you, use your machine name or IP address instead). You should see a machine-generated description of your service, like the one shown in Figure 10.1. Alternatively, you can just run the project: Running a Web Services project runs a browser and loads the .asmx file into it.

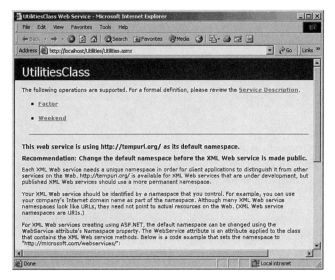

FIGURE 10.1 The .asmx file serves the information about the Web Service.

The .asmx file was generated for you when the project was created. It contains only a single line:

```
<%@ WebService Class=Utilities.UtilitiesClass %>
```

This directs ASP.NET to load the class called `UtilitiesClass` in the `Utilities` namespace. The methods in that class are the Web methods offered by your Web Service.

Just as your class is in a C++ namespace, supported by the .NET Framework, so your Web Service can be in a namespace. That way if there are several Utilities Web Services, they can be distinguished. By default, your Web Service is in a namespace called tempuri.org, and when you load it, the browser reminds you that this should be changed to a real namespace before the application is deployed. To do so, add an attribute to the class declaration in UtilitiesClass.h, so that the class definition starts like this:

```
[System::Web::Services::WebServiceAttribute(
    Namespace="http://gregcons.com/vcdotnetkickstart")]
public __gc
    class UtilitiesClass : public System::Web::Services::WebService
{
```

Namespaces for Web Services are generally based on domain names, because they are globally unique. There is no requirement that any particular server exist at the domain name you enter, or that the path following the domain name correspond to an actual path on the server. It's simply a way to construct a string that won't conflict with a string chosen by another developer. If you are building this application yourself, change my domain name (gregcons.com) to your own domain.

After adding the attribute, build and run the application again. The warning message about the Web Services namespace will be gone.

The Web page lists the Web methods offered by the Web Service: Factor() and Weekend(). The name of each is a link. Click the link for Factor and you'll see more details about it, and have an opportunity to call the service straight from the Web browser. Enter test values for i and d and click Invoke. A new browser window appears with the result, expressed in XML, of the Web method. For example, if you enter 3 for i and 1.5 for d, you see XML like this:

```
<?xml version="1.0" encoding="utf-8" ?>
<boolean xmlns="http://gregcons.com/vcdotnetkickstart">true</boolean>
```

The answer, true, is wrapped in a boolean element. The results from a Web Service call are always wrapped in XML for you. When you use a Web Service from an Visual C++ application, you don't need to write code to parse the XML and get the results; it's done for you. But this same Web Service can be used by applications written in any development tool or environment, in any programming language, on any operating system. All that's required is the capability to make an HTTP request of a specific URL, passing the parameters in the GET or POST, optionally wrapped in SOAP XML, and then to parse the XML that's returned from the Web Service. This is what makes Web Services a technology that changes the way software is built. They can be written in almost any language, and used from any language, without requiring any interaction between the environments beyond the most simple and generally available—to make an HTTP request, to build XML, and to parse XML to get the information it contains.

Consuming a Web Service in Managed C++

Writing the code to make the HTTP request, packaging up the parameters, and parsing the XML would not be hard. But when you write an application in Visual C++, consuming a Web Service is actually even simpler.

The concept of adding references in managed C++ is extended to include adding a Web reference. This is a reference to a Web Service. When you add it, a proxy class is generated that has one method for each Web method in the Web Service. Your code calls methods of this proxy class, and the calls are handled by the proxy class, which packages the parameters, makes the HTTP request, and parses the result XML for you.

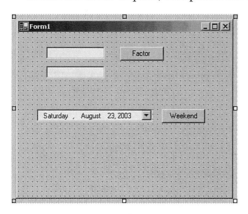

FIGURE 10.2   The client user interface tests both Web Services.

Follow these steps to create a Visual C++ application that uses the Web Service created earlier in this chapter. First, create a Windows Forms Application called UseUtilities. Drag two text boxes and a button onto the form, grouped together in the top half. Change the name of the first text box to intText and remove the default text. Change the name of the second text box to doubleText and remove the default text. Change both the name and the text of the button to Factor. Drag a date time picker and a button onto the bottom half of the form. Leave the name of the date time picker as dateTimePicker1. Change the name and the text of the button to Weekend. The final interface should resemble Figure 10.2.

Double-click the Factor button to edit the handler code. This handler will call the Web Service, and to do so requires a reference to the Web Service proxy. Right-click the References node in Solution Explorer, and choose Add Web Reference. In the Add Web Reference dialog box, fill in the text box labeled URL with the URL to the .asmx file of the Web Service created earlier in this chapter:

```
http://localhost/Utilities/Utilities.asmx
```

Click the Go button and the Web Reference dialog box shows the same list of services the browser displays when you load this URL yourself. Change the Web Reference Name from localhost to Utilities and click Add Reference. Visual Studio will generate code for you, and you will see another node in Solution Explorer labeled Utilities, along with an entry, Utilities.h, under Generated Files.

Calling the Web Service consists of creating an instance of the proxy class, and then calling a method. Add these lines to the click handler for the Factor button:

```
private: System::Void Factor_Click(System::Object *  sender,
                                   System::EventArgs *  e)
{
    Utilities::UtilitiesClass* ws = new Utilities::UtilitiesClass();
    int i = intText->Text->ToInt32(NULL);
    double d = doubleText->Text->ToDouble(NULL);
```

```
    if (ws->Factor(i,d))
        MessageBox::Show(S"The double is a factor");
    else
        MessageBox::Show(S"The double is not a factor");
}
```

The first line of code creates the proxy object. Then the numbers are extracted from the text boxes. The `ToInt32()` and `ToDouble()` methods both take a pointer to an `IFormatProvider`, because numerical formats can vary. For example, the number written as 1.234 in North America is written as 1,234 in Europe. A format provider assists the conversion process by holding format rules such as the currency symbol, the punctuation symbol that indicates the decimal point, and so on. Passing `NULL` to these functions instructs them to use the format provider set up on the machine where the code is running.

Build and run this code, and enter some combinations of integer and double that should return `true` (for example, 2.5 is a factor of 5) and others that should return `false` (for example, 3.1 is not a factor of 5). Ensure you get the expected behavior.

Working with a `DateTime` object is no harder than working with integer and double variables. Switch back to a design view of Form1.h and double-click the Weekend button. Enter this code:

```
private: System::Void Weekend_Click(System::Object *  sender,
                                    System::EventArgs *  e)
{
    Utilities::UtilitiesClass* ws = new Utilities::UtilitiesClass();
    DateTime dt = dateTimePicker1->Value;
    if (ws->Weekend(dt))
        MessageBox::Show("It's the weekend!");
    else
        MessageBox::Show("Not the weekend yet.");
}
```

This code creates an instance of the proxy object, and passes the value from the date time picker to the `Weekend()` method.

Describing Web Services with WSDL

If you type the click handler code yourself, you'll notice the IntelliSense helping you to choose the Web methods of the Utilities Web Service and reminding you of the parameters the methods take. This information comes from the WSDL (Web Services Description Language, pronounced wiz-dull) that describes the Web Service itself. To see the WSDL for this chapter's sample Web Service, bring up a browser and point it to the Web Service .asmx file again, and then click the Service Description link. You'll see XML describing the Web

Service in a machine-readable way that is, with a little effort, also human-readable. For example, try to read this excerpt:

```
<s:element name="Factor">
<s:complexType>
<s:sequence>
  <s:element minOccurs="1" maxOccurs="1" name="i" type="s:int" />
  <s:element minOccurs="1" maxOccurs="1" name="d" type="s:double" />
  </s:sequence>
  </s:complexType>
  </s:element>
<s:element name="FactorResponse">
<s:complexType>
<s:sequence>
  <s:element minOccurs="1" maxOccurs="1" name="FactorResult"
        type="s:boolean" />
  </s:sequence>
  </s:complexType>
  </s:element>
```

The first element describes the parameters for a call to Factor. There is to be exactly one element (minOccurs is 1 and maxOccurs is 1) called i, of type int. There is to be exactly one element called d, of type double.

The second element, FactorResponse, describes the return value from the Web method. It is of type boolean.

The WSDL for the Utilities method goes on to describe the Weekend element and then goes through the SOAP required to make the same calls. It's all there, suitable for use by any development tool (or hardworking developer) to ensure that the parameters passed to and returned from the Web methods are the expected types.

There's no need to create XML, parse XML, understand SOAP, or even know what WSDL is to use a Web Service. It's all handled for you behind the scenes.

Discovering Web Services

Adding a Web reference when you know the URL of the .asmx file is simple enough. But if you didn't write the Web Service, how do you know the URL? That's where discovery comes in.

When you add a Web reference by typing a URL and clicking Go, the large area in the middle of the Add Web Reference dialog box displays information about the Web Service located at that URL. But before you enter a URL, that area contains useful links to help you find a Web Service:

- Web Services on the local machine

- Browse UDDI Servers on the local network

- UDDI Directory

- Test Microsoft UDDI Directory

The first link works with IIS to find Web Services on your own computer. Auxiliary files called *discovery documents,* with the extension .disco, assist in this process. The other links rely on UDDI, Universal Description Discovery and Integration, to find Web servers that offer Web Services. UDDI is a cross-vendor initiative to publish information about Web Services in a way that can be used from a variety of development environments and operating systems. There are public UDDI servers on the Internet, which hold information about Web Services offered to anyone. You can also set up an enterprise UDDI server, available only to computers on your own network, that holds information about your internal Web Services. There are also test directories for you to experiment with.

Try adding another Web reference to the UseUtilities project. Right-click the References node in Solution Explorer, and choose Add Web Reference. Click the link to Web Services On The Local Machine. You should see all the Web Services you have created—even those created in languages other than Visual C++. Click the Back button, and then click UDDI directory. Enter a keyword under Service Name and see what's out there. For example, Figure 10.3 shows some of the services registered with UDDI with the word *weather* in the service name.

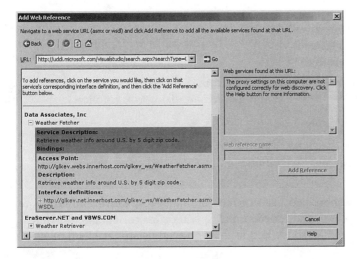

FIGURE 10.3   UDDI helps to find publicly available Web Services.

You can try adding references to these services, reading the WSDL that describes them, or just letting Intellisense show you what objects, methods, and parameters are available to you. Experiment a little—and think of how much work you can save leveraging an existing Web Service instead of writing your own from scratch.

Writing a Web Service in Unmanaged C++

Can you write a Web Service in unmanaged C++? Yes, you can. A tool called ATL server supports very high-performance Web Services. It shouldn't be your first choice for ordinary Web Services, because it's a little harder to work with than the techniques shown earlier in this chapter. For example, strings are handled as BSTR types, and memory is not managed for you.

Implementing the Factor() Web method of the Utilities Web Service in ATL Server can serve two purposes in this chapter: demonstrating how to use ATL Server to write a Web Service, and demonstrating how a Web Service client (UseUtilities) can switch Web references and still access the Web Service in the same way, although the implementation might change dramatically.

In Visual Studio .NET 2003, create a new project. Choose ATL Server Web Service for the project type, and name it ATLUtilities. Click Finish to create the solution with all the default options. Two projects are created: ATLUtilities and ATLUtilitiesIsapi. The ATLUtilities project defines the ATLUtilitiesService namespace, and within that, a class, CATLUtilitiesService, and an interface, IATLUtilitiesService. The interface defines the Web methods and the class implements them. A HelloWorld() method has already been created for you.

In ATLUtilities.h, find the interface definition, which starts with __interface. Further down the file, find the code for the class. You can see the way that methods are implemented, and the use of attributes to reduce the coding required.

To add the Factor method to the project, right-click IATLUtilitiesService in Class View, and choose Add, Add Method. Fill out the Add Method Wizard dialog box as follows:

1. Enter **Factor** for the method name.

2. Enter the first parameter: choose SHORT from the drop-down box for Parameter Type, select the In check box for Parameter Attributes, enter **i** for the Parameter name, and click Add.

3. Enter the second parameter: choose DOUBLE from the drop-down box for Parameter Type, select the In check box for Parameter Attributes, enter **d** for the Parameter name, and click Add.

4. Enter the return value: choose VARIANT_BOOL* from the drop-down box for Parameter Type, select the Retval check box for Parameter Attributes, enter **result** for the Parameter name, and click Add.

5. Click Finish.

Visual Studio will add the method to the interface and class, and open the implementation file, ATLUtilities.cpp, for you to fill in the skeleton method that was generated for you. Add this code:

```
int j = (int)( i / d);
*result = (j*d == i);
return S_OK;
```

Add the [soap_method] attribute to ATLUtilities.h, before the declaration of Factor() in the ATLUtilitiesService class. This ensures that Factor() is exposed as a Web method.

Now, change UseUtilities so that it uses ATLUtilities for the Factor method. In the UseUtilities project, add a Web reference. Click the link to browse Web Services on your machine. You'll see a new category now, Discovery Documents, with ATLUtilities listed there. ATL Server doesn't generate an .asmx file, but it makes a discovery file that can be used to add the reference. Click ATLUtilities to select it, and click View Service to see the methods that are offered. You should see Factor() listed along with HelloWorld().

Change the name of the reference from the machine name to ATLUtilities, and click Add Reference. In the click handler for the Factor button, find this line:

```
Utilities::UtilitiesClass* ws = new Utilities::UtilitiesClass();
```

Change it to this:

```
ATLUtilities::ATLUtilitiesService* ws =
    new ATLUtilities::ATLUtilitiesService();
```

Make no other changes to the application. Build it and run it, and it will work just as before—even though it is now using a version of the Factor Web method that was built with a completely different tool. The client application is insulated from details like the implementation of the Web Service.

Because client applications aren't affected by your choice of development tool, you're free to choose the tool that's best for you. Comparing the managed C++ and ATL Server version of Factor(), the ATL Server version is clearly more difficult to write and maintain. It works with COM types such as BSTR and VARIANT_BOOL, and returns an HRESULT instead of using exceptions. You should be comfortable writing COM applications in unmanaged C++ using other ATL tools in order to work in ATL Server. The bottom line is that you should use ATL Server only when you have already implemented your Web Service in managed C++ and found that it doesn't meet your required performance levels. You can then re-implement it in unmanaged C++ for maximum speed, and know that your clients need only change the Web reference, and not any of the other code in the client.

Calling a Web Service from Unmanaged C++

If you need to write a new application that uses a Web Service, you will probably write it in managed C++. But what if you have an existing unmanaged C++ application, and you want to enhance it to use a Web Service?

Create a Win32 console application called UnManUseUtilities. Add a Web reference to the Utilities project using the same URL to the .asmx file as before, http://localhost/Utilities/Utilities.asmx.

Edit UnManUseUtilities.cpp so that it reads as follows:

```
// UnManUseUtilities.cpp : Defines the entry point for the console application.
//

#include "stdafx.h"

#include <iostream>
using namespace std;

int _tmain(int argc, _TCHAR* argv[])
{
    ::CoInitialize(NULL);
    { //brace brackets for scope only
    UtilitiesClass::CUtilitiesClass ws;
    int i = 3;
    double d = 1.5;
    bool result;
    ws.Factor(i,d,&result);
    if (result)
        cout << "1.5 is a factor of 3" << endl;
    else
        cout << "1.5 is not a factor of 3" << endl;
    i = 4;
    d = 1.7;
    ws.Factor(i,d,&result);
    if (result)
        cout << "1.7 is a factor of 4" << endl;
```

```
    else
        cout << "1.7 is not a factor of 4" << endl;
    } // forces destruction of ws
    ::CoUninitialize();
    return 0;
}
```

This code starts and ends with a call to `CoInitialize()` and `CoUninitialize()`, because access to Web Services from unmanaged C++ is offered through COM. The proxy object that is created by this code must be cleaned up before `CoUninitialize()` is called, so there is a set of brace brackets here just to establish that scope and trigger the destruction of the proxy object.

Inside the brackets, this code creates the proxy object and calls its `Factor()` method. Notice that even though this is the very same managed Web method that was called from managed code earlier in this chapter, the signature of this unmanaged proxy is different from the signature of the managed proxy—it takes three parameters, and the third is passed by address so the function can change it. This code is not as simple to write or maintain as the managed code equivalent, so unmanaged code should probably not be your first choice, but it's by no means impossibly hard for you to use a Web Service from unmanaged code.

In Brief

- Writing a Web Service from managed C++ is supported by a project type in Visual Studio. This generates all the supporting files to describe and discover your Web Service.

- Consuming a Web Service from managed C++ requires only that you add a Web reference to the service, which can be written in any programming language and can run on any operating system.

- Writing a Web Service in unmanaged C++ is more difficult than writing one in managed C++ but offers very high performance for those services that need it.

- Using a Web Service in unmanaged C++ is only slightly more complex than using one from managed C++, and is very similar to using a COM component.

Writing a Data Layer in Managed C++

Database Concepts

Simply put, a database is a collection of information, typically organized as a collection of records. Each record is composed of fields, and each field contains information related to that specific record. For example, suppose you have an address database. In this database, you have one record for each person. Each record contains six fields: the person's name, street address, city, state, ZIP code, and phone number. A single record in your database might look like this:

```
NAME: Jane Customer
STREET: 16 Maple Dr.
CITY: Indianapolis
STATE: IN
ZIP: 46290
PHONE: 800-555-1212
```

Your database will contain many records like this one, with each record containing information about a different person. To find a person's address or phone number, you search for the name. When you find the name, you also find all the information that's included in the record with the name.

This example uses a flat database. For home use or for small businesses, the simple flat database model can be a powerful tool. However, for large databases that must track dozens, or even hundreds, of fields of data, a flat database can lead to repetition and wasted space. Suppose you run a large department store and want to track some information about your employees, including their name, department, manager's name, and so on. If you have 10 people in Sporting Goods, the name of the Sporting Goods manager is repeated in each of those 10 records. When Sporting Goods hires a new manager, all 10 records have to be updated. It would be much simpler if each employee record could be related to another database of departments and manager names.

A relational database is like several flat databases linked together. Using a relational database, you can not only search for individual records, as you can with a flat database, but also relate one set of records to another. This enables you to store data much more efficiently. Each set of records in a relational database is called a *table*. The links are accomplished through *keys*, which are values that define a record. (For example, the employee ID might be the key to an employee table.)

The sample relational database that you use in this chapter was created using Microsoft Access. The database is a simple system for tracking employees, managers, and the departments for which they work. The Employees table (see sample data in Table 11.1) contains information about each store employee; the DeptManagers table (see sample data in Table 11.2) contains information about each store department's manager; and the Departments table (see sample data in Table 11.3) contains information about the departments themselves. (This database is very simple and probably not usable in the real world.) The database is included with the sample application for this chapter; copy the file somewhere onto your own computer.

TABLE 11.1

Employees Table

EMPLOYEEID	EMPLOYEENAME	EMPLOYEERATE	DEPTID
236	Anderson, Maggie	8.95	COSMETICS
247	Anderson, Richard	6.53	MENSCLOTHING
242	Calbert, Susan	9.03	ENTERTAINMENT
250	Greene, Nancy	6.55	SPORTING
243	Hanley, Frank	7.25	HARDWARE

TABLE 11.2

DeptManagers Table

DEPTID	MANAGERID
COSMETICS	236
ELECTRONICS	239
ENTERTAINMENT	242

TABLE 11.3

Departments Table

DEPTID	DEPTNAME	LOCATION
COSMETICS	Cosmetics	3rd Floor
ELECTRONICS	Electronics	4th Floor
MENSCLOTHING	Men's Clothing	1st Floor

Typically a database is used to answer business questions such as

- How many employees do we have?

- What is the highest and lowest pay rate in our firm?

- What is Richard Anderson's work location?

- Do any employees earn more than their own manager?

Some of these questions can be answered by looking in a single table: The Employees table contains all the employees and their pay rates. Others require combining tables. Finding where Richard Anderson works involves finding his department ID, MENSCLOTHING, and then finding that department's location, 1st Floor. To answer the pay rate question, you would loop through each employee, noting their department ID, using the DeptManagers table to find the department manager's employee ID, from there going back to the Employees table to determine the manager's pay rate, and comparing it to the pay rate of the employee.

The questions answered by this chapter's samples are simple, but you can easily adapt these same techniques to more complicated manipulations of more complicated databases.

The ADO.NET Class Library

ADO.NET is far more than just a managed version of ADO. It represents a different and more scalable way of approaching database access, ideal for use in a data layer that might be supporting hundreds or thousands of users, and yet a way that also works well for a single user application.

ADO.NET hinges around two classes: the DataSet and the DataReader. If you're familiar with XML programming, you can think of these as equivalent to DOM and SAX. The DataSet, like DOM, gathers all the information together into an easily accessible structure and then closes the data source. You can work with the data, shuffle it around, add and remove entries, get some information from the beginning, jump ahead to the end, jump back to the middle, and even put data back to the source when you're finished with it. The DataReader, like SAX, is used to process information as you read it from the source. It's often referred to as one-way-one-way access; you can only go through the data by starting at the beginning and reading to the end (one way) and you can only read information from the source, you can't put updates back into the source (one way).

A `DataSet` contains a collection of `DataTable` objects, which can be related to each other through `DataRelation` objects. Each `DataTable` contains a collection of `DataRow` objects, and at the same time a collection of `DataColumn` objects. What a `DataSet` does not contain is any information about where the data came from. `DataSets` don't fill themselves; instead they are filled by a companion object called a `DataAdapter`. A `DataAdapter` holds four commands: one for reading from the database, one for inserting records, one for deleting records, and one for updating information. Generally the latter three commands are not used (if you're not updating the information back to the data source) or are machine-generated from your `Select` command, the one that reads from the database.

A `DataSet` can be bound to a variety of controls in a user interface, such as a data grid. You can easily persist it as XML, and it's perfect for passing from layer to layer, even from machine to machine. Although it's by no means a small or light-weight class, it is full of functionality that is needed in almost every data-enabled application.

Filling a `DataSet` and Binding to a Control on a Form

Single-tier data access applications are popular sample and starter applications, but they don't fill many niches in software development. This especially applies to examples in which all the database interaction code is right in the event handler for the button click. It's just too hard to maintain that kind of application. In this section, the solution has two projects: one with the user interface and one with the database code. You could build the database code into a separate class library project in its own solution, using the techniques of Chapter 6, "Writing a Class Library in Managed C++," and even share the database code among several applications.

You could move all this database code into a Web Service (as in Chapter 10, "Writing and Consuming a Web Service"), and then change the user interface code to use the Web Service. This design would then become a distributed application built on Web Services. Alternatively, you could use .NET Remoting (as in Chapter 14, "Moving Layers to Different Machines with .NET Remoting") to move the database project onto another computer, creating a distributed application built on .NET Remoting. The more modular your application is, the simpler the job of pulling part of it onto another machine becomes.

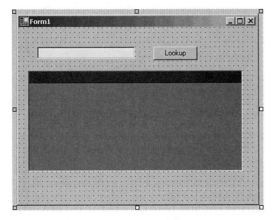

FIGURE 11.1 Creating a simple user interface.

Creating the User Interface

Create a Windows Forms application called EmployeeUI. Drag on a text box, and then change the Text property to an empty string and the name to employeeName. Drag a button next to it, and then change the text and the name to Lookup. Drag a data grid underneath them and resize it to take up most of the dialog box. The form should resemble Figure 11.1.

Creating the Data Layer Project

Before you write the Click handler for the Lookup button, you must write the data layer class that will provide the database access. In Solution Explorer, right-click the entire solution and choose Add, New Project. Select a Class Library (.NET) and name it EmployeeData. Right-click EmployeeData in Solution Explorer, and choose Add, Add Class. Choose a Generic C++ class.

Name the class Employee and click Finish on the Generic Class Wizard. In Employee.h, add a namespace declaration (you can copy it from EmployeeData.h), and change the class definition to make it a public, garbage-collected class:

```
namespace EmployeeData
{
    public __gc class Employee
    {
    public:
        Employee(void);
        ~Employee(void);
    };
}
```

This class needs a Lookup() method that takes a string, represents an employee name, and looks that name up in the database, returning a data set holding all the records in the database that matched the name. Add the declaration to the class definition:

```
DataSet* Lookup(String* name);
```

Add these using statements to the top of the file, after the pragma:

```
using namespace System;
using namespace System::Data;
```

Add this stub for the Lookup function to Employee.cpp:

```
DataSet* Employee::Lookup(String* name)
{
    DataSet* ds = new DataSet("Employees");
    return ds;
}
```

Add a reference to System.Xml.dll (on the .NET tab of the Add Reference dialog box) so that this code will compile (the DataSet class defines some interfaces that are defined in the System.Xml assembly), and then enter this code. At the top of Employee.cpp, add a using statement:

```
using namespace EmployeeData;
```

Finally, remove the EmployeeData.cpp and EmployeeData.h files: They aren't needed in this solution. Right-click each of them in Solution Explorer and choose Remove. Build the solution to make sure there are no typing errors.

Handling the Connection String

The Lookup()method will use a DataAdapter to fill ds before returning it. To create a DataAdapter, you need a connection to the database. To create a connection, you need a connection string. It's a bad idea to hard-code connection strings in many different functions throughout an application. There are two reasons for this:

- If the database name, location, or authentication technique ever changes, you will have to find and change the connection string in many places within your code.

- The built-in connection pooling in ADO.NET works only if all the connection objects that are created use identical connection strings. If the strings vary a little, even in the order of the parameters inside them, the connections won't be pooled and your application will run more slowly.

It's appealing, then, to have a variable that holds the connection string, and to set that once, perhaps in the constructor, and use it throughout this data layer component. Expand the class definition in Employee.h, adding these lines after the declaration of Lookup:

```
private:
    String* ConnStr;
```

Add this line to the body of the `Employee` constructor:

```
ConnStr = "Provider=Microsoft.Jet.OLEDB.4.0;Data
➥Source=E:\\Working\\Kick Start\\deptstore.mdb";
```

Make sure you change the path to match the location where you copied the Access file earlier. Now you can use this connection string throughout the data layer.

Using a Configuration File

If you want the connection string to be a property of the data layer, keeping it in a member variable that is set in the constructor makes a lot of sense. But what if you ever need to change it? Using a hard-coded string like this would require you to edit the source code and recompile the application, not to mention redistributing the application and redeploying it, whenever the connection string changes. A better approach than hard-coding is to use a configuration file.

Configuration files for ASP.NET applications have received plenty of publicity, but it's a lesser-known feature of regular Windows applications. A configuration file is a collection of XML that can be edited by a user, and read by the application to determine settings such as connection strings. Unfortunately, you can't add a configuration file to your class library, but it can read the application's configuration file.

To add a configuration file to the application, right-click the `EmployeeUI` project in Solution Explorer and choose Add, Add New Item. Select Configuration File (app.config) and click Open. Edit the file so that it reads like this:

```
<configuration>
  <appSettings>
    <add key="connstr" value="Provider=Microsoft.Jet.OLEDB.4.0;
➥Data Source=E:\Working\Kick Start\deptstore.mdb" />
  </appSettings>
</configuration>
```

The idea behind a configuration file is that whenever you build the solution, this file will be copied to EmployeeUI.exe.config in the same folder as EmployeeUI.exe. This configuration file controls the behavior of the application at runtime, and changes to this file take effect without your having to rebuild the solution. For a C++ project, you have to arrange this copy step yourself. Here's how:

1. Bring up the properties page for the `EmployeeUI` project.

2. Expand the Build Events folder and select Post-Build Event.

3. Choose All Configurations from the Configurations drop-down box at the top of the dialog box.

4. Click next to Command Line and a ... symbol appears. Click that symbol.

5. Click the Macros button to display a list of useful shortcuts.

6. You could enter the entire post-build string as literal text, but it would need to be edited if you changed the name of the application, or even switched between Debug and Release builds. You are aiming for the string `copy app.config Debug\EmployeeUI.exe.config` or `copy app.config Release\EmployeeUI.exe.config` but it should be built from placeholders.

7. Type the words **copy app.config** into the empty white box in the Command Line dialog box. Enter a space. Double-click `ConfigurationName` in the list of macros. Enter a backslash. Double-click `TargetFileName` in the list of macros. Type **.config** immediately after it in the command line.

8. Click OK in the Command Line dialog box. The command-line property should now be

```
copy app.config $(ConfigurationName)\$(TargetFileName).config
```

9. Click OK on the properties page.

The next step is to use the entry that you added to the configuration file.

Edit the constructor for `Employee` so that it uses the configuration settings. Replace the line of code that set the value of `ConnStr` with this line:

```
ConnStr =
   Configuration::ConfigurationSettings::AppSettings->get_Item("connstr");
```

The `ConfigurationSettings` class represents the contents of the configuration file, and the static `AppSettings` property of the class represents the contents of the `<appSettings>` element within the file. The `get_Item()` method takes a key and returns the corresponding value.

Writing the `Lookup()` Method

With the connection string issue settled, all that remains to complete this data layer is to write the `Lookup()` method. The steps this method will complete are as follows:

1. Create a new empty data set.

2. Build the query string.

3. Create the data adapter.

4. Use the data adapter to fill the data set.

5. Return the data set.

When you're trying to get information from a database, there's a lot than can go wrong. Your connection string might not be right, you might not have permission to access the database, your query might contain a syntax error, and so on. It's very important to surround database code in a try/catch block so that you can get as much information as possible if anything goes wrong.

Enter this code for the Lookup() method:

```
DataSet* Employee::Lookup(String* name)
{
    DataSet* ds = new DataSet("Employees");

    StringBuilder* query = new StringBuilder();
    query->Append("SELECT * FROM Employees WHERE EmployeeName Like '%");
    query->Append(name);
    query->Append("%'");

    OleDbDataAdapter* adapter = new OleDbDataAdapter(query->ToString(),
                                                     ConnStr);

    try
    {
        adapter->Fill(ds,"Employees");
    }
    catch (OleDbException* e)
    {
        Console::WriteLine("OleDbException caught while filling the dataset");
        Console::WriteLine(e->Message);
    }
    return ds;
}
```

There are several points to notice about this code:

- It uses a StringBuilder to build the SQL statement from the string that was passed in.

- The SQL statement uses the LIKE clause and surrounds the name with % characters to find strings that contain the name *string*.

- There's no need to open or close the connection; the adapter takes care of that. You just pass the connection string to the adapter constructor.

- The adapter fills the data set; data sets cannot fill themselves.

Using the Data Layer from the UI

Before the user interface code can use the data layer, you must add a reference to that data layer. Right-click the References node under EmployeeUI in Solution Explorer and choose Add Reference. Select the Projects tab and add a reference to EmployeeData.

In the design view for Form1.h, double-click the Lookup button to edit the handler. Add this code to the method:

```
private: System::Void Lookup_Click(System::Object *  sender,
                                   System::EventArgs *  e)
{
    EmployeeData::Employee* emp = new EmployeeData::Employee();
    DataSet* ds = emp->Lookup(employeeName->Text);
    dataGrid1->DataSource = ds->Tables->get_Item(0);
}
```

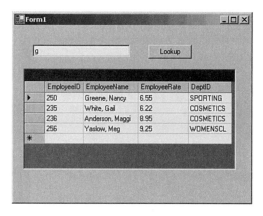

FIGURE 11.2   The application searches for employees by name.

All the database work is delegated to the data layer. Here in the user interface, the handler creates an instance of the Employee object from the data layer, calls its Lookup() method, and binds the returned data set to the data grid for display.

Build and run this application. Enter a short string of letters in the text box and click Lookup. You should see some results in the grid. Figure 11.2 shows the results of searching for names that contain the letter G in the sample database provided with this chapter.

This application demonstrates how simple it is to separate your user interface from a data layer or other class library that provides services to the user interface. It also uses a configuration file to maximize the flexibility of the deployed application.

Using a Data Reader for Quick One-Way Access

If the user isn't going to update the information you retrieve from the database, you might get better performance by using a data reader instead. A data reader is not as flexible as a data set—for example it can't be passed between machines or returned from a Web Service as a data set can—but it can substitute nicely for the data set that was used in the previous section. It can't be bound to a data grid, but not all applications benefit from a data grid anyway. In this section, a console application uses a data reader to look up employee names.

SHOP TALK

TWO DATA GRID CONTROLS

You might have heard somewhere that you can bind a data reader to a data grid. This is partially true. There are two data grids in the libraries that come with the .NET Framework: the WinForms data grid and the ASP.NET data grid. They appear very similar, but the way they work internally has a number of differences. An ASP.NET data grid will bind to a data reader, but a WinForms data grid will not.

Should you feel slighted, as a WinForms developer, that the WinForms team didn't add this feature to their data grid whereas the ASP.NET team did? Not really. The ASP.NET data grid simply creates a temporary DataTable (usually contained in a data set), reads the entire contents of the data reader into the temporary table, and then binds the data grid to the table. This eliminates any performance savings you might have achieved by using a data reader instead of a data set.

Creating the Console Application

Add another project to the solution; select a .NET Console Application and call it EmployeeConsole. This project needs a reference to the data layer; add a reference as before and again use the Projects tab of the Add Reference dialog box, and then select EmployeeData.

You will add code to the console application to use a new method of the Employee class to read from the database with a data reader.

Writing the New LookupReader() Method

Open EmployeeData.h and add another method to the Employee class:

```
IDataReader* LookupReader(String* name);
```

There is only one DataSet class no matter where your data comes from; all the specialization is in the adapters. There are adapters for SQL, for OleDB, and so on. The Lookup() method used an OleDbDataAdapter, and if you changed your data source, the changes required to your code would be confined to the Lookup() method, because it returns a DataSet with no source-specific information in it.

In contrast, there are many data reader classes: OleDbDataReader, SqlDataReader, OracleDataReader, and so on. If you were to write to LookupReader() to return an OleDbDataReader, and then later you needed to change your database implementation, your changes would ripple through to the calling code and perhaps even further. Returning a database-specific data reader is not a good idea. Instead, take advantage of the fact that all the data readers implement the IDataReader interface and declare that LookupReader() returns an IDataReader. The OleDbDataReader is an IDataReader, as are all the others, so any future changes to LookupReader() will not change the return type of the method and the changes won't affect any other code.

The code for LookupReader() is very similar to the Lookup() method, but you must create the connection and command objects yourself instead of passing strings to an adapter constructor. Add this code for the method:

```
IDataReader* Employee::LookupReader(String* name)
{
    StringBuilder* query = new StringBuilder();
    query->Append("SELECT * FROM Employees WHERE EmployeeName Like '%");
    query->Append(name);
    query->Append("%'");

    OleDbConnection* conn = new OleDbConnection(ConnStr);
    OleDbCommand* SelectCommand = new OleDbCommand(query->ToString(),conn);
    conn->Open();
    return SelectCommand->ExecuteReader(Data::CommandBehavior::CloseConnection);
}
```

Because your code opens the connection, it should close it. However, a data reader is not disconnected like a data set. You can't close it until you have read all the data, and you can't close the connection without closing the data reader. That means that this code can't close either the data reader or the connection. The data reader is returned to the calling code, which can close it, but that calling code has no access to this connection object. Passing the CloseConnection constant as the second parameter of ExecuteReader() tells the data reader "when you close, close your own connection at the same time." This ensures the connection will not be left open when the calling code is finished with the data reader. Leaving connections open when you are finished with them can have a significant impact on the performance of your application, because it sabotages the built-in connection pooling in ADO.NET.

Getting and Using the Data Reader from the Console Application

With the new method added to Employee, add code to the main() function to prompt the user for a name, pass the name to LookupData(), and then read and echo the contents of the data reader. Edit EmployeeConsole.cpp so that it reads like this:

```
// This is the main project file for VC++ application project
// generated using an Application Wizard.

#include "stdafx.h"
#using <mscorlib.dll>

using namespace System;
using namespace System::Data;
```

```
int _tmain()
{
    Console::WriteLine(S"Enter a name or part name");
    String* name = Console::ReadLine();
    EmployeeData::Employee* emp = new EmployeeData::Employee();
    IDataReader* dr = emp->LookupReader(name);
    while (dr->Read())
    {
        Console::WriteLine("{0}\t {1}\t {2}\t {3}",
            dr->get_Item(0),
            dr->get_Item(1),
            dr->get_Item(2),
            dr->get_Item(3));
    }
    dr->Close();
    return 0;
}
```

The data reader has a Read() method that returns false when there is no more to read, but otherwise points itself to the next record. You can access the fields using get_Item(), which takes a numerical index or a string—pass the field name if you use the string. When you're finished with the data reader, close it. As discussed earlier, this will also close the connection.

Configuration Files Revisited

The configuration file that was added to the Windows Forms application does not control the console application. You need to add an application file to the console application project, and a custom post-build event as before. However, the copy is a little different. Enter the property as

```
copy app.config ..\$(SolutionName)\$(ConfigurationName)\$(TargetFileName).config
```

This ensures the config file ends up in the EmployeeUI folder where it belongs.

Finally, you need to change the startup project. The EmployeeUI project is bolded in Solution Explorer to show you that when you run the solution (for example, by pressing F5), you will actually run the EmployeeUI project. Right-click EmployeeConsole in Solution Explorer and choose Set As Startup Project to arrange for F5 to run the console application. Then build and run the project. Enter a name or part of a name. Here is a sample run:

```
Enter a name or part name
g
250     Greene, Nancy   6.55    SPORTING
235     White, Gail     6.22    COSMETICS
```

```
236     Anderson, Maggie       8.95    COSMETICS
256     Yaslow, Meg     9.25   WOMENSCLOTHING
Press any key to continue
```

This console application demonstrates one of the values of a separate data layer; it can support multiple applications. This console application could easily have used the data set from Lookup() by iterating through the rows of the data set, but the data reader code is easier to write and executes more quickly. Now the data layer has two useful functions, and application developers can use whichever is best for each project.

Updating the Database with a Data Set

The two sample applications shown so far have been read-only: Each found the records matching a criteria (part of the employee name) and displayed them. Many applications offer their users the capability to update the database as well as display records. Data sets and data grids are well suited for this task.

Modifying the Data Layer

Add another function to the Employee class in the data layer called Update. This is the declaration to add to the class definition in Employee.h:

```
void Update(DataSet* newrecords);
```

The code for this new method belongs in Employee.cpp. It looks like this:

```
void Employee::Update(DataSet* newrecords)
{
    OleDbDataAdapter* adapter = new OleDbDataAdapter("SELECT * FROM Employees",
                                                      ConnStr);
    OleDbCommandBuilder* cb = new OleDbCommandBuilder(adapter);
    adapter->Update(newrecords, "Employees");
}
```

The adapter used for the update needs all four commands: select, insert, update, and delete. A data set keeps track of all the changes made to it (for example by a user working with a data grid). When the adapter saves the changes back to the database, it works with the data set to

- Insert into the database (using the insert command) all the records marked in the data set as new.

- Update all the records marked as changed.

- Delete all the records marked as deleted.

To create an adapter with all four commands, this code first creates an adapter with a `select` command, very similar to the `select` command used in the `Lookup()` method. It then creates an associated `OleDbCommandBuilder` object which will build the three other commands automatically. With the commands in place, getting all the user's changes into the database is simply a matter of calling the `Update()` method of the adapter. The second parameter, `"Employees"`, is the name of the table within the data set—this corresponds to the name given to the table when it was filled in the `Lookup()` method.

Modifying the User Interface

Add a button to `Form1`, next to the Lookup button, and change both the text and the name to `Update`. Double-click the button to add and edit the handler for the click event.

The next step is to change the `DataSet` instance, `ds`, used in the `Lookup` click handler from a temporary local variable to a member of the `Form1` class. Add these lines before the function definitions in Form1.h:

```
private:
    DataSet* ds;
```

Change the line in the `Lookup` click handler that fills the data set so it no longer declares the variable:

```
ds = emp->Lookup(employeeName->Text);
```

Enter this code for the `Update` click handler:

```
private: System::Void Update_Click(System::Object *  sender,
                                   System::EventArgs *  e)
{
EmployeeData::Employee* emp = new EmployeeData::Employee();
emp->Update(ds);
ds->Clear();
employeeName->Text = "";
}
```

This code creates an instance of the data layer object, uses it to update the data set back into the data source, and then clears the data set and the text box. The reason it's so simple is only partly because the data layer is doing the work—after all, the `Update()` method in `Employee` is pretty short, too. It's really the power of the adapter and the data set working together that makes this application so quick to put together.

Build and run the application (don't forget to make `EmployeeUI` the startup project again) and try changing someone's pay rate or name. To delete a record, click in the left margin to select the whole record and press Del. To add a record, type values in the blank row at the bottom of the data grid, and then move the cursor to another row when you're finished.

Make sure you type the right kind of data for each field (for example, a number in the Pay Rate field), because this simple application has no error checking.

When you've made some changes, click Update, and then search again, using a criteria that should find the changed records (or would find deleted ones if they weren't deleted), and make sure you see your changes. You can even close the application and open the database in Access to confirm your changes went through.

Data Sets and XML

A `DataSet` object is not only a collection of tables, each with rows and columns. You can also think of it as an XML document, and work with it as though it were XML. The `DataSet` class has methods that produce and read XML with little or no work on your part.

Getting XML from a `DataSet`

To see how quickly you can create XML from a database, add another button to `EmployeeUI`, and change the text to `Write XML` and the name to `WriteXML`. Double-click the button to edit the click handler, and add this code:

```
private: System::Void WriteXML_Click(System::Object *  sender,
                                     System::EventArgs *  e)
{
    ds->WriteXml("db.xml");
}
```

How hard is that? The data set will write itself out to a file as XML; all you need to do is provide a filename.

Build and run the application, enter a search string, click Lookup, and when the results appear, click Write XML. Browse to the project folder for `EmployeeUI` and you should see that a new file, db.xml, has appeared. Drag this file into Visual Studio to open it and see the XML. For example, entering **GR** in the text box, the XML generated looks like this:

```
<?xml version="1.0" encoding="utf-8"?>
<Employees>
  <Employees>
    <EmployeeID>250</EmployeeID>
    <EmployeeName>Greene, Nancy</EmployeeName>
    <EmployeeRate>6.55</EmployeeRate>
    <DeptID>SPORTING</DeptID>
  </Employees>
</Employees>
```

You might notice there are two <Employees> tags, one inside the other. The outer one comes from the name of the data set, which was set in Lookup(). The inner one is the name of the table. If the data set held several tables, it would write them all out inside the outer <Employees> tag.

Filling a Database from XML

The same simplicity comes into play when you use an XML file to fill a data table. To see it at work, add another button to Form1 with a name of AddXML and the text set to Add From XML. Double-click the button to edit the handler, and then add this code:

```
private: System::Void AddXML_Click(System::Object *  sender,
                                   System::EventArgs *  e)
{
    DataSet* newemployees = new DataSet("NewEmployees");
    newemployees->ReadXml("newemployees.xml");
    EmployeeData::Employee* emp = new EmployeeData::Employee();
    emp->Update(newemployees);
}
```

This code creates an empty data set, fills it from a file called newemployees.xml, and then uses the data layer to get the new records into the database.

Here is a sample XML file. Enter this XML into a file called newemployees.xml and place the file in the EmployeeUI project folder.

```
<?xml version="1.0" encoding="utf-8"?>
<EmployeeList>
  <Employees>
    <EmployeeID>301</EmployeeID>
    <EmployeeName>Smith, John</EmployeeName>
    <EmployeeRate>7.02</EmployeeRate>
    <DeptID>MENSCLOTHING</DeptID>
  </Employees>
  <Employees>
    <EmployeeID>302</EmployeeID>
    <EmployeeName>Lee, Alice</EmployeeName>
    <EmployeeRate>7.55</EmployeeRate>
    <DeptID>SPORTING</DeptID>
  </Employees>
</EmployeeList>
```

It's important that none of the `EmployeeID` values in this XML file are already in use in the database, because an exception is thrown if you try to add a record with a non-unique key. Build and run the application, click the Add From XML button, and then enter a search name of Smith. Click Lookup—you should see that John Smith has been added. Similarly, look up Alice Lee.

Working with XML and data sets is almost ridiculously easy. When you have a powerful data access layer and are using a data grid in your user interface, database applications come together remarkably quickly.

In Brief

- ADO.NET features two very different classes that, between them, handle most common database programming situations.

- The `DataSet` class represents a table or tables held in memory and is disconnected from its data source. A `DataSet` can be bound to a data grid or other controls, and can persist itself to and from XML.

- The `DataReader` class is ideal for one-way-one-way database access and is faster than a data set for simple database reads. In a WinForms application, it can't be bound to a data grid, but the contents can be written to the console or into a text box quickly.

- Configuration files are an excellent place to keep connection strings, because changing a configuration file doesn't require the application to be recompiled.

Writing a Windows Service

What Is a Windows Service?

A Windows service is an application without a user interface that runs independently of any user-started applications. Typically a service starts automatically when the computer starts—even if a user does not log on to the computer. Think of them as background processes that keep things humming smoothly.

There are two ways to see the services that are running on your own machine. The first is under Computer Management. Right-click the My Computer icon on your desktop and choose Manage, and then expand Services and Applications. Click the Services node and you'll see the services running on your machine, as in Figure 12.1.

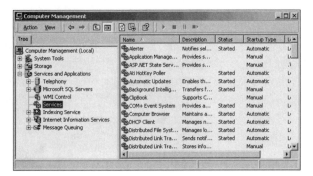

FIGURE 12.1   The services running on your computer are listed under the Services node in Computer Management.

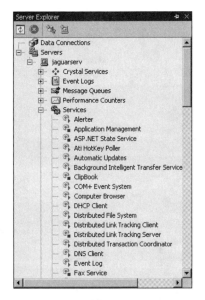

FIGURE 12.2   You can see and control services from within Visual Studio.

As a developer, you'll like the convenience of using the Server Explorer in Visual Studio .NET to view and control your services. If it's not already open, open it by choosing View, Server Explorer. Expand the Servers node, and then your own machine, and then Services. As in Figure 12.2, you'll see the same list of services as you would see under Computer Management, without having to bring up a separate tool.

Many services are referred to as servers. HTTP or Web servers, mail servers, and ftp servers all run as services on a Windows machine, as does the print server, any fax software you have installed, and similar applications. They wait in the background for requests or events to occur, and then they handle those requests or events in some way.

Another important category of services provides maintenance duties for another application. Consider an application that displays information, such as internal company announcements. Each piece of information has an expiry date, and after this date it is deleted. The job of deleting expired information is handled by a service that runs in the middle of the night, looks through all the information in the system, and deletes any with expiry dates before the current date. This ensures that expired information is always deleted, and doesn't impose any performance delays on the application that displays information to the user. This architectural choice is an excellent one for applications used by many users.

SHOP TALK

SERVER EXPLORER

So many programmers I talk to don't even realize the Server Explorer exists. It's a tremendous time saver, giving you access to all your services, SQL databases, performance counters, and event logs. In Visual Studio 6 and earlier, I would often have three or four other applications open, and would switch back and forth between them as I developed and debugged my applications. Now it's "one-stop shopping" with the Server Explorer. If you haven't used it, building this chapter's sample application should give you plenty of opportunities. I strongly encourage you to try it out.

Creating a Simple Windows Service in Managed C++

The sample service in this chapter will check Web sites for you to be sure they are serving pages. It will make extensive use of a configuration file, because it has no user interface. The configuration file will control

- The URLs to check

- An email address to notify if a site is down

- How often to check

The service will check the URLs when it starts, and then sleep for the specified period of time. If any URL doesn't respond, an email will be sent and an entry will be added to the event log. Email and event logs are excellent ways for applications without a user interface to notify an administrator of problems that need intervention.

Creating the Skeleton of the Service

Start by creating the project. Create a Windows Service (.NET) project called URLChecker. Because a service doesn't have a user interface, the view that opens (of your user interface) is not very useful. Click the link to switch to code view.

A class has been generated, called URLCheckerWinService, which inherits from ServiceBase in the System::ServiceProcess namespace. This class has two useful methods: OnStart() and OnStop(). You add code to these methods to actually implement the service.

Services that react to events thrown by others don't need a loop construct; the OnStart adds the service to the list of listeners for a particular event and then you write the corresponding event handler. This chapter's service, however, will use a loop. The OnStart() method creates a new thread which loops until a control variable makes it stop. It has to loop in a separate thread so that OnStart() can return control to the code that called it.

Add these private variables to the class, just before the definition of OnStart():

```
private:
    bool stopping;
    int loopsleep; //milliseconds
    Thread* servicethread;
```

Add a function to the class:

```
void CheckURLs()
{
    loopsleep = 1000; //milliseconds
    stopping = false;
    while (!stopping)
    {
        Threading::Thread::Sleep(loopsleep);
    }
}
```

This is the function the thread will call. It loops until it is told to stop, through the control variable stopping. This function is just a skeleton to begin with and will expand later in this chapter. Add code to OnStart() and remove the TODO comment, so that it reads like this:

```
void OnStart(String* args[])
{
    Threading::ThreadStart* threadStart =
                    new Threading::ThreadStart(this,CheckURLs);
    servicethread = new Threading::Thread(threadStart);
    servicethread->Start();
}
```

This code uses a helper class called ThreadStart to hold the delegate representing CheckURLs. The ThreadStart object is passed to the constructor of a Thread() object, and finally OnStart() starts the thread. This kicks off the loop. To be sure that the loop will stop, implement OnStop() as follows:

```
void OnStop()
{
    stopping = true;
}
```

Although this service doesn't do anything yet, it can be installed, started, and stopped.

Setting Properties and Adding an Installer

Switch back to the empty design view of your service, right-click the background, and choose Properties. Change the name for URLCheckerWinService to URLChecker. Then right-click the background again and choose Add Installer. A new file is created and opened in design view, showing a service process installer and a service installer.

The service process installer has only one property of interest: the account under which the service will run. Click serviceProcessInstaller1 to select it, and then open the Properties window. By default, the Account property is User, which means that the installer will prompt for an ID and password when you install the service, and the service will run with that user's privileges. It's more useful to run the service under a system account. Changing the Account property to LocalSystem will run the service as a privileged account. Use this only if you need it; LocalService is a less-privileged choice for services that don't need to pass credentials to another machine, and Network Service is another nonprivileged account that can authenticate to another machine. Although this service contacts other machines, it doesn't need to authenticate, so LocalService is a good choice if you are installing the service on a Windows 2003 machine. To support a variety of operating systems, use the older LocalSystem account.

The service installer is used to control the way the service runs, and you have three choices: Manual, Automatic, and Disabled. An Automatic service starts whenever the machine is restarted. A Manual service can be started on request. A Disabled service cannot be started. A user can change the startup type with Computer Management or Server Explorer, but other code cannot start the service. Leave this property set to Manual.

Installing and Testing the Service

In order to test the service, you must install it. Services written in Visual Basic or C# can be installed using a utility called installutil.exe, but this utility has trouble loading C++ assemblies. The wizard generates a main() function for this service that you can use to install the service. Open a command prompt and change directories to the Debug folder beneath the project folder. Make sure you have built the project, and then execute its main function like this:

```
urlchecker.exe -Install
```

Expand the Services node in Server Explorer and scroll down to the bottom, where you should see URLChecker preceded by a symbol made from a gear wheel and a small red square. Right-click it and choose Start. After a small delay, the red square becomes a green triangle. Right-click it again and choose Stop. You have demonstrated that your service can be installed successfully, and can process both Start and Stop commands without errors. Now it's time to add code so that the service does something useful.

Once the service is installed, you don't need to reinstall it or update or refresh anything when you make changes to your code. Just stop the service in Server Explorer, change your code, build the project, and start the service again. Your new code will execute. (If you forget to stop the service before building, you'll get a fatal link error because the linker will be unable to open your .EXE file.)

Checking a URL

To change the service so that it checks URLs, first add a configuration file to the project. Configuration files are discussed in Chapter 11, "Writing a Data Layer in Managed C++," where a configuration file holds a connection string for database access. Right-click the project in Solution Explorer, and choose Add, Add New Item. Select a Configuration File and click Open. Enter XML so that the configuration file reads like this:

```
<configuration>
  <appSettings>
    <add key="urls" value="http://www.gregcons.com http://www.microsoft.com" />
    <add key="email" value="you@yourdomain.com" />
    <add key="minutesinterval" value="2" />
  </appSettings>
</configuration>
```

Make sure you change the email address to one that will reach you. If you want, add some more URLs. Leave a space between each URL, and don't forget to include the http:// specifier. Add a postbuild step, as first discussed in Chapter 11, to copy the configuration file to the output directory. The command line should read like this:

```
copy app.config $(ConfigurationName)\$(TargetFileName).config
```

Add this code at the beginning of CheckURLs(), just before the loop:

```
//get config info from file
String* URLString =
      Configuration::ConfigurationSettings::AppSettings->get_Item("urls");
String* delims = S" ";
Char delimiter[] = delims->ToCharArray();
URLs = URLString->Split(delimiter);
email = Configuration::ConfigurationSettings::AppSettings->get_Item("email");
interval = Configuration::ConfigurationSettings::AppSettings->
      get_Item("minutesinterval")->ToInt16(NULL);

//set lastrun to force an immediate check
lastrun = DateTime::Now - TimeSpan(0,interval+1,0); //hours, minutes, seconds
```

This code could go in the OnStart() method, but you can't debug a service until it is started, so you want as little code as possible in OnStart(). Because this code is before the loop, it will only execute once anyway.

This code retrieves the list of URLs from the configuration file and uses Split() to separate it at spaces. It also retrieves the email address and the interval at which the URLs should be checked.

You might be tempted to change the Sleep() call at the bottom of the loop to sleep for however many minutes the configuration file requested, but that will leave your service unable to respond to stop requests until it wakes up. An unresponsive service can interfere with shutdown and other system processes. It's better to leave the loopsleep value at one second, and use a saved time to track when URLs were last checked. This variable, called lastrun in this sample, starts at a value small enough to ensure the URL checking will happen immediately when the service starts running. The calculation uses the TimeSpan helper class, which simplifies date and time arithmetic significantly.

Add these member variables to the class:

```
DateTime lastrun;
String* URLs[];
String* email;
int interval; //minutes
```

Change CheckURLs() to use the information from the configuration file and attempt to retrieve information from each URL in turn. Edit the body of the loop so that it reads like this:

```
if (DateTime::Now > lastrun + TimeSpan(0,interval,0))
{
    lastrun = DateTime::Now;
    for (int i = 0; i < URLs->Length; i++)
    {
        try
        {
            Net::WebRequest* req = Net::WebRequest::Create(URLs[i]);
            req->Method = "HEAD";
            Net::WebResponse* resp = req->GetResponse();
        }
        catch (...)
        {
            //couldn't reach server - notify someone
        }
    }
}
Threading::Thread::Sleep(loopsleep);
```

This code determines whether it's time to check URLs, and if it is, it sets lastrun and then goes through all the URLs in the array. Notice that the array, declared with square brackets just like an old-style C++ array, has a property called Length that can be used to set up this loop. The WebRequest class is used to get the headers only by setting the Method to HEAD. This saves time, because there's no need to read the entire page returned from the server; you just want to confirm there's a page to return.

If this service was a link-checker, it might be interested in whether the Web server returned a page for that URL, or a 404 error, or some other kind of response. But this service is simply confirming that the server exists and responds. If the server doesn't exist, the GetResponse() method throws an exception, which this code catches and uses as the trigger to notify the administrator that one of the monitored Web sites is down.

Sending Email

The SmtpMail class in the System::Web::Mail namespace represents a mail message. The simplest way to use it is with the static Send() method, which takes four string parameters:

- The email address from which the message will appear to come

- The email address to which the message will be sent

- The subject line for the message

- The body of the message

Add a reference to System.Web.dll and then edit the catch block in CheckURLs to read as follows:

```
catch (Exception* e)
{
    Text::StringBuilder* body = new Text::StringBuilder(S"");
    body->Append(S"URLChecker could not reach ");
    body->Append(URLs[i]);
    body->Append(Environment::NewLine);
    body->Append(e->ToString());
    Web::Mail::SmtpMail::Send(S"urlchecker@yourdomain.com",
                              email,
                              S"URL Checker failure report",
                              body->ToString());
}
```

If there is no SMTP server running on your machine, set the shared Web::Mail::SmtpMail::SmtpServer property to the IP address or fully qualified name of your mail server, such as mail.yourdomain.com, before calling Send(). Also, make sure you change the From address to your own domain when you edit this code.

You can test this service now. Simply edit the configuration file so that it contains at least one URL that will not return a page. For example, if there's a computer on your network that does not have a Web server installed, use that computer's IP address. If you plan to try making up a domain name, check in a browser first to see whether there is a server at that domain or not. Stop the service, rebuild the solution (so as to trigger the post build step that copies the configuration file), and start the service. Wait for at least as long as your interval time, and then check your mail. You should receive a message that reads like this (with a different URL):

```
URLChecker could not reach http://205.210.50.4
System.Net.WebException: The underlying connection was closed: Unable to
➥connect to the remote server.
   at System.Net.HttpWebRequest.CheckFinalStatus()
   at System.Net.HttpWebRequest.EndGetResponse(IAsyncResult asyncResult)
   at System.Net.HttpWebRequest.GetResponse()
   at URLChecker.URLCheckerWinService.CheckURLs() in
➥e:\urlchecker\urlcheckerwinservice.h:line 94
```

Stop the service, or you'll continue to get email every few minutes.

Adding Event Log Entries

Sending email is one way a service can notify the administrator of a problem. The Event Log is another way. Because it's easy to use, and works even when your Internet connection cuts you off from your email, why not add event logging to URLChecker?

Before the loop in CheckURLs(), add these lines:

```
Diagnostics::EventLog* log ;
if (! Diagnostics::EventLog::SourceExists("URLCheckerService") )
    Diagnostics::EventLog::CreateEventSource("URLCheckerService",
                                             "URLCheckerLog");
log = new Diagnostics::EventLog("URLCheckerLog");
log->Source = "URLCheckerService";
```

This sets up an event source called URLCheckerService and a custom event log called URLCheckerLog. It then creates a EventLog object that can write to URLCheckerLog and sets the source to URLCheckerService.

Add this line at the end of the catch block, after the lines that send the email:

```
log->WriteEntry(body->ToString(),Diagnostics::EventLogEntryType::Error);
```

That's all it takes to add event logging to your service! Stop the service, build it, and start it again. Wait for the email to reach you, and then scroll up in Server Explorer to the EventLogs node. Expand it, and then expand URLCheckerLog (the log name) beneath it, and finally URLCheckerService (the source name) beneath that. You see at least one error entry, identified with an X on a red background as in Figure 12.3.

FIGURE 12.3   The service has added entries to its own event log.

The Server Explorer only shows the first few characters of the log entry. To see the whole entry, use the Event Log section under Computer Management. You might have to close and re-open Computer Management to refresh the list of Event Logs. Expand Event Viewer, and then select URLCheckerLog. You will see the log entries: Double-click one for the details, as in Figure 12.4.

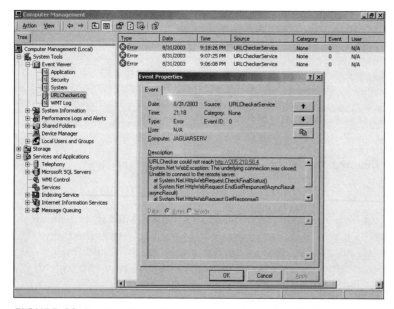

FIGURE 12.4   The details of the event log entries are available from the Event Viewer.

Debugging a Service

Debugging a service is not just a matter of pressing F5. You must attach the debugger to the running service, and you can only attach it after the service is started. Especially if you want to debug the code at the beginning of the `CheckURLs()` method, you'll find it helpful to slow the code down a little by inserting this line at the very top of the function:

```
Threading::Thread::Sleep(2*60*1000);
```

This causes the service to pause for two minutes, which should be long enough for you to attach to the process. Set a breakpoint on the line immediately after this one, stop the service, and build it. Then move quickly to attach to the process, as follows:

1. Start the service.

2. Choose Debug, Processes.

3. Make sure the Show System Processes check box is selected.

4. Scroll the Available Processes box to the bottom and select URLChecker.exe.

5. Click Attach.

6. On the Attach to Process dialog box, ensure Common Language Runtime and Native are selected, and then click OK.

7. Click Close.

8. Wait for execution to pause at your breakpoint.

If more time elapses than the pause you added, try setting a breakpoint on this line:

```
while (!stopping)
```

Control should reach this line once per second, giving you a chance to step through the loop. If you need more time to attach the debugger, stop debugging, stop the service, change the line of code that sleeps the service so that it sleeps longer, and repeat the attachment steps.

Once the debugger is attached to the service, you can do everything you normally would do: step through code, examine variables, and most importantly, see error messages and exceptions. When your service is not attached to a debugger, messages directed to the user (such as exception dialog boxes) are not shown; there is no one to show them to. When you are debugging, you see these messages. This should dramatically ease the difficulty of getting a more complex service working.

In Brief

- A service runs in the background, without an associated user session. It can even start running when no user has logged on to the machine.

- A server must be installed before it can be used. Add an installer to your project, and then run the application with the -Install option. This need only be done once.

- Because a service has no user interface, it must use non-interactive methods of communication such as sending email, writing to the event log, or writing to files on the hard drive when errors occur.

- To send email, use Web::Mail::SmtpMail.

- To write to the event log, use Diagnostics::EventLog. Set the log name and source before writing an entry.

- To debug a service, insert a pause in the function called by OnStart(), start the service, and attach the debugger to the running process.

Strengthening Your Managed Applications with Security and Encryption

Understanding Encryption Techniques and Technologies

Encryption has long been considered an advanced topic, but the .NET Framework makes it remarkably simple to encrypt and decrypt data within your applications. This is especially important for mobile code, which can rely on passwords or other information that is stored within your code or within a configuration file. You might also want to prevent hand-editing of documents saved by your application; this is especially true of applications used for financial purposes. Imagine if the tax collectors gave you an application to calculate your own taxes, and you could lower your tax owing with Notepad!

Although it's simple to use cryptography (the science of ciphers, codes, encryption, and decryption) in a .NET application, it's important to understand some of the principles before you begin. Some techniques can be overkill for your application; others can be useless if you don't use them in the correct combination.

Ciphers, Plaintext, and Ciphertext

Before you start adding encryption to your application, there are a few words you need to know:

- A code replaces words with other words or with numbers; modern cryptography doesn't use codes much any more

- A cipher replaces a number with another number; because any piece of text can be represented as numbers (bytes), most modern cryptography techniques use ciphers

- Plaintext is a string written in its original, plain form: a password or secret message

- Ciphertext is the transformed, encrypted version of plaintext

Encryption is the process of transforming plaintext into ciphertext. If a "bad guy" gets the ciphertext, it can't be used against you. Of course, if the "bad guy" is able to transform the ciphertext back into plaintext, whatever it was you wanted to prevent is probably going to happen after all. Preventing decryption by interceptors is a big part of why encryption is used in applications, but it's not the only reason for encryption and decryption.

Confidentiality, Integrity, and Authentication

There are three desires that are generally satisfied with the use of some form of cryptography: confidentiality, integrity, and authentication. To explain these terms, consider a conversation between two entities that is taking place in public: It could be a person ordering a book over the Internet, or two people passing notes in a high school classroom.

- Confidentiality means that no eavesdropper can learn the sender's secret information.

- Integrity means that the sender's information is not changed between leaving the sender and reaching the destination.

- Authentication means that the destination is absolutely sure the message is from the sender.

These same three concepts apply to information that is not passed as a message in the usual sense; for example if a user stores information on the hard drive, confidentiality addresses that user's worry that someone else would be able to read the stored information. Integrity addresses the program developer's worry that a user could hand-edit the stored information without the checks and balances the application provides. Authentication addresses the issue of whether or not the user is indeed authorized to use the application, or to read or write files.

Symmetric and Asymmetric Cryptography

Cryptography is generally split into two branches: symmetric cryptography and asymmetric cryptography. In symmetric cryptography there is one key, and algorithms exist to encrypt or decrypt information using that key. The correspondents must agree on a shared secret key in some nonpublic manner, such as a private meeting, a disk in a courier envelope, or a telephone conversation. In asymmetric cryptography, each user has a two-part key; a public part known to everyone (including eavesdroppers) and a private part known to no one else (not even the destination of the message). These two keys are the opposite of each other: If the sender applies a private key to encrypt something, anyone can apply that sender's public key to decrypt it. If someone intends a message for a particular recipient, it can be encrypted with the recipient's public key; the recipient just applies the private key to decrypt it.

Consider the requirement for confidentiality. If two people have agreed on a symmetric key and encrypt everything they send, they can be sure that the key prevents outsiders from eavesdropping. Of course, how can you agree on a secret key with an individual (or entity, such as an online store) with whom you have no nonpublic interaction? Confidentiality can also be assured using asymmetric cryptography. Encrypting information with your own private key doesn't protect confidentiality, because anyone can decrypt them with your public one. But if the sender encrypts using the recipient's public key, confidentiality is assured: Only the recipient knows the private key.

Integrity can also be protected with both methods, and both rely on a related technology known as *hashing*. A hash takes a long and complex string or series of numbers and reduces it to a single number. A good hash does so in a way that comes close to guaranteeing that two different strings or series of numbers will never hash down to the same result. A cryptographically useful hash is also very difficult to invert: If you obtain the hash result, you can't use it to determine the original series of numbers.

How does a hash protect integrity? The sender sends not only the message, but a hash of the message as well. Any change to the message would mean that the hash value sent along would no longer match the hash from the new message. But a hash alone can't ensure integrity if the "bad guy" who intercepts and changes the message can calculate a hash result for the new message, and send a new one along with the new message. If the sender and recipient are using symmetric cryptography, the sender encrypts the message and its hash. The recipient decrypts them, determines what the hash should be, and compares it to the hash that was sent. Because the interceptor can't read the combined message, a replacement message can't be slipped in as before; although the interceptor might be able to change some bits in the message, the recipient will know right away that the message received is not what was sent. The same logic applies with asymmetric cryptography, except that the sender encrypts everything with the recipient's public key, knowing that only the recipient can decrypt it with the matching private key.

What about authentication? In symmetric cryptography, if you receive a message that makes sense when it is decrypted with the shared secret key, you are confident that it came from the only other person who knows that shared secret key. But that's not the case with the asymmetric approaches described so far. The sender encrypts the message with the recipient's public key, but everyone knows the recipient's public key; that means anyone can write a message to the recipient and claim it's from some other sender. Proving it's from a particular sender involves the sender's private key at some point.

You can include some simple text, such as the sender's name, encrypted with the sender's private key. The recipient would apply the sender's public key, and if the result is the sender's name, the message must have come from the sender. The problem with this is that the recipient can save the ciphertext (the sender's name encrypted with the sender's private key) and paste it into some future message, successfully posing as the sender. The text to be encrypted with the sender's private key has to be different for every message, so that it can't ever be reused. The perfect candidate for this is the hash of the message. It's been calculated anyway, and it will be different for every message.

To summarize, in order for a symmetric cryptography user to create a message with confidentiality, integrity, and authentication, the sender first constructs a message, and then computes a hash. The sender then glues together the message and the hash, and encrypts the whole thing with the secret shared key. The recipient decrypts with the secret shared key and recomputes the hash for the message as received. If the hashes match, the recipient knows that this message is from the sender, that it has not been changed in transit, and that no one has learned anything from it in transit.

In order for an asymmetric cryptography user to create a message that will have confidentiality, integrity, and authentication, the sender must construct a message and compute a hash. The sender glues together the message, the hash, and the hash encrypted with the sender's private key, and then encrypts the whole thing with the recipient's public key. The recipient decrypts everything with the private key, and extracts the message. The recipient recomputes the hash for the message as received. As with symmetric cryptography, if the hashes match, the message has not been changed. The recipient goes on to decrypt the third part with the sender's public key: if the result matches the hash then the message is definitely from the sender. The encrypted hash has no way to pose as the sender later because no other message will have that same hash value.

Cryptography in the .NET Framework

In many ways, security is an ongoing battle between those who want to keep information secret, and those who want to learn other people's secrets. Some encryption algorithms have been cracked in shockingly short amounts of time. Perhaps no encryption algorithm will stand forever. That presents an interesting challenge to the designers of a package of classes to support encryption and decryption.

The classes that are used to implement cryptography within your applications are in the `System.Web.Cryptography` namespace. This contains two important classes: `SymmetricAlgorithm` and `AsymmetricAlgorithm`. These abstract classes are the base classes for classes named for the various encryption algorithms that ship with the .NET Framework. In version 1.1, these are

- DES, RC2, Rijndael, and TripleDES: symmetric algorithms

- DSA and RSA: asymmetric algorithms

The twist is that the class called `System.Web.Cryptography.TripleDES` does not implement the TripleDES algorithm. It's a base class for a class called `TripleDESCryptoServiceProvider`, which actually provides the implementation. This allows several implementations of a particular algorithm to co-exist within the library, while exposing their common structure and properties to your code.

To keep your code as robust as possible, avoid using the names of the implementation classes. Each of the base classes has a `Create()` method that returns a new instance of the current default implementation class. For example, this line creates an instance of the `RijndaelManaged` class without naming it:

> **CLASS NAMES**
>
> The names of the implementation classes that ship with the .NET Framework are built from the name of the algorithm and a clue about the way the class is implemented. Classes with names that end with `CryptoServiceProvider` use the CryptoAPI library that ships with Windows. Classes with names that end with Managed are written in managed code, usually C#.

```
Rijndael* r = Rijndael::Create();
```

A using namespace statement would be needed for this line to compile.

When you use the `Create()` method, you are making it simpler to drop in new and better implementations of an algorithm in the future. Install the new class into the library and make it the default implementation (or more realistically, upgrade to some hypothetical new version of the library that contains new classes and defines some of them to be the new default implementations for selected algorithms). Your code will then use the new implementations without any code changes, and without even a recompile.

Encrypting Information

The encryption classes don't have methods with names like `Encrypt()` or `Decrypt()`. Instead they work by reading from and writing to streams using companion objects called encryptors and decryptors, and special streams known as crypto streams. To encrypt information that is going into a file, you create an ordinary file stream, and then layer a crypto stream on that file stream, and write to the crypto stream. The data is encrypted as it is written. To encrypt one string into another string, you create a memory stream associated with the output stream, and then layer on a crypto stream and write to the crypto stream, which encrypts as it writes to the memory stream, which you can then get into the string.

Encrypting into a File

Here's a simple console application that prompts for a string, and then encrypts it and writes it into a file:

```
Console::WriteLine(S"Enter a sentence");
String* plaintext = Console::ReadLine();
unsigned char stringbytes __gc[] =
      Text::ASCIIEncoding::ASCII->GetBytes(plaintext);
FileStream* fs = new FileStream("secret.txt",FileMode::Create);
Rijndael* rijndael = Rijndael::Create();
ICryptoTransform* transform = rijndael->CreateEncryptor();
CryptoStream* cs = new CryptoStream(fs, transform, CryptoStreamMode::Write);
cs->Write(stringbytes,0,stringbytes->Length);
cs->Close();
fs->Close();
```

The samples in this chapter are console applications. You're most likely to use these techniques in a class library, probably a business layer component.

This code gets a string from the user and then converts it into an array of bytes. Pay special attention to the way the garbage-collected array of unsigned characters is declared:

```
unsigned char stringbytes __gc[]
```

Experienced C++ programmers are often frustrated trying to remember where to place the __gc modifier when declaring a garbage-collected array.

Having created the array, this code opens a file in the project directory called secret.txt. Of course, you don't need to hard-code the filename, but it keeps this sample simpler to use a hard-coded name.

The next step is to create an implementation instance by calling the static Create() method of the Rijndael class. This generates a random key and initialization vector to be used for the encryption.

A call to `CreateEncryptor()` creates an encryptor that can be passed to the constructor of the crypto stream. The layering means that bytes will go from the byte array to the crypto stream to the file stream, and finally to the file on the hard drive. All the code needs to do is to write to the crypto stream that's wrapped around the file stream. The final step is to close both streams.

You run this console application and enter a short sentence, such as this:

```
Shh! Don't tell anyone!
```

> **THE RIJNDAEL ALGORITHM**
>
> Rijndael is a symmetric cryptography algorithm that was chosen as a replacement for DES. The default implementation is written in C# and comes with the base class libraries when you install the .NET Framework. The other symmetric algorithms leverage the Windows CryptoAPI library, and different machines may have different versions, with varying key lengths, depending on the version of Internet Explorer or even the country in which the software was installed. Using Rijndael in this sample eliminates difficulties caused by CryptoAPI versioning issues or key length issues.

Browse to the secret.txt file and open it in Notepad. You'll see content similar to this (the exact characters depend on the key and initialization vector, and yours will differ):

```
VÛÇ⁻ojÁùpy n ( 8¦IŸõ ¶'ñZk +Ðy
```

This is the encrypted text. It's just that simple to encrypt information before you save it.

Arrangements for Keys

Because Rijndael is a symmetric algorithm, anyone who wants to decrypt the contents of secret.txt will need the key and initialization vector that were used to encrypt this text. Symmetric algorithms always rely on a shared secret. You can, for example, write the key into a text file called key.txt and the initialization vector into another file called iv.txt—but that would hardly be secure, especially if you kept them in the same folder as secret.txt. However, if you emailed key.txt and iv.txt to someone, and then later emailed secret.txt, the person would be able to decrypt secret.txt. Unfortunately, so would anyone else who could access your correspondent's email.

You have a variety of options for making the key available. You can choose more obscure filenames, you can save the files onto a disk and courier it directly to the person who is going to read the file, you can even print the key and the initialization vector, fax the printout to your colleague, and get your colleague to retype the files by hand—because that way nothing can be intercepted through email or over the network. Because the initialization vector is only 16 bytes long, and the key only 32 bytes long, you can even read them over the phone to your colleague for retyping. There are many options to choose from, and they all rely on a shared secret.

In the sample for this chapter, you'll see another version of the shared secret technique: The key and the initialization vector are actually in secret.txt—unencrypted! Because they are arrays of numbers, they look like the same gibberish as the rest of the encrypted data. Add these two lines before the line that creates the crypto stream:

```
fs->Write(rijndael->IV,0,rijndael->IV->Length);
fs->Write(rijndael->Key,0,rijndael->Key->Length);
```

These write the initialization vector and the key out directly, using the file stream, not the crypto stream. That means later they can be read back before a decrypting crypto stream has been created. This might feel a little dangerous, like leaving the key to your house under the doormat, but it doesn't have to be. Obviously you don't email a file like this to someone and explain in the message how it was encrypted, with what algorithm, and where the key and initialization vector are stored. You can deliver that information in person: Or if you are writing the application that stores and also the application that reads, don't tell anyone, just use the information. And of course, you can make it safer by mixing it up a bit. Just because this sample uses the initialization vector followed by the key doesn't mean you need to. Flip them around. Or put some meaningless characters between them. Write one of them twice, just to be confusing. As long as only you know the secret—what order they are in, what they're padded with, and so on—only you will be able to decrypt the file.

After making this change and running the application again, try entering the same sentence you encrypted before. The secret.txt file should still contain a lot of strange characters, but it will be a little longer now.

Decrypting Information

Decrypting the file is simply the reverse process. You again create an implementation instance, and then read the real initialization vector and key from the file and replace the random values that were generated by the call to Create(). With these in place, create a crypto stream and wrap it around the file stream, and then read from it. The information is decrypted as you read.

Here's snippet from a console application that reads secret.txt and decrypts it:

```
Rijndael* rijndael2 = Rijndael::Create();
FileStream* fs2 = new FileStream("secret.txt",FileMode::Open);
unsigned char  realIV __gc[] = new unsigned char __gc[rijndael2->IV->Length];
fs2->Read(realIV,0,rijndael2->IV->Length);
rijndael2->IV = realIV;
unsigned char  realKey __gc[] = new unsigned char __gc[rijndael2->Key->Length];
fs2->Read(realKey,0,rijndael2->Key->Length);
rijndael2->Key = realKey;
ICryptoTransform* transform2 = rijndael2->CreateDecryptor();
```

```
CryptoStream* cs2 = new CryptoStream(fs2,transform2,CryptoStreamMode::Read);
StreamReader* sr = new StreamReader(cs2);
String* plaintext2 = sr->ReadToEnd();
Console::WriteLine(plaintext2);
sr->Close();
cs2->Close();
fs2->Close();
```

Here are the differences between this code and the code presented in the previous section:

- The file stream is created with a FileMode of Open, because this code reads the file.

- Two garbage-collected arrays of unsigned characters are created, one for the key and one for the initialization vector, and memory is allocated for them with new.

- The key and initialization are read directly from the file and then used to change properties of the implementation instance.

- The transform is generated by CreateDecryptor(), because the information is being decrypted as it is read.

- The crypto stream is in read mode rather than write mode.

- A stream reader is used to simplify the job of reading the stream into a string.

This code takes advantage of the fact the key and initialization vectors are always the same length in the Rijndael algorithm. As a result the length of the random key and initialization vector generated by Create() can be used to allocate space for the real values to be read from the file.

Test this code yourself. Use the sample from the encryption section to fill secret.txt with an initialization vector, a key, and some encrypted text. Then run this code to read secret.txt and write out the original text. You should see the sentence you originally entered.

If you changed the way the first sample saved the initialization vector and key, make sure you make the corresponding changes to this code.

Role-Based Security

Security and authentication involve a lot more than encryption. How do you make sure that the user who is running your application is authorized to do so? What if only certain users are allowed to save, or to change specific settings (such as a discount rate), or to use some part of the application? Role-based security lets you establish who is running your application, determine whether they are in a particular group, or even prevent them from using parts of the application if they are not in the group you want.

Determining Identity

The `System::Security::Principal` namespace contains classes that hold information about the user who is running the application (the identity) and extended details, such as Windows groups, about that identity (the principal). You should know that not all applications run under the identity of the user who runs them; for example, when you load an ASP.NET Web page, the code might run with your identity, or might run with a general anonymous privilege. When you run a console or WinForms application, it runs under your identity unless the application has arranged otherwise.

Here's a simple console application called `Roles` that demonstrates Windows identity and principal concepts:

```
using namespace System;
using namespace System::Security::Principal;

// This is the entry point for this application
int _tmain(void)
{
  WindowsIdentity* Identity = WindowsIdentity::GetCurrent();
  WindowsPrincipal* Principal = new WindowsPrincipal(Identity);

  //Print the values.
  Console::WriteLine("Principal Values for current thread:");
  Console::WriteLine("Name: {0}", Principal->Identity->Name);
  Console::WriteLine("Type: {0}", Principal->Identity->AuthenticationType);
  Console::WriteLine("IsAuthenticated: {0}",
                     __box(Principal->Identity->IsAuthenticated));
  Console::WriteLine();
  Console::WriteLine();
  Console::WriteLine("Identity Values for current thread:");
  Console::WriteLine("Name: {0}", Identity->Name);
  Console::WriteLine("Type: {0}", Identity->AuthenticationType);
  Console::WriteLine("IsAuthenticated: {0}", __box(Identity->IsAuthenticated));
  Console::WriteLine("IsAnonymous: {0}", __box(Identity->IsAnonymous));
  Console::WriteLine("IsGuest: {0}", __box(Identity->IsGuest));
  Console::WriteLine("IsSystem: {0}", __box(Identity->IsSystem));
  Console::WriteLine("Token: {0}", Identity->Token.ToString());
  return 0;
}
```

The first line of this code gets the identity under which the application is running. That should be you, because the application doesn't contain any code to change the identity. Then it gets a principal based on that identity. The remainder of the code illustrates some useful properties of the identity and principal objects. Notice the use of __box to wrap up the Boolean values, and the `ToString` method to convert nonstring values to strings.

When you run this application, the output should resemble this:

```
Principal Values for current thread:
Name: YOURDOMAIN\you
Type: NTLM
IsAuthenticated: True


Identity Values for current thread:
Name: YOURDOMAIN\you
Type: NTLM
IsAuthenticated: True
IsAnonymous: False
IsGuest: False
IsSystem: False
Token: 304
```

Once you know who is running your code, you can write security code of your own, comparing the name of the identity or principal with a list of authorized users that you have stored somewhere. But that will require you to write code to manage user lists: adding and deleting users, changing their authority code, and so on. It's a lot less work to leverage Windows groups. Even if they aren't in use by the people who'll be running the application, it's less work to teach people to use Windows groups than to write your own equivalent administration section.

Testing for Roles

A role is a general concept in identity-based authentication, and Windows groups are one way to assign and test roles. (There are others, such as COM+ roles, that are out of scope for this chapter.) A role generally corresponds to a job title, such as a manager, or a privilege level, such as an administrator. Some roles contain only one user, others many more. A user can be in any number of roles.

USING YOUR DOMAIN AND MACHINE NAMES

Most role names contain strings that are particular to your installation, such as your domain name, or your machine name. The sample code uses the placeholders YOURDOMAIN and YOURMACHINE. Make sure you substitute appropriately.

This code determines whether a user is in a particular Windows group:

```
String* role = "YOURDOMAIN\\Domain Users";
if (Principal->IsInRole(role))
    Console::WriteLine("You are a domain user");
else
    Console::WriteLine("You are not a domain user");


role = "BUILTIN\\Administrators";
if (Principal->IsInRole(role))
    Console::WriteLine("You are an administrator");
else
    Console::WriteLine("You are not an administrator");


role = "YOURMACHINE\\Experts";
if (Principal->IsInRole(role))
    Console::WriteLine("You are an Expert on this machine");
else
    Console::WriteLine("You are not an Expert on this machine");
```

When this code runs, the output is similar to this:

```
You are a domain user
You are an administrator
You are not an Expert on this machine
```

Notice the three prefixes in the role strings:

- YOURDOMAIN is a domain name. Use this prefix when you're referring to a group that has been created on your domain controller.

- BUILTIN refers to built-in groups such as Administrators, created when you install Windows.

- YOURMACHINE is a machine name. Use this prefix when you're referring to a local group.

You can test this code by creating a local group using Computer Management, and adding yourself to it. Right-click My Computer on your desktop and choose Manage. Expand the Local Users and Groups section, and then click Groups. Figure 13.1 shows a list of groups on a typical machine.

Choose Actions, New Group to create a group. Name it Experts, and click Add to add users to it. Add yourself. Click Create to finish creating the group. Then log off Windows and log back on to update your security profile, and run the application again. Now you should be told you are an Expert. (And don't forget about the logging off and logging on. You'll do a lot of that when you're testing security code.)

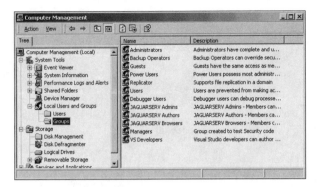

FIGURE 13.1 You can create users and groups on your own machine.

You can use tests of `IsInRole()` to decide whether to enable or disable a button in a graphical user interface, or to decide whether some action the user has taken should be logged. Once groups have been set up that represent that various kinds of users in your system, you can check to see which kind of user (what authority level) is running the code.

One approach is to throw a security exception when the wrong kind of user tried to do something. If you want to do that, you're better off using permissions sets than coding the test and the throw by hand.

Using Permissions Sets

A permissions set is a representation of what a particular user or role is allowed to do. Permission sets can be used imperatively or declaratively, the documentation likes to say, which means you can either call a function or add an attribute.

To demonstrate the imperative use of permissions set, add an unmanaged (generic C++) class to the `Roles` project and call it `AccessControlled`. That generates this class definition:

```
class AccessControlled
{
public:
    AccessControlled(void);
    ~AccessControlled(void);
};
```

Edit the implementation file to look like this:

```
#include "StdAfx.h"
#using <mscorlib.dll>
#include "accesscontrolled.h"
```

```
using namespace System;
using namespace System::Security::Permissions;
using namespace System::Security::Principal;

AccessControlled::AccessControlled(void)
{
    AppDomain::CurrentDomain->SetPrincipalPolicy(
                            PrincipalPolicy::WindowsPrincipal);
    //String* role = "BUILTIN\\Administrators";
    String* role = "YOURMACHINE\\Experts";
    PrincipalPermission* p = new PrincipalPermission(0,role);
    p->Demand();
}

AccessControlled::~AccessControlled(void)
{
}
```

The first line of this constructor is vital: Without it the code will compile but will always react as though you are not in the group. The call to `SetPrincipalPolicy()` instructs the framework to create `WindowsPrincipal` objects by default.

The code creates a `PrincipalPermission` object that represents being in a particular role. (The role names used in this example follow the same rules as those used for `IsInRole()`.) The first parameter is 0 here, to indicate that any user identity is acceptable. You can pass in a string representing a specific user if you want, in which case you are preparing to demand that a particular user be running the application and that the user be in the group.

Having created a `PrincipalPermission` object, the code goes on to demand that the individual running this application meet the conditions in that object. If the demand fails, a security exception will be thrown.

Add these lines to the main function in Roles.cpp to create an `AccessControlled` object, triggering a call to the constructor:

```
AccessControlled* ac = new AccessControlled();
Console::WriteLine("created the access controlled object");
```

Remember to add an #include statement at the top of Roles.cpp (after the one already there) to bring in accesscontrolled.h.

When you are a member of the Experts group on your machine, this code runs without incident. When you are not, it throws a `SecurityException`, like this one:

```
Unhandled Exception: System.Security.SecurityException:
    Request for principal permission failed.
    at System.Security.Permissions.PrincipalPermiss
ion.Demand()
    at AccessControlled.__ctor(AccessControlled* )
in e:\roles\accesscontrolled.cpp:line 15
    at main() in e:\roles\roles.cpp:line 54
```

While testing, remember you must sign off and sign on again for your new group membership to take effect.

The other way to use `PrincipalPermission` is as an attribute, declaratively. This requires the class to be garbage collected, because only managed classes can have attributes. Add another generic class called `ManagedAccessControlled` to the project and edit the class definition to read like this:

```
using namespace System::Security::Permissions;
[PrincipalPermissionAttribute(SecurityAction::Demand,
                              Role = "BUILTIN\\Administrators")]
__gc class ManagedAccessControlled
{
public:
    ManagedAccessControlled (void);
    ~ManagedAccessControlled (void);
};
```

Edit the main function again, but the call to `SetPrincipalPolicy()` can't be in the constructor, because it must be called before the attempt to construct the `AccessControlled` object. Add these lines to the main (and don't forget the #include at the top):

```
AppDomain::CurrentDomain->SetPrincipalPolicy(PrincipalPolicy::WindowsPrincipal);
ManagedAccessControlled* mac = new ManagedAccessControlled();
Console::WriteLine("created the managed access controlled object");
```

The constructor itself does not need any security code. No one can create or use a `ManagedAccessControlled` object unless they are in the specified role.

You can use role-based security throughout your applications, determining whether a user is in a role or not, even preventing access to parts of the application by unauthorized users. Your class library will be more secure if you use the techniques from this section to control who uses the application.

In Brief

- Encryption and decryption are supported in the .NET Framework using an extensible and configurable class library.

- Symmetric and asymmetric encryption and decryption are supported by the Base Class Libraries.

- To encrypt information, write it to an encrypting crypto stream. To decrypt information, read it from an decrypting crypto stream.

- Role-based security lets you leverage Windows groups to determine whether a user is authorized to perform a specific activity.

- Using attributes to enforce role-based security requires little or no coding, yet ensures that only authorized users can use the restricted parts of an application.

Moving Layers to Different Machines with .NET Remoting

Writing a Class That Will Be Available Through Remoting

In many ways, the .NET runtime is a parallel concept to COM: It allows two or more applications or components to interact while they are executing. .NET remoting is a parallel concept to DCOM: It allows two or more applications or components to interact while executing on different computers.

The mechanics of creating and using a remoted class are remarkably simple. If you have experience with DCOM or CORBA, don't expect .NET remoting to be similar: There's very little difference between writing a pair of classes that will interact remotely, and writing a pair of classes that will interact on the same machine.

The base class libraries include a class called MarshalByRefObject, in the System namespace. A remoted class must inherit from this class. Because a managed class can inherit from only one class, you might have to adjust your design to allow MarshalByRefObject to be the base class for your remoted class.

TWO COMPUTERS

Remoting involves communications between two computers. To build and test the sample code in this chapter, you need two computers, each with the .NET Framework (version 1.1) installed, and a connection between the two.

To build this chapter's example, create a .NET project, a class library called Greeting. Add a generic C++ class called Greeter. Remove the generated constructor and destructor from Greeter.h and Greeter.cpp, and then edit the class definition to read like this:

```
namespace Greeting
{
    public __gc class Greeter: public MarshalByRefObject
    {
    public:
        String* Greet(String* name);
        String* Greet();
        Data::DataSet* Records();
    };
}
```

You can offer any methods you want from a remoted class, of course. These examples show how to pass and return strings, and how to return a data set. Remoted objects are typically in business or data layers, which makes these return types typical.

Edit Greeter.cpp to include these implementations of the functions:

```
using namespace Greeting;

String* Greeter::Greet()
{
    return "Hello!";
}
String* Greeter::Greet(String* name)
{
    Text::StringBuilder* ret = new Text::StringBuilder(S"Hello, ");
    ret = ret->Append(name);
    ret = ret->Append(S"!");
    return ret->ToString();
}
Data::DataSet* Greeter::Records()
{
    Data::DataSet* ds = new Data::DataSet();
    ds->ReadXml("c:\\people.xml");
    return ds;
}
```

Of course, a method in a data layer that returns a data set would normally fill it from a database. In order to make this example work on a variety of machines, it just reads a file of XML. The connection between XML and data is discussed in Chapter 11, "Writing a Data Layer in Managed C++." Using a file of XML like this is a great way to prototype an application that involves data.

In order for this code to compile, add a reference (using the .NET tab of the Add Reference dialog box) to System.Web.dll. In order for it to run, you'll need a file of XML. Add one to the project by right-clicking Greeting in Solution Explorer and choosing Add, Add New Item, and then selecting XML File. Name it people.xml and edit it to read like this:

```
<?xml version="1.0" encoding="utf-8"?>
<people>
  <person>
    <name>Kate Gregory</name>
    <website>www.gregcons.com</website>
  </person>
  <person>
    <name>Joe Somebody</name>
    <website>www.somewhere.org</website>
  </person>
  <person>
    <name>Sue Whoever</name>
    <website>www.wherever.net</website>
  </person>
</people>
```

Save the file, and then copy it to the c:\ folder. You'll need it there when you test these classes on your development machine, before deploying them to a second machine.

Finally, delete Class1, defined in greeting.h, because you have no need for it. Build the solution to confirm that there are no errors. This is a straightforward class library; the only thing that sets it apart from any other class library is that the Greeter class inherits from MarshalByRefObject.

Writing a Remoting Client

The client can be any kind of application: console application, Windows application, Windows service, and so on. In this section, you'll create a Windows application to use the remoted class. Add a new Windows Forms project called GreetingClient to the same solution.

As first discussed in Chapter 4, "Building Simple User Interfaces with Windows Forms," you use the toolbox to build a simple user interface on the blank form that is generated for you. Add the following controls:

- A button called Greet with text of *Greet*

- A label called Greeting with its text set to an empty string

- A button called GreetName with text of *Greet Name*

- A text box called NameBox with its text set to an empty string

- A button called GetRecords with text of *Get Records*

- A data grid called RecordsGrid that is docked to the bottom of the form

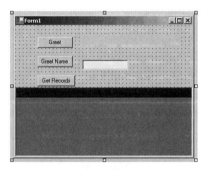

FIGURE 14.1 Creating a user interface for a client that uses the remoted interface.

The completed form should resemble Figure 14.1.

Add a reference (using the Project tab) to the Greeting project, and then edit the code, adding this private variable:

```
Greeting::Greeter* greet;
```

Add this line to the constructor, after the call to InitializeComponent():

```
greet = new Greeting::Greeter();
```

The handlers for the three buttons will each use this variable to call methods of the remoted class. At the moment, it's not remoted—that's simpler to do once you know the client is working. Debugging across remoting is a little more difficult than ordinary debugging.

Continue to develop the client by double-clicking the Greet button in Design View, and then editing the handler to use the remoted object, so that it reads like this:

```
private: System::Void Greet_Click(System::Object *  sender,
                            System::EventArgs *  e)
{
   Greeting->Text = greet->Greet();
}
```

This code puts the return value from the Greet() method into the Text property of the label on the form.

Similarly, add this code for the GreetName handler:

```
private: System::Void GreetName_Click(System::Object *  sender,
                                      System::EventArgs *  e)
{
   Greeting->Text = greet->Greet(Namebox->Text);
}
```

This code uses the text from the text box and passes it to the overload of Greet() that takes a String*, and then puts the result in the Text property of the Greeting label.

The button handler for the third button will fill the data grid. Double-click the button and edit the handler to read like this:

```
private: System::Void GetRecords_Click(System::Object *  sender,
                                       System::EventArgs *  e)
{
   Data::DataSet* ds = greet->Records();
   RecordsGrid->DataSource = ds->Tables->get_Item(0);
}
```

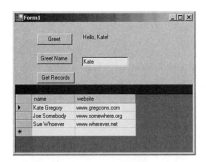

To test this code, right-click GreetingClient in Solution Explorer and choose Set As Startup Project. This will ensure that the Windows form runs when you run the solution. Build the code to ensure there are no errors, and then start debugging by pressing F5. Click the Greet button; you should see Hello! next to the button. Enter a name in the text box and click the Greet Name button; the label should change to greet that name. Finally, click the Get Records button; the data grid should fill in, as in Figure 14.2.

FIGURE 14.2   Testing the client application while the class library is still on the same machine.

Once you've established that the client and the class library work together, it's time to add remoting to it.

Hosting the Remoted Object and Configuring the Client

The class library cannot be remoted on its own; you need to build an application that will run on the second machine and accept requests for the remoted class. This application can be a Windows application, a console application, or a Windows service. The application must be running in order for remoting requests to be fulfilled; the runtime will not start the application when requests for the remoted class come in. If you write a service, as discussed in

Chapter 12, "Writing a Windows Service," you can arrange for it to start automatically whenever the server is booted, even if nobody logs on. That can make it simple to have your remoted objects available. In this section, you'll create a Windows application, because it's simple to write and control. Then you'll adjust the client to use the remoted object.

Creating and Configuring the Server Application

Even though the application will be deployed on a separate machine, you can create it within the same solution that already contains the class library and the client application. Add a Windows application called GreetingServer to the solution. Add a button named Listen, with text of *Listen*, and a label set to an empty string. This button will start the listener that provides access to the remoted object. Double-click the button and edit the handler to read like this:

```
private: System::Void Listen_Click(System::Object *  sender,
                                    System::EventArgs *  e)
{
   Runtime::Remoting::RemotingConfiguration::Configure(
              "GreetingServer.exe.config");
   ListeningLabel->Text = "Listening";
}
```

You don't need to write code to listen for requests or to serve out the requested objects. All this code does is load the remoting configuration from the configuration file. Right-click the project in Solution Explorer and choose Add, Add New Item, and select a configuration file. Then edit app.config to read like this:

```
<configuration>
   <system.runtime.remoting>
      <application>
         <service>
            <wellknown
               mode="Singleton"
               type="Greeting.Greeter, Greeting"
               objectUri="Greeter"
            />
         </service>
         <channels>
            <channel ref="tcp" port="9555" />
         </channels>
      </application>
   </system.runtime.remoting>
</configuration>
```

There are two important tags (or elements) in this configuration file: the service tag and the channels tag. Services, in other words remoted objects, are offered in two ways: as well-known objects and as activated objects. Well-known objects are offered by the server, and the client code is expected to know the name and ask for them by name. The server takes it from there. Activated objects are discussed later in this chapter, in the "Choosing Lifetime and Lifecycle Options Appropriately" section. A single hosting application can host multiple remoted objects by having multiple tags within the service element.

The wellknown element has three attributes: the mode, the type, and the objectUri. Using Singleton for the mode causes a single object to be created the first time the client code requests the object, and for the object to persist and be used for every request that follows. Using SingleCall for the mode causes a new object to be created for each method call that comes from the client, and then disposed when the call ends. It's more expensive than Singleton and should be used only when you know you will need it. The type attribute identifies the class (using the format *Namespace.ClassName*) and assembly (the DLL, without the .DLL extension) that is being exposed to remoting. The objectUri attribute defines the name that will be used by the client code to refer to this object. It doesn't need to match either of the names used in the type attribute, but it makes life simpler for those using this object if you keep the object name the same, as this example does.

The channels tag defines the mechanisms over which this server will be offering objects. There are two protocols provided by the .NET Framework: TCP and HTTP. Although most introductory examples feature HTTP, most developers with remoting experience actually find TCP simpler to use. This example shows that it certainly isn't complicated. Using HTTP involves IIS; using TCP does not. The channel tag has two attributes: ref sets the protocol, and port is a port that you choose fairly arbitrarily. Use a large number (between 9000 and 10,000 is good) that you don't believe is already in use on your server for some other remoting application.

When the configuration file is complete, add a post-build event, following the process first discussed in Chapter 11, but using this command line:

```
copy app.config "$(TargetPath).config"
```

When you build several projects in the same solution, the executable files associated with the project all go to a Debug or Release folder under the solution folder, not under the project folder. This command uses the full path and name of the executable being created, and adds the string .config, to build the location and filename to be used when copying app.config. Unlike the relative paths used in some other copy commands involving app.config in other chapters, this path is absolute. If your project folder's complete path involves a folder with spaces in the name (and there are plenty in a path like C:\Documents and Settings\ yourname\My Documents\Visual Studio Projects, which is quite likely the folder where your projects are created), the copy command will fail without the double quotes around the copy target.

Because you're relying on a post-build event to copy the configuration file for you, you'll need to rebuild the application when you change the configuration file. If you prefer, you can edit app.config manually and then apply the same edits to GreetingServer.exe.config to avoid having to build the application.

DON'T LOSE YOUR EDITS

If you edit only GreetingServer.exe.config to make a configuration change, the next time you build your project, the contents of app.config will be copied over your changes. Never edit GreetingServer.exe.config without making the same changes to app.config.

Notice that you don't need to change anything in your class library to make your class remoted. Once it inherits from `MarshalByRefObject`, it's remotable. The only code you write is the single line in the application that loads the configuration file. The real work is getting the configuration file right. That can be a lot of work; when the configuration file is wrong the error messages are rarely helpful. Work slowly and methodically when you are changing a remoting configuration file and trying to solve errors.

Changing the Client to Use the Remoted Object

Just as the class library needed very few changes to become a remoted library, so the client code needs very few changes to use the remoted object. Again, a configuration file does the heavy lifting. In the constructor of the `Form1` class, before the line that creates a new `Greeter` object, add this line:

```
Runtime::Remoting::RemotingConfiguration::Configure("GreetingClient.exe.config");
```

Add a configuration file to the `GreetingClient` project, and edit it to read like this:

```
<configuration>
   <system.runtime.remoting>
      <application>
         <client>
            <wellknown
               type="Greeting.Greeter, Greeting"
               url="tcp://111.222.33.44:9555/Greeter"
            />
         </client>
      </application>
   </system.runtime.remoting>
</configuration>
```

Make sure that you replace the IP address in this file with the IP address of the second machine, where you plan to deploy the remoted object and server application. The numbers after the IP address are the port: They must match the port in the server application's configuration file. The last part of the `url` attribute must match the `objectUri` attribute in the server application's configuration file, and the type attributes in the two files must match. You don't need a channels element in the client configuration file.

Add a post-build event to the `GreetingClient` project, with this command line:

```
copy app.config "$(TargetPath).config"
```

There is an unfortunate side-effect of building several executable projects under the same solution; the debugger doesn't seem to know where to find things. To work around this, set the working directory for the debugger to match the location of all the executable and configuration files. Open the properties page for the `GreetingClient` project, and select Debugging. As in Figure 14.3, set the `WorkingDirectory` attribute to `$(TargetDir)`.

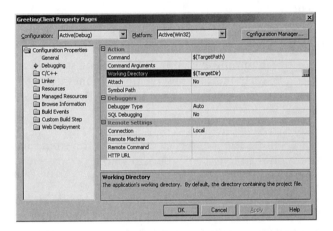

FIGURE 14.3 Setting the working directory for debugging, to ensure that the configuration file is found.

Build the solution and make sure both configuration files were copied to the Greeting\Debug folder.

Deploying to the Remote Machine

Copy greetingserver.exe, greetingserver.exe.config, and greeting.dll to a working folder on the other machine. It doesn't matter what the folder is called, and it doesn't have to be under wwwroot. Also copy people.xml to the root of the C drive on that machine, because the code looks in that hard-coded location. You don't need to copy any other files, edit any of the files you copy, or configure anything on the other machine.

On the remote machine, double-click greetingserver.exe to run it. Click the Listen button. When the Listening text appears, return to your client machine and press F5 to run the client under the debugger. Click each button in turn and confirm it is still working. That's how simple remoting is.

Perhaps you suspect that the client code is still using the local version of the `Greeter` object that it used during testing. You can easily prove that it's not. Stop debugging, and edit Greeter.cpp, changing the `Greet()` method to read like this:

```
String* Greeter::Greet()
{
    return "Hey, it's me!";
}
```

DEBUG LOCALLY

It can be awkward to make changes to a project that uses remoting when it is spread across two machines. A debug cycle that involves copying files from the development machine to the production server quickly becomes annoying. If you comment out the call to `Configure()` in the constructor of the client's form object, you'll be using the local version of the `Greeter` class, which will make development go much more quickly if you are expanding. Just remember to restore the line when you are ready to test the fully-deployed solution.

Build the solution and run it, and then click the Greet button again. You'll see `"Hello!"`, not the new text, proving that it's the remote version that's being called.

Once everything's working, it's a good idea to break it on purpose so you can see what happens. Try each of these tasks in turn, returning everything to a working state after each one, and observe the error messages you receive:

- Close the server application, and then run the client and click a button.

- Remove people.xml from the root of C on the server and click each of the three buttons in turn. See how the exception thrown on the server comes back to you?

- Edit one of the configuration files so that the port in each is not the same.

- Edit the client configuration file to use the wrong IP address.

- Edit the `type` attribute in the server configuration file to point to a non-existent assembly.

- Edit the `type` attribute in the server configuration file to point to a non-existent class within an existing assembly.

Seeing these error messages under controlled conditions should make the debugging process a little simpler when you're using remoting on your own projects.

Communication Over Remoting

When the client application wants to tell the remoted object something, there's no problem: just call a method. The implementations in the remoted class can do anything, including updating the database, adding entries to an event log, and so on. But what if something happens on the server that the client application should know about?

For example, you might write a client application used by order takers. It might submit orders to the server application using remoting, and get price lists and availability by calling some other methods of a remoted class from time to time. How can the server application notify the clients of the remoted objects that it's time to get a new price list—or even push a price list back down to them? The answer lies with .NET events.

Basics of .NET Events

Events are a simple and robust notification technique used within the .NET runtime much as Windows messages were used by Windows programmers before .NET existed. For example, when the user clicks a button on a GUI, an event is generated. A method in your code handles that event and reacts to the button click. This behavior is extensible—you can add and react to your own events. You can even do this over the remoting boundary.

To keep the example as simple as possible, this section adds a custom event to the server application that is raised by clicking a button. The client application will handle the event by displaying a message box.

Long ago, C and C++ programmers arranged event callbacks using function pointers. These were extremely powerful, but like so much C++ power they could be hard to use. The .NET Framework supports a type-safe function pointer implementation called a *delegate*, and does so across programming languages. Events and delegates combine to create an easy-to-use publish-and-subscribe mechanism. Event sources keep a list of handlers that might be interested in the events they raise, and with a single line of code the source can raise the event to all the handlers at once.Event listeners create a delegate object and pass it to the source to add to the list of handlers. It's all made as simple as possible, and it all works beautifully over remoting.

Changes to the Remoting Server

To use .NET events on the server, the client creates an appropriate delegate and passes it to the server, which adds it to a list of handlers. These handlers will then be invoked when the user clicks a button on the server form.

There are a number of steps involved in adding events to a remoted application. You can complete them in whatever order you prefer, but the application will not be usable until they have all been done. The steps are as follows:

- Define the delegate to be passed from the client to the server.

- Define a class, available to the server, that represents the event handler on the client.

- Add the event handler list to a suitable class on the server, in this case the existing Greeter class.

- Change the Greeter class so that the server application can reach the instance that was created for the remote client.

- Add a button to the server form.

- Code a handler for the button click that alerts all listeners.

- Change the server remoting configuration file to support two-way communication.

- Implement a handler in the client for the event that comes from the server.

- Change the client remoting configuration file to support two-way communication.

- Write code in the client that creates a delegate and passes it to the server to be added to the list.

Each of these steps is described in detail in this section.

Defining a Delegate

A delegate is often described as a type-safe function pointer. A delegate that represents a function that takes a String* can't be used to point to a function that takes different parameters. Similarly, a delegate that represents a function that returns a String* can't be used to point to a function with a different return type. The signature and return type of the function are part of the definition of the delegate. This is why delegates are called type-safe.

When working with events, both the code that raises the event (the event source) and the code that handles the event (the event sink) define a delegate. This is not an object or an instance, but rather an idea or definition. In managed C++, you define a delegate with the __delegate keyword. Add this line to Greeter.h in the Greeting project, before the namespace definition:

```
public __delegate void RemoteAlert(String* str);
```

Any function that takes a String* and returns void can be used to create a RemoteAlert delegate representing that function. The server-side code just works with the delegate and need not be aware of the name or details of the function that was used to create it. This definition is in the Greeting assembly so that the other applications in the solution can all access it.

Defining the Event Handler Base Class

The event handler is a function that matches the signature of the delegate: In this example it must be a void function that takes a String*. The client application implements a class to hold this function, and passes a reference to an instance of the class up to the server, to be added to the list of event handlers maintained there. The class must be known to the server code, either because the server code includes a header file that defines it or because the server code has a reference to an assembly that defines it.

SHOP TALK

WHY USE INHERITANCE WITH EVENT HANDLERS?

The requirement that the handler class be known to the server causes trouble for many developers who are using remoting. They discover that events appear to work only when the server application and client application are in the same folder—in other words, when they are not really using remoting. Many have discovered that copying the client application to the remote server machine also enables events to work properly over remoting. Copying a client application to the server machine, even though it runs on a client machine, feels awkward. It also sets you up for frustrating debugging or maintenance work, because you might have to copy files again and again, and forgetting to copy might make the application fail even though there's nothing wrong with the code.

The technique I show in this chapter looks awkward at first glance. But it works, and even better it works without your having to copy the client application to the server machine. It's worth learning.

To make the event handler class known to the server, without the server having a reference to the entire client application, use a base class for the handler class. Define the base class in the class library, as part of the Greeting namespace. The server can add a reference to the class library and it will then gain access to the definition of this base class. The client will implement a class that inherits from this base class, and pass a reference to it (as a base class pointer) to the server. The server does not need to know about the specific base class that was implemented in the client application. This lessens the coupling between the client and the server and simplifies deployment and maintenance.

Add a class to the Greeting solution and name it RemoteHandlerBase. Edit remotehandler-base.h so that it reads like this:

```
#pragma once
using namespace System;

namespace Greeting
{
public __gc class RemoteHandlerBase: public MarshalByRefObject
    {
    public:
        void Alert(String* s)
        {
            HandleAlert(s);
        }
    protected:
        virtual void HandleAlert(String* s)=0;
    };
}
```

The class must inherit from `MarshalByRefObject`, because instances of a class derived from it will be passed from the client to the server, to be added to the handler list. It has two methods: `Alert()` and `HandleAlert()`. `HandleAlert()` does the actual work (it handles the `Alert` event when it is raised), and it's pure virtual in this base class. An implementation will be provided in any class that derives from `RemoteHandlerBase`. `Alert()` must be nonvirtual, and it just calls the virtual `HandleAlert()`function; the compiler will ensure that the appropriate derived class version is executed.

Changing the Greeter Class

The `Greeting` class library has grown from one class to two to support events. The next step is to change the `Greeter` class so that it maintains a list of events, and so that the server application can access a `Greeter` instance to raise an event.

Revise the class definition in Greeter.h so that it reads as follows:

```
public __gc class Greeter: public MarshalByRefObject
    {
    public:
        __event RemoteAlert* RemoteAlertEvent;
        String* Greet(String* name);
        String* Greet();
        Data::DataSet* Records();
        static void Alert(String* s);
        Greeter();
    private:
        static Collections::ArrayList* greeters=0;
    };
```

The new lines to be added are in bold text.

The `RemoteAlert` variable is decorated with the `__event` keyword. This indicates that it is actually a list of event handlers that match the `RemoteAlert` signature. New event handlers can be added to this list with the += operator. The `Greeter` class needs no code to manage or maintain this list; that code is all generated for you behind the scenes when you use the `__event` keyword.

The `Alert` method is a static method: When it is called it will invoke all the handlers for all the `Greeter` objects that have been created. This is not the only way to use events in remoting; a different application might have a nonstatic `Alert` method, so that each `Greeter` object alerted its own listeners. However, in this example application, the client object has one `Greeter` instance, obtained through remoting, and the server application has no reference to that object. Using a static method to access all instances provides access to the client's `Greeter` object from within the server application.

A constructor is added to the `Greeter` class so that it can maintain an instance list. This is the static variable called `greeters`. As each `Greeter` object is created, it will add itself to the list. That is how the `Alert()` method can reach all the `Greeter` objects that have been created.

In Greeter.cpp, add this implementation of the constructor:

```
Greeter::Greeter()
{
    if (!greeters)
        greeters = new Collections::ArrayList();
    greeters->Add(this);
}
```

The `ArrayList` collection is an array that will grow itself as more items are added. It's easy to use; this code just adds another `Greeter` reference to the list.

Next, add this implementation of `Alert()`:

```
void Greeter::Alert(String* s)
{
    for (int i=0; i < greeters->Count; i++)
        (static_cast<Greeter*>(greeters->get_Item(i)))->RemoteAlertEvent(s);
}
```

This code loops through the `ArrayList`, using `get_Item()` to access each item in the list in turn. The item is cast to a `Greeter*` (ArrayList keeps the collection as `Object*` references) and then this code raises each `Greeter`'s event. The events are raised by calling the `RemoteAlertEvent` member variable as though it were a function. (It's actually an instance of a class, generated by the __event keyword, that overrides the (operator, also called the function call operator.) Whether one event handler has been added to the list, or several, the list of events will take care of notifying each handler in turn that the event has been raised, and passing along the parameter: in this case a `String*` that was passed to `Alert()`.

Modifying the Form

Using the toolbox, drag another button onto `Form1` of the server application. Change the name and text to `Alert`. Double-click it to edit the button click handler, and add this code:

```
private: System::Void Alert_Click(System::Object *  sender,
                                  System::EventArgs *  e)
{
  Greeting::Greeter::Alert("The server Alert button was clicked");
}
```

This handler just calls the static `Alert()` method of the `Greeter` class, which as you've already seen will raise the `Alert` event to all the handlers that were added to the event lists in any `Greeter` objects that were created.

Changing the Server Configuration File

In this example application, remoting is controlled through a configuration file. To enable event handling, and passing callback references from client to server, the configuration file must be changed slightly.

Find this element in the app.config file in the `GreetingServer` project:

```
<channel ref="tcp" port="9555" />
```

Replace it with this expanded version:

```
<channel ref="tcp" port="9555">
   <serverProviders>
      <formatter ref="binary" typeFilterLevel="Full" />
   </serverProviders>
</channel>
```

This change is required in version 1.1 of the .NET Framework and up; older samples or articles that cover remoting will not mention it. Security settings in version 1.1 do not support callbacks by default, because they might represent a vulnerability. Client code is letting server code decide to trigger the execution of client code. You have to deliberately turn the feature on.

Implementing the Client Event Handler

Add a class called `RemoteHandler` to the `GreetingClient` project. This class inherits from `RemoteHandlerBase` and implements the `HandleAlert()` method. Edit remotehandler.h so that it reads like this:

```
#pragma once
using namespace System;
namespace GreetingClient
{
public __gc class RemoteHandler: public Greeting::RemoteHandlerBase
   {
   protected:
       void HandleAlert(String* msg);
   };
}
```

Because `RemoteHandler` inherits from `RemoteHandlerBase`, which in turn inherits from `MarshalByRefObject`, instances of this class can be passed over remoting by reference. These references are used to invoke the `HandleAlert()` method when the event is raised.

Edit remotehandler.cpp, adding this implementation of HandleAlert():

```
namespace GreetingClient
{
void RemoteHandler::HandleAlert(String* msg)
    {
        Windows::Forms::MessageBox::Show(msg,"Alert from server");
    }
}
```

This method is part of the client application. The message box it displays will appear on the screen of the client computer when the Alert button is clicked on the server computer.

Changing the Client Configuration File

Just as the remoting configuration file for the server application required changes to support events over remoting, so does the remoting configuration file for the client. Open app.config in the GreetingClient solution, and after the <client> tag that is already there, add this element:

```
<channel ref="tcp" port="0">
   <serverProviders>
      <formatter ref="binary" typeFilterLevel="Full" />
   </serverProviders>
</channel>
```

As in the server configuration file, this element takes care of the security restrictions, making it clear that you are deliberately using callbacks over remoting and that you trust the server application to trigger execution of parts of the client application. The <channel> element specifies a port of 0, which means that any available port can be used.

In the constructor for the Form1 class in GreetingClient, add this line after the call to Configure:

```
Runtime::Remoting::Channels::ChannelServices::RegisterChannel(
   new Runtime::Remoting::Channels::Tcp::TcpServerChannel("callback", 9556));
```

This line sets up the listening channel on which the callbacks will come. Choose a port that is not the same as the port in the configuration file, and that you are confident is not already in use on the network.

Creating a Handler and Adding It to the List on the Server

The constructor for the client Form1 is where the event handler will be passed to the server. As soon as the form is created, this client will be listening for Alert events from the server. Add these lines after the line that creates a Greeter object:

```
RemoteHandler* rh = new RemoteHandler();
Greeting::RemoteHandlerBase* rhb =
            static_cast<Greeting::RemoteHandlerBase*>(rh);
greet->RemoteAlertEvent += new RemoteAlert(rhb, &RemoteHandler::Alert);
```

This code creates an instance of the `RemoteHandler` class, defined here in the client. It then casts that instance to a `RemoteHandlerBase*`, because the server is only aware of the `RemoteHandlerBase` class. (`RemoteHandlerBase` is in the `Greeting` assembly, and the client has a reference to that assembly, so client code knows about both `RemoteHandler` and `RemoteHandlerBase`.) The final line of this code snippet creates a delegate using the special C++ syntax. The first parameter to the delegate constructor is a pointer to the object, and the second parameter uses the pointer-to-member syntax to create a function pointer. Once constructed, the delegate is added directly to the event handler list in the `Greeting` object by accessing the `public` variable and using the += operator.

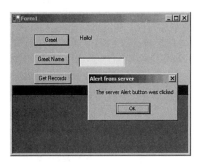

FIGURE 14.4 The client application displays a message box when it receives an event from the server.

Build the application, and copy greetingserver.exe, greetingserver.exe.config, and greeting.dll to a working folder on the other machine. Make sure the client configuration file contains the name or IP address of that other machine. On the second machine, run the server application by double-clicking it and then click the Listen button. On the local machine, start the client application, either by double-clicking the .EXE or by pressing F5 in Visual Studio. You can confirm that the buttons (Greet, Greet Name, and Get Records) still work as before. Then go to the remote machine and click the Alert button on the server. A message box like the one in Figure 14.4 should appear on the client machine. Nothing should appear to happen on the server machine.

Using events involves a certain amount of setup (changing configuration files, creating a base class for the event handler, adding event handler lists to a class, and so on), but once this infrastructure is in place, you can add as many custom events and handlers to your system as you want. The server can then notify all the client applications about changes or updates whenever they happen.

Choosing Lifetime and Lifecycle Options Appropriately

The example in this chapter created a remoted class called `Greeter`. `Greeter` is a well-known object, meaning that client applications ask for it by name. The alternative to a well-known object is a client-activated object. Well-known objects are activated on the server when a method of the object is first called (constructing the proxy object on the client does not create an object on the server). If the object is a Singleton, as in this chapter's example, it is not destroyed when the call returns, but waits on the server. All subsequent method calls (from any and all clients that are connecting to this server) are handled by this server object. If calls stop coming in, the object does not wait forever; eventually it is cleaned up on the server. You can control the amount of time that a Singleton object will exist after the last call it handles with a <lifetime> element in the configuration file, within the <application> element. Here is an example <lifetime> element:

```
<lifetime
    leaseTime = "10M"
    sponsorshipTimeOut = "2M"
    renewOnCallTime = "2M"
    LeaseManagePollTime = "10s"
/>
```

This element has four attributes:

- leaseTime—After this much time has elapsed since the creation of the object without a call for it, the cleanup process will begin. The default value is five minutes. Use zero ("0M") to achieve an infinite lifetime for the object.

- sponsorshipTimeOut—The cleanup process begins with a call to every remote client that has been using the object, asking if they still want it. (All this code is behind the scenes; you don't need to write anything to handle it.) The amount of time specified in this attribute controls how long the server will wait for an answer before assuming the client is no longer running and therefore is finished with the object. The default value is two minutes.

- renewOnCallTime—After the object is in use, this is the amount of time that will elapse after each call before cleanup will begin. The default value is two minutes.

- LeaseManagePollTime—How often the lease manager checks to see whether lifetimes have elapsed. Default is 10 seconds.

In all these attributes, a number followed by M indicates a number of minutes, and a number followed by S indicates a number of seconds.

If the object is SingleCall, it is cleaned up after every call and does not persist between calls. You must decide whether Singleton or SingleCall is the right lifetime option for your application. In this example, the Greeter object holds a list of event handlers, so it must continue to exist between calls—that makes Singleton the right choice. In another application, calls might be infrequent and stateless, making SingleCall the right choice.

Client-activated objects provide an alternative to well-known objects and allow multiple remoted instances of a class to exist at the same time. With well-known objects, either one instance exists and is shared by all clients, or one instance is created and then destroyed for each method call, with no state persisting between calls. The client-activated approach allows you to create an object that lives between calls and can hold state, and to create a different instance for each client that is using the application. Use `type=activated` instead of `type=wellknown` in the configuration file. The lifetime is still governed in the same way; when the client that created a particular instance hasn't used it for a while, the lease may expire and the object may be cleaned up. Use the same `<lifetime>` element to control the lifetime of an activated object as shown for a well-known object.

SHOP TALK

REMOTING VERSUS WEB SERVICES

Web Services, covered in Chapter 10, "Writing and Consuming a Web Service," allow client code to execute code on a remote machine over the Internet. It's reasonable to wonder what the difference is between the two and under what circumstances you would choose one over the other.

Web Services are an excellent way for unrelated applications to communicate. For example, an application written by Company A can use a Web Service exposed by Company B to place an order for products or services. The Web Service is completely self-describing, and because Web Services rely on cross-platform standards like HTTP and XML, there's no need for the two firms to be using the same programming language, operating system, or data formats.

Remoting is useful in more tightly-coupled scenarios. XML can be verbose, and Web Services use XML to describe everything. Each time you call a Web Service that returns a data set, it also sends you the schema for that data set, just to be sure that the data is self-describing. In contrast, two applications that communicate using remoting are rather like an old married couple who can finish each other's sentences. The example in this chapter relies on conveniences such as both client and server applications having a reference to the `Greeter` class library. These shared definitions allow the applications to exchange information in a more compact manner.

Which should you use? If you are writing only half the application, and relying on a business partner to write the other half, agree to use Web Services and you need not agree on anything else. If you're writing a distributed application, with both halves developed by the same team, consider remoting. It's convenient and efficient.

In Brief

- A remoting application consists of two applications (Windows applications, console applications, or Windows services), one on each computer.

- Remoting behavior is controlled by a configuration file for each application. Settings in these two files must correspond for remoting to work.

- Once remoting is configured, making the calls is no different from using local objects.

- Remoting supports events, allowing notifications to flow from machine to machine with very little effort.

- Remoting and Web Services each serve their own purpose in distributed development, with remoting more appropriate for applications with both client and server developed by the same team.

Building Advanced User Interfaces in Managed C++

Extending Windows Controls

The Windows Forms controls presented in Chapter 4, "Building Simple User Interfaces with Windows Forms," can be used to create rich and varied user interfaces. Think of these controls as the starting point for your applications. You can build all your forms from the WinForms controls alone, but you are by no means restricted to them.

You can create a single control of your own that inherits from one of the WinForms controls, and extends the library functionality. Alternatively, you can create your own controls by pulling together two or more WinForms controls into a WinForms user control. This collection of controls and code can be placed onto any other form, and works as a self-contained piece of the user interface.

To build this chapter's samples, start by creating a WinForms application called AdvancedUI. In a separate instance of Visual Studio.NET, create a Windows control library project called control. These two solutions will form the basis of the examples shown throughout this chapter.

Extending a Library Control

A class that inherits from a WinForms control need only provide the extra functionality you choose to add; the basic functionality is all inherited from the base class with no coding required by you. To demonstrate how simple it can be, this section shows how to build a text box that accepts only numbers. There are two ways to achieve this: one is to react to each keystroke and discard anything that's not a number, and the other is to wait until the control loses focus and then validate the text it holds. The second approach validates entries that are pasted in as well as those that are typed, so it's a better approach.

Start by adding a generic C++ class called NumbersOnlyTextBox to the control project, and edit NumbersOnlyTextBox.h so it looks like this:

```
using namespace System;
namespace control
{
    public __gc class NumbersOnlyTextBox :
        public System::Windows::Forms::TextBox
    {
    };
}
```

Leave NumbersOnlyTextBox.cpp as a stub file that just brings in the header file. You can't just delete it, or else the class won't be compiled as part of compiling the project. It should look like this:

```
#include "StdAfx.h"
#include ".\numbersonlytextbox.h"
#using <mscorlib.dll>
```

Because this text box inherits from System::Windows::Forms::TextBox, it has all the properties and methods of that class. There are no mandatory steps involved in inheriting from text box, but in order to give this text box different behavior than the library TextBox class, you have to write some code that implements that behavior.

Whenever a form is submitted or accepted, a Validating event is raised. All controls can override the OnValidating() method to validate themselves. In addition, many controls have a Valid property (get_Valid() in C++ syntax) that can be used to determine whether a control is valid. Because this control will have this property, you can use it in the override of OnValidating(). Add the entire method inside the class definition:

```
protected:
    void OnValidating(System::ComponentModel::CancelEventArgs* e)
    {
        if (!Valid)
            e->Cancel = true;
    System::Windows::Forms::TextBox::OnValidating(e);
    return;
    }
```

When the content of the text box is not valid, this code cancels the event that triggered the validation, which for a text box is usually switching focus to another control or clicking a button that causes validation.

The next step is to write the `Valid` property. It can rely on a helper method called `IsValid()`. Add this code inside the class definition:

```
public:
    [System::ComponentModel::Browsable(false)]
     __property bool get_Valid()
    {
        return IsValid(Text);
    }
```

The attribute on this property keeps it from appearing in the Properties window for the control when it's used in the designer. By default, the properties you write are added to the Properties window. This is great for design-time properties, but not helpful for a runtime read-only property like `Valid`.

The last step in creating this control is to write `IsValid()`, which works with any string rather than only with the text property of the control. Add this method inside the class definition:

```
private:
    bool IsValid(String* Contents)
    {
        Regex* re = new Regex("\\d*");
        Match* m;
        m = re->Match(Contents);
        bool test = m->Success
                && m->Index == 0
                && m->Length == Contents->Length;
        if (!test)
            System::Windows::Forms::MessageBox::Show("enter only numbers here");
        return test;
    }
```

For this code to compile, you need to add this line at the top of the file:

```
using namespace System::Text::RegularExpressions;
```

The `IsValid()` method relies on the regular expressions support in the .NET Framework to confirm that the string consists entirely of digits (0–9). You could construct a more complex regular expression that could handle characters such as – and .; this expression will match positive integers of any length. It ensures that in addition to finding the pattern (\d represents a digit and * means any number of them) the pattern begins at the start of the string and lasts until the end of the string. This ensures that strings like 1a and b2 will rejected even though they contain digits.

To use this control, first build it and correct any errors. Then switch to the instance of Visual Studio in which AdvancedUI, the WinForms project, is open. Add a reference to the controls assembly (you have to browse from the .NET tab on the Add Reference dialog box).

Use the toolbox to drag two text boxes onto the form. Right-click on the surface of the form and choose View Code to open form1.h. About half way down the file, find this line:

```
private: System::Windows::Forms::TextBox *  textBox1;
```

Change it to read like this:

```
private: control::NumbersOnlyTextBox *  textBox1;
```

Expand the InitializeComponent() method, and find this line:

```
this->textBox1 = new System::Windows::Forms::TextBox();
```

Change it to read like this:

```
this->textBox1 = new control::NumbersOnlyTextBox();
```

Build the project and switch back to the designer; you should still see two text boxes on the form. If there is a problem with the changes you made to the code, the upper text box will disappear. When you correct the code, you will again see the text box in the designer. Run the project, and try using Tab to move to the second text box while the first still holds the default text, textBox1. You should get an error message from the control itself. Confirm that the second text box allows you to type whatever you want and does not produce error messages.

Creating a User Control

When you created the control project, a user control was generated for you with the rather unfortunate name of controlControl. It's quite difficult to change the name, and simpler just to remove it and add a new one with a better name. Remove controlcontrol.h and controlcontrol.cpp from the project, and then right-click the project in Solution Explorer and choose Add, Add New Item. Select Windows User Control. Name the control PhoneNumber.

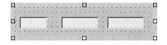

FIGURE 15.1   Placing three text boxes on the user control.

A blank design surface appears, much like the empty form in a Windows Forms project. Drag three text boxes onto the surface, set the text property of each to an empty string, and then resize the text boxes and the surface until your control resembles Figure 15.1.

Open the code for form1.h and change the declaration and the creation of each text box to be a `control::NumbersOnlyTextBox`, as in the previous section. Even though this user control is in the same namespace as the text box class you've defined, the designer doesn't recognize the class unless you provide the namespace explicitly. The declarations should end up reading like this:

```
private: control::NumbersOnlyTextBox *  textBox1;
private: control::NumbersOnlyTextBox *  textBox2;
private: control::NumbersOnlyTextBox *  textBox3;
```

The `InitializeComponent()` method should start like this:

```
void InitializeComponent(void)
{
    this->textBox1 = new control::NumbersOnlyTextBox();
    this->textBox2 = new control::NumbersOnlyTextBox();
    this->textBox3 = new control::NumbersOnlyTextBox();
    this->SuspendLayout();
```

At this point you can use this user control on a form, but it's going to be more useful if it does more than just hold the three text boxes. For example, why not expose a `Text` property that combines the three text boxes, and saves a little bit of coding for all the applications that use the `PhoneNumber` control? Add this method to the class definition:

```
public:
__property String* get_Text()
{
    System::Text::StringBuilder* sb = new System::Text::StringBuilder();
    if (String::Compare(textBox1->Text,"") != 0)
    {
        sb->Append("(");
        sb->Append(textBox1->Text);
        sb->Append(") ");
    }
    sb->Append(textBox2->Text);
    sb->Append(" ");
    sb->Append(textBox3->Text);
    return sb->ToString();
}
```

Build the project to make sure there are no errors, and then switch back to the `AdvancedUI` project.

You could add a `PhoneNumber` control to the form by dragging some other control on and then editing the behind-the-scenes code, as you did in the previous section for the

NumbersOnlyTextBox, but there's no obvious choice for a control that's close to a PhoneNumber control. At this point it's best to add the control to the toolbox so you can drag it on to the form like any other control. Here's how to do so:

1. Open Form1.h in the designer.

2. Select the My User Controls tab.

3. Right-click the empty part of the toolbox, and choose Add/Remove Items.

4. On the Customize Toolbox dialog box, select the .NET Framework Components tab and click Browse.

5. Browse to control.dll in the control folder and click Open.

6. Scroll through the list of controls and make sure NumbersOnlyTextBox in the control namespace and PhoneNumber in the control namespace both have a selected check box on the left.

7. Click OK to add these controls to the tab.

Once the PhoneNumber control is on the tab, you can drag one onto the form like any other control. (You can try a NumbersOnlyTextBox, too, if you like.)

Drag on a PhoneNumber and a button. Change the name and the text of the button to Phone, and double-click it to add a click handler. Add this code to that handler:

```
private: System::Void Phone_Click(System::Object *  sender,
                                   System::EventArgs *  e)
{
    String* msg = S"Phone control text: ";
    msg = msg->Concat(phoneNumber1->Text);
    MessageBox::Show(msg);
}
```

Build the application and run it. Notice which text boxes allow you to enter arbitrary text and which demand numbers. Click the Phone button to see the Text property of the control in use, as shown in Figure 15.2.

That's how simple it is to add your own controls to an application, whether they are an extension of a library control with inheritance, or an aggregation of several controls, with useful properties of the combined controls layered onto the aggregation.

FIGURE 15.2   The text property of the user control simplifies coding for the forms that use the control.

Using Drag and Drop

By default, a form and the controls on it do not support drag and drop. A text box will support copy and paste with Ctrl+C and Ctrl+V, but will not allow you to drag a little piece of text onto the text box. It will also not allow you to grab the text in a text box and drag it elsewhere.

Making a Control a Drop Target

Changing a control on your form so that it can act as a drop target requires three steps:

1. Change the `AllowDrop` property to `True`.

2. Write code to handle the `DragEnter` event.

3. Write code to handle the `DragDrop` event.

Open Form1 of the `AdvancedUI` project in the designer, and select `textBox2`, the ordinary text box. In the Properties window, find the `AllowDrop` property and change it to `True`. Then click the lightning bolt at the top of the Properties window to display events. Find `DragEnter` in the list and double-click it to add a handler. Add code to the handler so that it reads like this:

```
private: System::Void textBox2_DragEnter(System::Object *  sender,
                             System::Windows::Forms::DragEventArgs *  e)
{
    if (e->Data->GetDataPresent(DataFormats::Text))
        e->Effect = DragDropEffects::Copy;
    else
        e->Effect = DragDropEffects::None;
}
```

This code uses the `DragEventArgs` parameter to change the cursor style as the user drags something over `textBox2`. If the data being dragged is text, the familiar copy cursor is displayed. If it's any other format, the slashed circle icon that indicates you can't drop your data here is displayed.

If you've shown the user a copy cursor, there is every chance the user will let go of the drag and drop over `textBox2`. That will trigger a `DragDrop` event. Back in the designer, use the event view of the Properties window to add a handler for `DragDrop`, and then edit its code to read like this:

```
private: System::Void textBox2_DragDrop(System::Object *  sender,
                             System::Windows::Forms::DragEventArgs *  e)
{
    textBox2->Text = e->Data->GetData(DataFormats::Text)->ToString();
}
```

The single line of code inside this handler just gets the data that was dropped, makes sure it's a string, and puts it into the Text property of the text box. Notice that even though this is the DragDrop handler for textBox2, you could put the data wherever you wanted. It's up to you to write a meaningful and consistent user interface.

Build the project and run it to test dragging and dropping. Open some other application (Word, Notepad, or Internet Explorer will all do) and highlight some text. Click and hold to drag the text, and drag it over the form as it runs. You should see the "No Drop" icon (the slashed circle) as you drag the text scrap over the background of the form, or any of the controls other than textBox2. When you drag over textBox2, the cursor will change to the arrow with a small + that indicates a copy. Let go, and the text you dragged appears in the text box.

Now try dragging something else. For example, open Windows Explorer and drag a file over the surface of the application. Even as you drag it over textBox2, the cursor doesn't change, because this application doesn't accept files as drag-and-drop data.

Try one more test before closing the application. Try dragging information out of one of the text boxes: highlight the text with the mouse, and then click and drag. Nothing happens. Although textBox2 has been enabled as a drop target, none of the boxes has been enabled as a drag source.

Making a Control a Drag Source

Enabling a text box as a drag source is a little trickier than enabling one to be a drop target. The first decision to make is which user behavior will start the dragging? It's usually a click-and-hold on the mouse, so you will handle the MouseDown event in the text box. But, of course, users click the mouse in a text box for many reasons other than to drag and drop. When you add a handler for the MouseDown event in the form itself, you prevent ordinary mouse behavior from happening in that text box—including such simple tasks as selecting the text you might want to drag! There are some complicated ways around it: A simple one is to support dragging from your text box with a right-click and drag rather than a left-click.

In the designer for Form1, select textBox1 and switch to the Events view in the Properties window. Double-click MouseDown to add a handler. Edit the handler so it reads like this:

```
private: System::Void textBox1_MouseDown(System::Object *  sender,
                              System::Windows::Forms::MouseEventArgs *  e)
{
    if (e->Button == System::Windows::Forms::MouseButtons::Right)
        textBox1->DoDragDrop(textBox1->Text, DragDropEffects::Copy);
}
```

That's all it takes to hand the contents of your text box to the framework, ready to be dropped on a waiting drop target, on this same application or another one. Build and run the project, type a number into the upper text box, and then select the number and right-click and drag it into the lower text box. It's a nice intuitive interface. Also, try dragging into Notepad or some other drop-target application, just to demonstrate to yourself that it works.

It's actually simpler to drag from other kinds of controls, such as list boxes, than from a text box, because the act of clicking the mouse on those controls doesn't wipe out the user's selection. Experiment a little, and you'll be ready to add full mouse support to all your Windows applications.

Using GDI+

GDI+, the latest version of the Windows graphics design interface library, enables you to add eye-popping graphics to your applications with very little code. Often a GDI+ application can draw an image from scratch more quickly than it would draw a saved bitmap or JPEG of that image.

You can use the techniques in this section to draw an image on the background of a form, to build a specialized control, or to produce other kinds of graphical output such as a chart. Drawing in GDI+ involves three kinds of objects: pens, brushes, and text. All three draw on a surface represented by an instance of the `Graphics` class.

Getting a Graphics Object

Because all drawing requires a `Graphics` object, the first step in any drawing code is obtaining an instance. There are three ways to do so:

- If your drawing code is in a handler for the Paint event, perhaps for the background of a form or control, the second argument of the handler method is a `PaintEventArgs` pointer; it has a `Graphics` property your code can access.

- If your drawing code is in some other member function of a form or control, you can call its `CreateGraphics` method to reach the `Graphics` object associated with the form or control.

- To draw into an `Image` object (perhaps because your code is generating a JPEG), use the static `Graphics::FromImage()` method, passing in a reference to the `Image` object.

Once you have a `Graphics` object, you draw on it by calling methods of the `Graphics` class, and passing in drawing objects, such as pens or brushes, and coordinates that position the shape or line on the drawing surface.

FINDING COLOR NAMES

The `Color` structure has a number of colors defined as constants. You can see these in the online help, but many people won't be sure exactly what color AliceBlue or PapayaWhip really is. To see the colors with their names, use the same designer you use to build your WinForms application or control. Select a button, or the form background, and click next to the `BackColor` property in the Properties window. On the mini dialog box that appears, select the Web tab, which presents a huge number of colors along with their names. Make a note of the ones you like—the same names are used for the constants in the `Color` structure.

If there's a color you want to use that doesn't seem to exist as a predefined color constant, or if you want a color that's partially transparent, you can use the `FromArgb()` method of the `Color` class: It uses the opaqueness (a number from 0 to 255 where 0 is completely transparent) and the red, green, and blue values to create exactly the color you desire.

Drawing with Pens

Pens are used to draw lines. A pen has a width, a color, a style (for example solid or dashed), and end styles (called caps), such as arrows. To create a red pen two pixels wide, you pass the color and width to the constructor:

```
Drawing::Pen* p = new Drawing::
➥Pen(Drawing::Color::Red, 2);
```

With a `Graphics` object, you call its methods, passing in this pen. For example, to draw a line

```
g->DrawLine(p, 10, 10, 50, 50);
```

The four numbers in this function call are the x and y coordinates of the starting point, followed by the x and y coordinates of the end point. You can also construct `Point` objects and pass them to `DrawLine()`.

To draw a hollow shape, use `DrawRectangle`, `DrawEllipse`, or `DrawPolygon`. (A square is just a special case of a rectangle, and a circle is a special case of an ellipse.) You can also draw Bezier curves and other complex shapes.

Painting with Brushes

To fill a shape or area, you need a brush. A solid brush fills a shape with a single color, but there are also patterned brushes such as `HatchBrush` and `TextureBrush`, and you can fill a shape with a blend of colors using a single brush—if it's a `LinearGradientBrush` or `PathGradientBrush`. (`SolidBrush` and `TextureBrush` are in the `Drawing` namespace; the other brushes are in the `Drawing::Drawing2D` namespace.) The constructor for a `LinearGradientBrush` takes two points and two colors: The brush will fade from one color to the other through the rectangle.

Once you have a brush, you use methods of the `Graphics` instance to draw shapes on it: `FillRectangle()`, `FillEllipse()`, and `FillPolygon`, for example. If you want a different border around the shape, draw a hollow shape with a pen that's just slightly larger than the filled shape.

Here's an example of code that draws a rectangle on the surface of a form when a button on that form is clicked:

```
private: System::Void Draw_Click(System::Object *  sender,
                                   System::EventArgs *  e)
{
    Drawing::Drawing2D::LinearGradientBrush* b =
        new Drawing::Drawing2D::LinearGradientBrush(Point(0,00), Point(100,100),
                                    Drawing::Color::Red,Drawing::Color::Blue);
    Drawing::Graphics* g = CreateGraphics();
    g->FillRectangle(b, Rectangle(175,50,100,55));
    b->Dispose();
    g->Dispose();
}
```

Add a button to the Form1 surface and change the name and text to Draw. Double-click the button to edit the handler for the click event, and add this code to the handler.

If you're familiar with the MFC approach to drawing, you'll notice here that you don't need to save the old pen or brush before you draw and then restore it. The Framework takes care of the housekeeping, and makes sure your code doesn't interfere with other drawing code elsewhere in the application. It is a good idea, however, to clean up your Graphics object, as well as your pens, brushes, and so on when you're finished with them by calling Dispose().

Writing Text

Writing text is slightly more complex than drawing a hollow or filled shape: The DrawString method of the Graphics object takes the following parameters:

- The string to be written

- A Font object (which can be constructed using a face name and a size)

- A brush with which to fill in each letter

- The coordinates at which to start writing the string

- Optionally, a StringFormat object that can cause the text to be written on an angle, from right to left, or clipped slight differently than the default

These lines of code draw text on a Graphics object g, which has already been obtained:

```
String* text = "Red to Blue";
Drawing::Font* f = new Drawing::Font("Arial", 12);
Drawing::SolidBrush* b2 = new Drawing::SolidBrush(Drawing::Color::Black);
g->DrawString(text, f, b2, Point(175, 110));
f->Dispose();
b2->Dispose();
```

To see this code run, edit the Draw handler described in the previous section and add these lines just before the call to g->Dispose(). Build and run the application, enter a number in the upper text box to prevent validation errors, and click the Draw button to see the text underneath the gradient-filled rectangle.

Using GDI+ makes adding graphical touches to your applications much simpler than it has been in the past. You can create information-rich interfaces, or just impress your users by going beyond gray forms with gray buttons on them. Add some color, some shapes, and some alternative ways of communicating to the applications you build.

LANGUAGE, CULTURE, AND LOCALE

There are several words used in internationalization and localization that might need a little explaining. Let's start with internationalization: That's the overall process of realizing that an application might be used by people who read a different language than the developer creating the application, and might format dates and numbers differently as well. It's an architectural approach that you use from the beginning of a project, for example, by using `ToShortDateString()` instead of passing in a hard-coded date format. Localization is the job of making a new satellite assembly or resource file for a particular location. It is done once for each locale into which the application will be translated.

A locale is more specific than a language. English, for example, is spoken in many countries, but not identically so. Words such as *color* (which might appear on a button or menu item) are spelled differently in US English than in Canadian English, for example, and there are differences between French in France and French in Canada, or Spanish in the US and Spanish in Spain. A culture includes a language, a country, and a set of rules about formatting numbers, currency, times, and dates.

A Windows application uses two culture settings: one called `Culture`, used for dates and numbers, and the other called `UICulture`. Generally speaking, users can change `Culture` themselves on the Control Panel, but `UICulture` reflects the version of Windows the user has installed. If you bought the US English version of Windows, your `UICulture` is US English regardless of your Control Panel settings. You can install the Multilingual User Interface Pack, which among other things lets you change your `UICulture` from the Control Panel.

Internationalizing and Localizing a Windows Application

Although many (perhaps even most) commercial software users speak and read English, not all do. Those for whom English is a second language often prefer to use software that works in their own language. If you want to ship versions of your software that support more than one language, you need to think about internationalization and localization.

Designing for Internationalization

Windows has recognized the need for multi-language support for years, enabling users to set their locale and culture information on the Control Panel, and then using that information wherever possible in the user interface. Your application almost certainly leverages that power without knowing it. For example, when you convert a `DateTime` object to a string by calling its `ToShortDateString()` method, the format of the string depends on the user's culture settings. The same date might be represented as 03/04/2003 or 04/03/2003, depending on the user's location and settings. Similarly the number 1.234 in North America is written as 1,234 in Europe, and you don't have to write code to support this: When a number is converted to a string the local format rules are applied.

Support for different formats for numbers and dates is useful and convenient, but what about that form with buttons that read Add or Delete? What about your error messages and your prompts? There are many places within an application that reflect the language in which an application was developed. Building a WinForms application makes it simpler to support multiple languages and localization rules without writing a lot of code.

To build an application that supports multiple languages, you actually create multiple assemblies. The first contains all your executable code and one set of resources (text properties of controls and the like) prepared in the original language you used when developing the application. Satellite assemblies contain only the resources, translated into a different language or locale. The Framework checks the user's culture setting and loads the appropriate satellite assembly. If there is no satellite assembly corresponding to the user's setting, the original resources in the main assembly are used.

Localizing a Windows Application

To see how to localize a WinForms application, drag another button onto Form1 of the AdvancedUI project. Change the button's name to Hello and the text to Hello World. Double-click the button to add a handler, but don't add any code to the handler yet. Build the project and make sure it runs.

In the designer, select the entire form, and use the Properties window to change the Localizable property to True. Change the Language property of the form to French (Canada). Click the button and change the Text property to Bonjour Tout Le Monde. Lengthen the button to accommodate the text.

Build and run the application. Unless your copy of Windows is French Canadian, you should see Hello World on the button.

> ### CULTURE NAMES
>
> Culture names come in two parts: a language and a locale. The language part is the ISO standard two letter abbreviation: en for English, fr for French, de for German, and so on. The ISO list is available at
>
>   http://www.loc.gov/standards/
>   ➥iso639-2/englangn.html
>
> The locale part is also a standard two letter abbreviation: CA for Canada, US for the US, DE for Germany, and so on. The ISO list is kept up to date at (be sure to type this all on one line)
>
>   http://www.iso.ch/iso/en/prods-services/
>   ➥iso3166ma/02iso-3166-code-lists/list-en1.
>   ➥html

To simulate owning a French-Canadian copy of Windows, add this line to the Form1 constructor, before the call to InitializeComponent():

```
System::Threading::Thread::CurrentThread->CurrentUICulture =
    new System::Globalization::CultureInfo("fr-CA");
```

When you set your UICulture with this line of code, the application displays the French version of the button. You can see how simple it is to support multiple languages on your buttons and other form components with this technique. Follow these steps:

1. Code the entire application and test it. The user interface should be frozen before localization begins.

2. Set the Localizable property of the form to True.

3. Set the Language property of the form to the language in which you want to distribute the application.

4. Change the Text property of buttons, labels, and other form components to their equivalents in the new language. Resize and rearrange components, if necessary.

5. Repeat steps 3 and 4 for each language and locale you want to target.

Of course, this is only part of the story. What about your error messages and other strings? You don't set these in the designer, so you can't localize them this way. Instead you can keep them in a resource file, and create a different version of the resource file for each locale.

Adapting an existing application to get its strings from a resource file is quite a bit of work. That's why internationalization starts at the beginning of a project. Rather than adjusting the rest of the AdvancedUI project to use a resource file, this section shows you how to use a resource file in a new section of code.

Make sure that the Language property of Form1 is set to Default, and build the application. Right-click the AdvancedUI project in Solution Explorer and choose Add, Add New Item. Select an Assembly Resource File and name it Strings. The file is XML and it opens in the data view for you to edit. There are five columns in the resource file:

- name—The name of the resource. Avoid generic names such as ErrorMessage; take the time to decide on a naming convention for all the error messages, prompts, and so on that will be used in your application.

- value—The actual string to display. This first resource file is in your default language.

- comment—A place for the programmer to document this resource.

- type—Resources can be strings, but can also be binary files such as images or audio clips. For nonstring resources, enter a class name such as System.Drawing.Bitmap for the type.

- mimetype—For nonstring resources, the MIME type of the data, such as application/x-microsoft.net.object.bytearray.base64 for binary (Base64) data.

Enter Hello for the name and Hello World for the value of the resource. Save the resource file.

Add another resource file named Strings.fr-CA.resx. The name is important: The part immediately before the .RESX extension must match the language and locale combination for which you are localizing. The first part must match the resource file you already created. Make sure you provide the .RESX extension—because there is a dot in the filename, the wizard will not add the extension for you if you omit it. (It thinks .fr-CA is the extension.)

In the data view of the French Canadian resource file, enter a resource named Hello with a value of Bonjour Mes Amis. Save the resource file.

Open the code for Form1.h and scroll to the bottom, where the empty Hello_Click handler was added earlier. Edit the handler so it reads like this:

```
private: System::Void Hello_Click(System::Object *  sender,
                                  System::EventArgs *  e)
{
   Resources::ResourceManager* rm =
      new Resources::ResourceManager("AdvancedUI.ResourceFiles",
                         Reflection::Assembly::GetExecutingAssembly());
   String* greeting = rm->GetString("Hello");
   Windows::Forms::MessageBox::Show(greeting);
}
```

This code starts by creating a ResourceManager. The two parameters that are passed to the constructor are the resource file and the assembly. When you add .RESX files to your project, the build process converts them to a single resource file called <projectname>.ResourceFiles.resources. The first part of this name, <projectname>.ResourceFiles, is what you pass to the constructor to identify the resource file. The assembly to pass is the one that is currently executing, available from a static method of the Assembly class.

Once a ResourceManager instance is created, you use it to access resources such as strings. In a large application you might make the ResourceManager reference a member variable of the form, create it in the form Load event, and just use it in various button handlers. The GetString() method looks up a string, and takes the name as a parameter. This code just puts up a message box with that string.

Build and run the application. If your UICulture is still set to French Canadian by the extra line in the constructor, you will see the Bonjour Tout Le Monde button, and when you click it, the message box will read Bonjour Mes Amis. Comment out the line in the constructor, build and run the application, and you should see Hello World on the button and in the message box.

If you wanted to make a version of this application in another language, you would add another .RESX file, but make no changes to the code. That's how the .NET Framework can make localization feasible even for small applications and small development teams. Just remember that you must plan for internationalization from the beginning—finding every hard-coded string in your application and replacing it with a call to GetString() will be very tedious.

Being Localizable

It's natural to wonder why you have to set the Localizable property of the form to True. Shouldn't forms always be localizable? Making a form localizable means that you no longer make any assumptions about user interfaces, not even assuming that text runs left to right instead of right to left. The number of properties for each component that is set in InitializeComponent goes up dramatically when a form is localizable. For example, when you first add the Hello button to this application, these lines are added to InitializeComponent():

```
this->Hello->Location = System::Drawing::Point(112, 224);
this->Hello->Name = S"Hello";
this->Hello->TabIndex = 5;
this->Hello->Text = S"Hello World";
this->Hello->Click += new System::EventHandler(this, Hello_Click);
```

When the Localizable property of the form is set to True, this block of code changes to

```
this->Hello->AccessibleDescription =
    resources->GetString(S"Hello.AccessibleDescription");
this->Hello->AccessibleName =
    resources->GetString(S"Hello.AccessibleName");
this->Hello->Anchor =
    (*__try_cast<__box System::Windows::Forms::AnchorStyles * >
        (resources->GetObject(S"Hello.Anchor")));
this->Hello->BackgroundImage =
    (__try_cast<System::Drawing::Image * >
        (resources->GetObject(S"Hello.BackgroundImage")));
this->Hello->Dock =
    (*__try_cast<__box System::Windows::Forms::DockStyle * >
        (resources->GetObject(S"Hello.Dock")));
this->Hello->Enabled =
    (*__try_cast<__box System::Boolean * >
        (resources->GetObject(S"Hello.Enabled")));
this->Hello->FlatStyle =
    (*__try_cast<__box System::Windows::Forms::FlatStyle * >
        (resources->GetObject(S"Hello.FlatStyle")));
this->Hello->Font =
    (__try_cast<System::Drawing::Font * >
        (resources->GetObject(S"Hello.Font")));
this->Hello->Image =
    (__try_cast<System::Drawing::Image * >
        (resources->GetObject(S"Hello.Image")));
```

```
this->Hello->ImageAlign =
    (*__try_cast<__box System::Drawing::ContentAlignment *  >
        (resources->GetObject(S"Hello.ImageAlign")));
this->Hello->ImageIndex =
    (*__try_cast<__box System::Int32 *  >
        (resources->GetObject(S"Hello.ImageIndex")));
this->Hello->ImeMode =
    (*__try_cast<__box System::Windows::Forms::ImeMode *  >
        (resources->GetObject(S"Hello.ImeMode")));
this->Hello->Location =
    (*__try_cast<__box System::Drawing::Point *  >
        (resources->GetObject(S"Hello.Location")));
this->Hello->Name = S"Hello";
this->Hello->RightToLeft =
    (*__try_cast<__box System::Windows::Forms::RightToLeft *  >
        (resources->GetObject(S"Hello.RightToLeft")));
this->Hello->Size =
    (*__try_cast<__box System::Drawing::Size *  >
        (resources->GetObject(S"Hello.Size")));
this->Hello->TabIndex =
    (*__try_cast<__box System::Int32 *  >
        (resources->GetObject(S"Hello.TabIndex")));
this->Hello->Text = resources->GetString(S"Hello.Text");
this->Hello->TextAlign =
    (*__try_cast<__box System::Drawing::ContentAlignment *  >
        (resources->GetObject(S"Hello.TextAlign")));
this->Hello->Visible =
    (*__try_cast<__box System::Boolean *  >
        (resources->GetObject(S"Hello.Visible")));
this->Hello->Click += new System::EventHandler(this, Hello_Click);
```

As you can see, you should turn this property on only when you plan to localize your application.

In Brief

- You can write your own controls either by inheriting from a control provided in the Base Class Libraries, or by aggregating several controls into one new control. In both cases, your own code provides the unique behavior you desire.

- You can make a control into a drop target by setting its AllowDrop property to True and adding handlers for the DragEnter and DragDrop events.

- You can make a control into a drag source by adding a handler for a common event, such as a mouse click, and calling `DoDragDrop()` in that handler.

- GDI+ enables you to use sophisticated graphics such as blends and transparent colors with ease, using pens, brushes, fonts, and a `Graphics` object.

- Use the forms designer and the Properties window to make different versions of a form for different languages and cultures.

- Move error messages and other strings into a resource file to simplify the job of localizing your application.

Index

Symbols

\ (backslash), 55

. (dot), namespaces, 49

:: (double colons), namespaces, 49

<< operator, 34

_ (underscore), 9

A

Accept Button property, 84

accessing

automation servers, 173-174

databases. *See* ADO.NET Class Library

accounts, installers (Windows service), 225

Actions menu commands, New Group, 244

activated objects, 255

Active Template Library (ATL), unmanaged COM components, 150-153

adapters, OleDbDataAdapter, 213

Add Class command (Add menu), 32, 92, 207

Add Dataset Wizard, 77

Add Member Variable Wizard, 98, 154

C

How can we make this index more useful? Email us at indexes@samspublishing.com

cryptography

    asymmetric, 235-236

    decryption, 240-241

    encryption

        authentication, 234-236

        ciphers, 234

        ciphertext, 234

        confidentiality, 234-236

        hashing, 235-236

        integrity, 234-236

        keys, 239-240

        plaintext, 234

    encryption classes, 236

        files, 238-239

        streams, 237-239

    symmetric, 235-236

    symmetric algorithms, Rijndael, 239

CTime, unmanaged code, 15

culture names, localization, 283

cursor styles, changing, 277

custom marshalers

    C#, 144

    CleanUpNativeData() method, 142-143

    GetInstance() method, 141

    ICustomerMarshaler class, 140-141

    MarshalManagedToNative() method, 141-142

    writing, 139-140

Customize Toolbox dialog box, 276

D

data

    adding to DataGrid, 75-77

    managed

        boxing, 21-23

        garbage-collected classes, 16-20

        indeterministic destruction, 17

        managed libraries, 110-112

        pinning, 21-23

        value classes, 19-21

    unmanaged, 15-16

        boxing, 21-23

        managed libraries, 110-112

        pinning, 21-23

Data grid (toolbox control), 66

data grids

    ASP.NET, 213

    data readers, binding to, 213

    WinForms, 213

data layers, 91

    applications, creating, 87

    projects, creating, 207-208

    prototypes, creating without, 75

data layers (managed C++)

    ADO.NET Class Library

        data readers, 212-216

        DataReader class, 205

        DataSet class, 205-212

loader-lock bug, 113

Loki Web site, 112

loop constructs, Windows service, 223-224

M

machine names, roles, 243

main function, 34

managed applications

COM components, 158-160

creating, 37-39

running, 37

unmanaged class libraries, calling, 100-101

unmanaged DLL (Dynamic-Link Library)

custom marshalers, 139-144

import library, 135-136

PInvoke, 137-139

user interfaces

drag and drop, 277-279

GDI+, 279-282

internationalization, 282

localization, 282-287

Windows controls, 271-276

versus C#, 110

Web Services

consuming, 193-196

testing, 192

writing, 189-193

Windows, 9-10

Windows service, creating

configuration files, 223

email, 228-229

event log entries, 229-230

installations, 225-226

installers, 225

loop constructs, 223-224

setting properties, 225

tests, 225-226

URL checking, 226-228

URLCheckerWinService class, 223

Word, spell checking with, 183-184

GAC, 180

PIAs (Primary Interop Assemblies), 179-180

references, 179

sample applications, 180-182

managed class libraries

benefits/limitations, 103-104

calling, managed languages, 109-110

COM components, 160

interfaces, adding, 161-162

Registry entries, 163

testing, 164-168

type libraries, 162

type libraries, adding to GAC (Global Assembly Cache), 162-163

creating, 104-106

N

symmetric cryptography, 235-236

SymmetricAlgorithm class, 237

syntax. *See* code

System namespace

    System::Console class, 50-51

    System::DateTime class, 53-54

    System::String class, 51-53

    System::Stringbuilder class, 51-53

System::Collections namespace, 58

System::Console class, 50-51

System::DateTime class, 53-54

System::Double parameter, 104-106

System::IO namespace, 55

System::String class, 51-53

System::Stringbuilder class, 51-53

System::Text namespace, 55-58

System::Threading namespace, 58-60

T

tables, relational databases, 204

tabs

    Alphabetic, 71

    Categorized, 71

    Events, 72

    Projects, 106

    Properties, 72

    Property Pages, 72

    Solution, 32

    Windows Forms, 65

tags

    channels, 255

    service, 255

TCP protocol, 255

template-based libraries, 112

test harnesses, 29-30

    managed, managed class testing, 39-42

    running, 96

    unmanaged, unmanaged class testing, 32-35

    writing, 34-35

testing

    applications, 29

    COM components

        managed C++, 159

        managed class libraries, 164-168

    DLL (Dynamic-Link Library), 131-132

    managed classes, 39-42

    remoted clients, 253

    roles (role-based security), 243-245

    unmanaged classes, 32-35

    Web Services, managed C++, 192

    Windows service (managed C++), 225-226

text, writing (Graphics objects), 281-282

text boxes

    properties, 82

    toolbox control, 65

Text property, 66, 207

Thread objects, creating, 60

threads, 58-60

ToDouble() method, 195

Your Guide to Computer Technology

www.informit.com

KICK START

< QUICK >

< CONCISE >

< PRACTICAL >

Microsoft .NET Kick Start
Hitesh Seth
0-672-32574-8
$34.99 US / $52.99 CAN

ASP.NET Kick Start
Stephen Walther
0-672-32476-8
$34.99 US / $54.99 CAN

ASP.NET Data Web Controls Kick Start
Scott Mitchell
0-672-32501-2
$34.99 US / $54.99 CAN

Microsoft Visual Basic .NET 2003 Kick Start
Duncan Mackenzie, et al
0-672-32549-7
$34.99 US / $52.99 CAN

Microsoft Visual C# .NET Kick Start
Steven Holzner
0-672-32547-0
$34.99 US / $52.99 CAN

XQuery Kick Start
James McGovern, et al
0-672-32479-2
$34.99 US / $52.99 CAN

Radio UserLand Kick Start
Rogers Cadenhead
0-672-32563-2
$34.99 US / $52.99 CAN

XPath Kick Start: Navigating XML with XPath 1.0 and 2.0
Steven Holzner
0-672-32411-3
$34.99 US / $52.99 CAN